TRAFALGAR'S
Lost Hero

TRAFALGAR'S
Lost Hero

Admiral Lord Collingwood and the Defeat of Napoleon

MAX ADAMS

WILEY

John Wiley & Sons, Inc.

Published by John Wiley & Sons, Inc., Hoboken, New Jersey
Published simultaneously in Canada

First published in Great Britain in 2005 by Weidenfeld & Nicholson as *Admiral Collingwood: Nelson's Own Hero*

For general information about our other products and services, please contact our Customer Care Department within the United States at (800) 762-2974, outside the United States at (317) 572-3993 or fax (317) 572-4002.

Wiley also publishes its books in a variety of electronic formats. Some content that appears in print may not be available in electronic books. For more information about Wiley products, visit our web site at www.wiley.com.

Library of Congress Cataloging-in-Publication Data
Adams, Max, date.
Trafalgar's lost hero : Admiral Lord Collingwood and the defeat of Napoleon / Max Adams.
    p. cm.
Includes bibliographical references and index.
ISBN-13: 978-0-471-71995-3 (cloth)
ISBN-10: 0-471-71995-1 (cloth)
 1. Collingwood, Cuthbert Collingwood, Baron, 1748–1810. 2. Great Britain—History, Naval—19th century. 3. Great Britain—History, Naval—18th century.
  4. Admirals—Great Britain—Biography. 5. Trafalgar, Battle of, 1805. I. Title.
DA87.1.C7A35 2005
940.2'745'092—dc22
2005015434

Printed in the United States of America

10 9 8 7 6 5 4 3 2 1

For my son Jack, with love

Acknowledgements

My grateful thanks must go firstly to the Winston Churchill Memorial Trust, who generously funded my travels in Collingwood's wake and who have taken such a keen interest in the project. It also gives me great pleasure to thank those people who showed me such open hospitality and kindness on my travels. In Menorca, Senor Fransisco Pons Mantonari, who gave me the room next to Collingwood's, and much of his valuable time; in Antigua, Mrs Hyacinth Hale and members of the *Royal Naval Tot Club of Antigua*, especially Mark and Lindsay Kiesseling; in Boston, Bill and Wendy Westman and on Cape Cod, Sally Gardner; in Sicily, the Sarullo family of Palermo. Also to Stephen and Christina Stead for many kindnesses along the way.

Warwick Adams not only improved many technical aspects of the manuscript, but also provided Latin translations, constant encouragement and a finely tuned ear. Dr Christopher Cumberpatch devotedly read and improved drafts of the manuscript. Jim Gill made it possible. I am most grateful too, to Mrs Susan Collingwood-Cameron, the Admiral's great, great, great niece, for allowing me access to her papers. Mr Clive Richards very kindly allowed me to photograph his portrait of Mary Moutray. For their continued support I would like to thank Liz and Stefan Sobell, and Samantha and Neil Callon.

Northumberland

When England sets her banner forth
And bids her armour shine,
She'll not forget the famous North,
The lads of moor and Tyne;
And when the loving cup's in hand,
And honour leads the cry,
They know not old Northumberland
Who'll pass her memory by.

When Nelson sailed for Trafalgar
With all his country's best,
He held them dear as brothers are,
But one beyond the rest.
For when the fleet with heroes manned
To clear the decks began,
The boast of old Northumberland
He sent to lead the van.

Himself by *Victory*'s bulwarks stood
And cheered to see the sight;
"That noble fellow Collingwood,
How bold he goes to fight!"
Love, that the league of Ocean spanned,
Heard him as face to face;
"What would he give, Northumberland,
To share our pride of place?"

The flag that goes the world around
And flaps on every breeze
Has never gladdened fairer ground
Or kinder hearts than these.
So when the loving cup's in hand
And honour leads the cry,
They know not old Northumberland,
Who'll pass her memory by.

Sir Henry Newbolt

The wood engravings in this book are from
1800 Woodcuts by Thomas Bewick, edited by Blanche Cirker,
Dover Publications, New York 1962

Contents

Illustrations follow pages 114, 160, and 216

The Collingwood touch

Visitors to Menorca arriving in vast eight-decker cruise ships at the island's main harbour, Port Mahon, are disgorged at the bottom of the cliff on which the town perches. It is one of the great maritime arrivals. To reach the town, and for a magnificent view back across the harbour, they must climb a broad stone staircase which for three centuries has been called Pigtail Steps, after the hairstyles of generations of English sailors. At the beginning of Patrick O'Brian's novel *Master and Commander*, these are the steps from which Jack Aubrey looks out in vain to catch a glimpse of the *Sophie*, his first command.

This was where *Sophie*'s real-life counterpart, a tiny 14-gun sloop called *Speedy*, brought her famous prize, the 32-gun xebec frigate *Gamo*, in 1801, shortly before peace broke out in the Mediterranean and Menorca was returned to Spanish control after a century of British domination. Even today, the bars that line the waterfront have an air of the English navy about them: their massive timber roofs remind one of the 'tween decks of a first-rate ship of the line, and their walls are made of bricks brought out from England as ships' ballast. Most tourists come to Menorca for the reliable summer climate; some stay on and brave winter storms: the tramontana and the mistral. Few miss Mahon's peculiarly attractive hybrid architecture which lends it an atmosphere of eighteenth-century Portsmouth crossed with Catalan baroque: the town that gave the world mayonnaise.

Of the many English visitors who come here every year, a small number regularly book rooms at Collingwood House, a respectable establishment lying a mile out from the busy town centre just off the road to Es Castell, at the end of a drive whose palm trees shade it from the worst of the midday sun. Fransisco Pons Mantonari, an educated man from very old Menorquin stock, has owned Collingwood House for more than forty years. When he came across the place in 1961, in the days before package holidays were generally affordable, it had been owned by the German sculptor Waldemar Fenn, and was in a lamentable state: its reconstruction has been a labour of love. Little of the original furnishing remained, and its current comforts represent a life's work. After decades of Fascist rule all records and deeds had been lost, and only local oral tradition was left to permit the association with Admiral Lord Collingwood: battle commander, diplomat, wit and bosom friend and hero of Nelson. Eventually, however, an old military map[1] turned up which showed that the house had been called Collingwood House at least as early as 1813. So Mantonari called his new business the Hotel del Almirante, but kept its English name too.

Today, restored to Anglo-Balearic splendour, this house overlooking the deep waters of Mahon harbour is a cliff-top shrine to an English naval officer and statesman largely neglected by posterity. It attracts not just genteel couples of a certain age, but also enthusiasts of naval history. Every Thursday morning during the season Mantonari, accompanied by the magnificent red macaw which sits complacently on his shoulder, gives guided tours of the hotel for guests, and anyone else who is interested. At a quarter-past ten, a small crowd gathers under a sign outside which is painted with a likeness of Collingwood holding his telescope, but looks as though it ought to read 'Admiral Benbow'. Once inside, one could be forgiven for thinking this was somewhere in Devon or Cornwall: there is dark polished oak panelling, and thick carpet on the floor. A pendulum clock ticks.

Mantonari is a seasoned performer. As he guides visitors through the foyer, past an original letter of Collingwood's hanging on the wall (cunningly framed with glass both front and back on a hinged mount) he nods at a portrait of Nelson which overlooks the bottom of the stairs: an engraving of the tragic hero writing his last letter to Emma Hamilton before Trafalgar. Mantonari pretends not to allow the name of Nelson to be spoken in his hotel; and laughs. Next to Nelson is a picture of Collingwood. It doesn't have the melodrama of the Nelson portrait. Collingwood was not a melodramatic man. His portraits suggest a stern, if kindly, headmaster, with flowing white hair and piercing eyes that might be about to laugh or to admonish. Stripped of his uniform and medals he might even pass for a notary, or a family doctor. It is hard to imagine him screaming 'Fire!' at his gun crews in the midst of battle. He holds his chin in one hand, with a telescope under his other arm. The telescope might symbolise a memory of his obituarist: Collingwood's 'grey hair streaming to the wind with eyes like an eagle's, on the watch'.[2] The real telescope, still in the possession of his family, was no show-piece: it has been repaired with an oilcloth and tar bandage, and the lenses are clouded with the salt spray of the Mediterranean. The hand on the chin is there not to make him look thoughtful, which he does anyway, but to hide a fold of flesh that sagged increasingly as he aged: a man old before his time.

Biographers of Nelson have tended to paint the relationship between the two men as a sort of Holmes-Watson partnership, with

Collingwood cast as the doughty but dull Watson to Nelson's brilliant Holmes. Holmes might be an appropriate fictional double for Nelson: a bold, sometimes erratic, passionate genius, capable of inspiring adoration in both men and women; but Collingwood is hopelessly miscast as Watson. He was a better seaman than Nelson, a subtler diplomat, and despite his conservative politics, a naval reformer at least fifty years ahead of his time. What Collingwood lacked, and admired above all else in his friend, was the irresistible Nelsonian impetuosity that allowed his enemy no time to recover once he had made a mistake: England's Saviour had himself, with typical immodesty, called it the Nelson touch. If there is a fictional counterpart to Collingwood, it is Jack Aubrey, Patrick O'Brian's very human English epitome.

Nelson was ten years younger than Collingwood. They first met, according to Collingwood, in 1773, when Nelson was just fifteen, and immediately fell into 'habits of friendship'[3] that lasted until Nelson's death thirty-two years later. Apparently almost complete opposites in character, they became each other's hero. And when, at half-past four on the afternoon of 21 October 1805, Collingwood's journal recorded that Captain Hardy had informed him of the death of the Commander-in-Chief, we can be sure not only that England had lost her hero, but that Collingwood had lost his closest friend, as an eye-witness recounted in a letter home:

> [Admiral Collingwood is] as bold as a lion, for all he can cry! – I saw his tears with my own eyes, when the boat hailed and said my lord was dead.[4]

Next to Collingwood's portrait on the staircase at the Hotel del Almirante is an unsigned eighteenth-century cartoon in the style of Gillray, entitled *The English Lion dismembered*. It depicts the humiliating trial of Admiral Sir John Byng, whose squadron failed in 1756 to prevent the French from taking Menorca during the Seven Years' War. Byng was executed by firing squad: *pour encourager les autres*, as Voltaire put it; not that English naval officers needed much encouragement, for Byng was roundly condemned in the service. In the Georgian Royal Navy, commanders were expected to take on and beat a superior force. Byng's defence, satirised, went like this:

> With thirteen ships to twelve, says B..g
> It were a shame to meet 'em.
> And then with twelve to twelve a thing
> Impossible to beat 'em.
> When more to many, less to few
> And even still not right
> Arithmetic will plainly shew
> 'Twere wrong in B..g to fight

Further up the staircase is a picture of Collingwood's dog Bounce, beloved companion for nearly twenty years.[5] Bounce was an almost perfect naval dog: intelligent and faithful, a fine swimmer; a sympathetic soul and the only creature on a ship carrying eight hundred men that his master could properly confide in, but sadly intolerant of gunfire. During battle or live-firing exercises he would creep down to the safety of the orlop deck. The portrait, of recent date, depicts Bounce as a Jack Russell terrier; but this cannot have been the case, for when Collingwood first acquired the dog he wrote home to his sister, saying how much Bounce was admired and indulged by the men, and noting that he had already grown as tall as his master's writing table. An English sheepdog perhaps, or a Newfoundland; not a terrier. Mantonari tells his audience that Bounce is said to have come from Menorca, and may have been one of those piebald, flop-eared, rangy pointers known locally as rabbit dogs, famed for their almost human personalities. What a pity that in the summer of 1808

Bounce – aged eighteen – was too tired to go ashore with his master at Cadiz and 'have his picture taken'.[6]

Upstairs, in the lobby, guests and visitors are shown Mantonari's Titian: 'not a very good Titian, but it *is* a Titian'. He recounts the story of Collingwood's ghost, said to have been seen pacing through the house on quiet nights and fingering odd notes on the piano. He shows us the door to Collingwood's own room (No. 7), and points to the padded leather coverings on all the doors that lead off the lobby. For sound-proofing, perhaps, when Collingwood was in conference with his many officers, or with envoys, interpreters, local dignitaries and military personnel. These were the years after Trafalgar. His friend and comrade Nelson was dead, and Collingwood became virtual viceroy of the Mediterranean, dealing with a fleet of eighty ships and maintaining relations with deys, beys, pashas, sultans, kings and queens, generals and diplomats, from Cadiz to Constantinople; managing relations of literally Byzantine complexity.

Collingwood's staff consisted of a flag captain (Richard Thomas), a first lieutenant (the excellent John Clavell)[7] and a secretary (William Cosway, who later tried to marry one of his daughters, but was discouraged after a terrible coaching accident left him a cripple).[8] There were rear-admirals and captains too; but the number of men for whom he was responsible must have been in the region of twenty-five thousand, and such were the stakes – complete domination of Europe by Bonaparte; invasion of England; loss of Britain's colonies – that Collingwood himself admitted he was 'giddy with the multiplicities'.[9] He was what we would now call a control freak, never delegating to others what he could do himself. And meticulous: orders for fresh vegetables were given the same attention as letters to emperors. Economical, too. His out-of-pocket expenses claim for the entire Mediterranean fleet in the four years after Trafalgar amounted to a paltry £54.[10] And during that famous action, in the extraordinarily frightening heat of battle, he calmly retrieved a sail which had been shot away by the enemy, neatly folded it and stowed it in a locker for future use.

Collingwood House was conveniently situated. It lay a mile or so south-east of Port Mahon, the bustling capital of Menorca, and overlooked a secure anchorage: from his window the Admiral could see his flagship, the magnificent 110-gun three-decker *Ville de Paris*. It was also far enough away from the port to escape the noise of rowdy sailors on shore leave, and merchants and local dignitaries seeking favours. Everybody seemed to want his attention. To a request from the Spanish governor of the island that Collingwood put down a mutiny in the army garrison, he replied that really it was none of his business, though if the French prisoners escaped from the Lazaretto he would see to the matter.[11] But when he heard about the problems the church of Santa Maria was having with its organ, he saw an opportunity for diplomatic advantage. This grand church in the centre of town, opposite the *Ajuntament*, or town hall, had had an organ built: a magnificent affair of three thousand pipes. An elaborate, not to say over-elaborate, wooden housing had been ordered from Austria.

Austria in 1809 was at the centre of Napoleon Bonaparte's schemes for the conquest of Europe. Nevertheless, the housing was transported overland from Vienna to somewhere on the Italian coast, perhaps Genoa or Livorno. There it remained, with no merchant ship able or brave enough to run the gauntlet of the French fleet in Toulon. Collingwood sent a frigate to fetch it, and it would be no surprise if his carpenters helped install it. The organ can still be heard at full blast every day during the summer months, when incurious tourists pass by on their way to the shops.

Across the road in the *Ajuntament* are portraits of King George III and Queen Charlotte. They, like the bow and sash windows of many of the older houses, are a reminder that for most of the eighteenth century Menorca was a British possession. It was not an easy island to hold. Its numerous beaches and creeks made amphibious assault by an enemy relatively easy,[12] and so a large garrison was required to be stationed there. But the prize was the harbour: Porto de Máo as it is in Catalan. It was said that there were four safe ports in the Mediterranean: June, July, August and Mahon. It is a natural harbour, up to 100ft deep all along its three-mile length and almost up to the quayside (Collingwood himself surveyed it as a master's mate in 1771). It never silts up, its only disadvantage being that it is impossible to enter in a northerly wind, and difficult to leave in a southerly. Strategically, it allowed the British a base from which to watch the enemy fleet in its stronghold at Toulon: the blockade was a mainstay of naval policy in the French wars. The first British base was built at Mahon in the late seventeenth century, and even now the naval establishment on the north shore is physically little changed from Collingwood's day.

By the time Collingwood leased or bought his house in 1809, Menorca was back in the hands of the Spanish, ceded to them at the Treaty of Amiens seven years earlier. First a friend, then ally, then vassal of France, Spain had risen in revolt against Bonaparte in May 1808, and within months the British fleet was again able to shelter, repair and take on stores in Mahon. By this time Collingwood had been away from home for more than six years. From the start of the war in 1803, right through the Trafalgar campaign, his elevation to a barony – a 'barreny', he called it, worth thirty shillings a year[13] – and years of wearying blockade and fruitless chase, not once had he even seen the coast of England, let alone his precious vegetable patch and the simple pleasures of the 'quarterdeck walk' in his garden at Morpeth. He had inherited a coal mine at Chirton near North

Shields, and was trying to master its complexities from a distance of two thousand miles. And the world was moving on. Within three years, a few miles upriver from Collingwood's birthplace in Newcastle, William Hedley would present *Puffing Billy* to the world and launch the railway age.

Collingwood was desperate to see his wife, whom he adored but whose spending, now that she was a member of society, had long since outstripped his pay. He missed his two daughters, whose childhood had passed him by, and he had been worn to a thread by his unbroken six-year tour of duty. His repeated requests for leave had been turned down by an Admiralty deploying a combination of emotional blackmail and flattery. When he resigned his commission in February 1810 it was because he knew he was dying. What ultimately killed him, according to the doctor who conducted his post-mortem, was a stoppage of the pylorus, or inferior aperture of the stomach: cancer.[14] But it is legitimate to say that forty-four years of selfless duty to his country had worn him out. No sensational wounds, no last great victory, no martyrdom in battle.

His final illness, though debilitating and terribly painful, did not dull his sense of duty, nor did it dull his humour. With all his cares, he still took the keenest interest in his officers and men. In particular, he was famous in the navy for bringing on talent, both from the officer class and the lower ranks. Indeed, against the modern trend that meant an officer had to 'pass for a gentleman', Collingwood still preferred them, as he put it, 'to come through the port-hole not at the cabin window'.[15] Perhaps because it mattered to him so much, he was critical of those who did not respond to his encouragement, as he confided to his sister in April 1809:

> But you may have heard that I am reckoned rather queer in the promotion of young men. I advance a great many who have not a

friend to speak for them, while those I respect most in the world
sometimes plead in vain. Those who are diligent and promise to
be useful officers never miscarry. And if your friend is such an one
send him to me ...

Mrs Currel's son never can be a sailor: he has something very
odd in his manner, or rather he has no manner at all, but saunters a
melancholic for a week together, unnoticing and unnoticed, except
when I give him a little rally to make his blood circulate, and this I
do, not in the expectation that it will make him better in his profession, but merely for his health's sake.

It is a pity she had not put him apprentice to Jno. Wilson, the
apothecary; he might have gone on very wisely. His gravity would
have established his reputation as a learned doctor, and if he did
poison an old woman now and then, better do that than drown an
entire ship's company at a dash by running on the rocks.

[P.S.] Bounce desires his best respects to your dogs[16]

This is the wickedly sardonic side of his character, revealed almost
exclusively to his family, and especially to his sisters, in thirty-five
years of correspondence. In one letter, to John Davidson, he
described the Bedouin practice of towing prisoners behind galloping
horses, and regaled him with the story of a washerwoman who had
been abducted by them and whose headless body had later been
discovered: 'did not tow well, I suppose.'[17]

Collingwood's officers and crew admired him, above all, for
another side: his humanity and sense of justice, and his consummate skill in handling men and ships. Readers of O'Brian's *Ionian
Mission* will recognise as a classic Aubrey-ism the following anecdote,
recounted by Collingwood's first biographer, and son-in-law, G. L.
Newnham-Collingwood. A midshipman had reported one of the
ordinary seamen, a man who had been at sea for many years, for
swearing at him. The usual punishment for such a serious offence
was flogging. Collingwood wrote a letter to the young man, saying:

In all probability the fault was yours. But whether it were or not,
I am sure it would go to your heart to see a man old enough to be
your father, disgraced and punished on your account; and it will,
therefore, give me a good opinion of your disposition, if, when he
is brought out, you ask for his pardon.

When, after receiving this letter, the midshipman duly begged the
man off his punishment, Collingwood said to the sailor, though with
a show of pained reluctance:

This young gentleman has pleaded so humanely for you, that in the
hope that you will feel a due gratitude to him for his benevolence,
I will for this time overlook your offence.[18]

No wonder it was later said by one of his junior officers that a look
of displeasure from him was worse than a dozen lashes at the
gangway from another captain. This was the Collingwood touch.
Its essence was distilled in an anecdote of John Scott's (who, as Lord
Eldon, became Lord Chancellor) from around the time of the
Spanish Armament in 1790:

I met Lord Collingwood in the Strand: he was a school-fellow of
mine under Moises. I had not seen him in many years – he had been
so long on board Ship that he walked with difficulty – we shook
hands – I observed that tears flowed down his cheeks – I asked him
what so affected him – He said that a few days before, his ship's
company were paid off – that he had lost his children – all his family
– that they were dear to him, and he could not refrain from what
I had noticed.

I attended his funeral at St Paul's and was much affected by the
grief manifested by some Seamen who had served under him. I was
a Bearer, and a poor Black Sailor in Tears laid fast hold of my Arm,
and attended almost the whole Ceremony.[19]

One reason for this affection may have been that Collingwood hated flogging, and used the lash so little that he acquired a reputation for having banned its use on his ships. He found physical brutality hard to reconcile with his faith, and once said:

> I cannot for the life of me, comprehend the religion of an Officer, who prays all one day, and flogs his men all the next.[20]

He managed his crews so skilfully that Sir John Jervis advised captains who had particularly awkward seamen aboard to send them to him: 'Old Cuddy' would soon sort them out.

One of Collingwood's most celebrated attributes was his bravery, which first won him his promotion to lieutenant in the amphibious assault on Charlestown in 1775 (more usually known as the battle of Bunker's Hill). In three great fleet actions he distinguished himself, disdaining the enemy's fire; and in one case, at the battle of Cape St Vincent, he sailed into the chaos and destruction of a furious mêlée to rescue Nelson. He was 'as brave an old boy as ever stood'[21] and after Trafalgar the celebrated frigate captain Henry Blackwood wrote that he had 'fought like an angel'.[22]

His handling of ships was equally renowned. Without his tactical cunning Trafalgar might never have been fought. In August 1805, with a squadron of four, he saw off a French detachment of sixteen ships by a series of brilliant feints and ruses which enabled him to establish the crucial blockade of Cadiz that led directly to the action at Trafalgar (he had taken over command of the fleet from Nelson who was in England, resting). And when, finally, Collingwood emerged from Nelson's shadow after that battle to assume control of Mediterranean operations he showed that he was fully equal to the enormous diplomatic and strategic task that faced him:

> He was in truth the prime and sole minister of England, acting upon the sea, corresponding himself with all surrounding

States, and ordering and executing everything upon his own responsibility.[23]

Collingwood did have his detractors; not just lazy historians who have conflated his attributes with Nelson's to make a single hero; in his own day he was thought by those who did not know him to be a dour and unimaginative provincial. Captains like Thomas Fremantle and Edward Codrington compared him unfavourably with Nelson. But there is more than a hint of snobbery there, perhaps most acutely observed by Jane Austen, whose brothers were captains in the Royal Navy:

> A man is in greater danger in the navy of being insulted by the rise of those whose father, his father might have disdained to speak to … than in any other line.[24]

Although he was the son of a debt-ridden trader from a northern coal-town, Collingwood was probably the most erudite naval officer of his day: Thackeray held him up as the perfect English gentleman, and a senior diplomat admitted that he wrote better than any of them.

The harsh carmine pink exterior of the Hotel del Almirante follows old English naval tradition: an iron-oxide based paint used as a cheap timber preservative and said to ward off scurvy. To the north-east, on the other side of the harbour, lies another Georgian mansion. This is Golden Farm, said to have been Nelson's residence when he stayed in Mahon in 1799; probably the association is mythical, for in 1799 Nelson was busy with his Neapolitan *ménage à trois*, though he did indeed visit the island, and hated it.

Right next to the cliff edge a set of rock-cut steps winds down to the little cove called El Fonduco, where the deep purple-blue waters of the harbour still shelter fishing boats and where a cluster of houses seems to lean out over the quay. From the slipway here

Collingwood could be rowed out with little fuss to *Ville de Paris* in his barge. In the old days Bounce would swim behind, but in August 1809, at the age of nineteen and crippled, like his master, by rheumatism, the dog fell overboard in the night and was drowned. Collingwood wrote:

> He is a great loss to me. I have few comforts, but he was one, for he loved me. Everybody sorrows for him. He was wiser than [many] who hold their heads higher and was grateful [to those] who were kind to him.[25]

Collingwood, having been told by his doctor that a spell ashore might help his non-existent appetite and ease his sore limbs, tried riding a horse, but could not. On 22 February 1810 he resigned his command. On the 25th he walked his last few painful steps on land, down to the cove at El Fonduco, where he was rowed out to his flagship. *Ville de Paris* was windbound for a few days but finally, on 6 March, the wind came round to the west and she set sail for England. He told Captain Thomas he was dying, but reassured him that he was coming to his end comfortably, and with no regrets. He died at sea the following day.

On 28 April the *Newcastle Courant* reported:

> On Saturday last, the Nereus frigate arrived at the Great Nore, with the remains of the late Lord Collingwood. They are now lying in state, in the royal hospital for seamen at Greenwich, and are to be entombed in St Paul's cathedral, with those of His Lordship's illustrious friend and commander NELSON. A monument will be erected by the public, in the same place, in grateful memory of his services.

A magnificent monument to Cuthbert Collingwood by John Graham Lough stands looking out to sea at Tynemouth. Below it are mounted four cannon taken from *Royal Sovereign,* the flagship from which he was the first to open fire at Trafalgar. There is a cenotaph to him in St Nicholas' cathedral in Newcastle on which, every 21 October, a wreath is laid by his townsmen. A hundred yards away on the Side, the ancient street where he was born in 1748, a small bust set above a doorway looks down, mostly unnoticed by passers-by. In Morpeth the red brick townhouse that he lived in during those brief periods when he was not at sea, still stands. And in a thousand hedgerows across Northumberland grow the oak trees that he planted for the future security of his country. But for a sense of his abiding presence, there is nothing to beat the short walk from Collingwood House to the cliff and down the rock-cut steps to El Fonduco, where he climbed into his admiral's barge for the last time with the words, 'Flagship, Coxswain'.

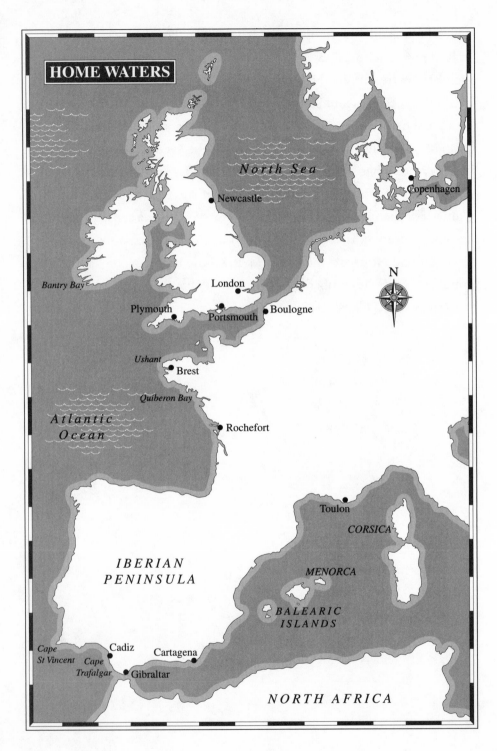

HOME WATERS

North Sea

Copenhagen

Newcastle

Bantry Bay

London

Plymouth   Boulogne
        Portsmouth

Ushant
        Brest

Quiberon Bay

Atlantic
Ocean   Rochefort

N

Toulon

CORSICA

IBERIAN
PENINSULA

MENORCA

BALEARIC
ISLANDS

Cape
St Vincent   Cadiz
       Cape   Cartagena
    Trafalgar
              Gibraltar

NORTH AFRICA

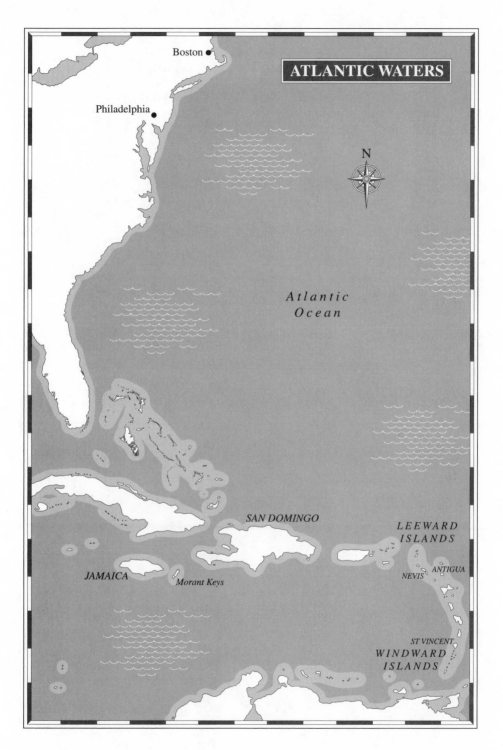

ATLANTIC WATERS

Boston

Philadelphia

N

Atlantic
Ocean

SAN DOMINGO

LEEWARD
ISLANDS

JAMAICA

Morant Keys

NEVIS

ANTIGUA

ST VINCENT

WINDWARD
ISLANDS

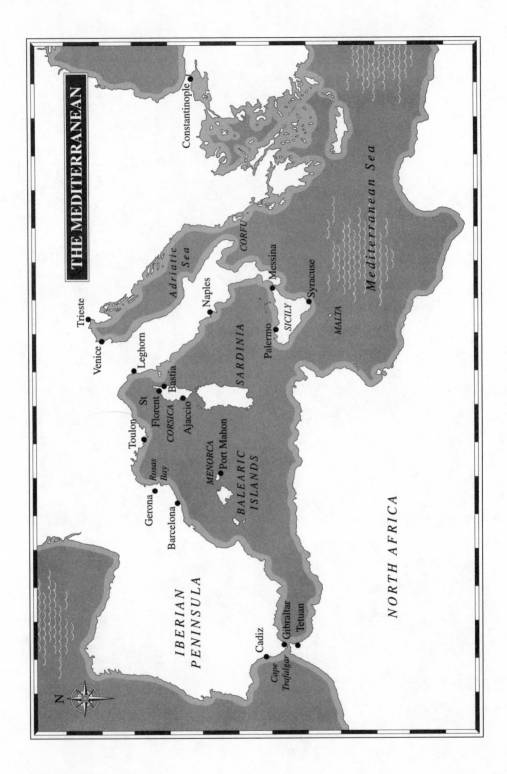

THE MEDITERRANEAN

Constantinople

Mediterranean Sea

Adriatic Sea

CORFU

Messina

Trieste

Venice

Naples

Syracuse

SICILY

Palermo

MALTA

Leghorn

Bastia

SARDINIA

St
Florent

CORSICA Ajaccio

Toulon

Port Mahon

*Rosas
Bay*

MENORCA

*BALEARIC
ISLANDS*

Gerona

Barcelona

NORTH AFRICA

*IBERIAN
PENINSULA*

Cadiz

Gibraltar

Tetuan

*Cape
Trafalgar*

N

CHAPTER ONE

A large piece of plum cake
1748-1771

In the wars against France that began in 1793 and, with a short break in 1802, ended at Waterloo twenty-two years later, Britain had four supreme commanders in the field. By chance, each succeeded his predecessor for reasons of declining health (or death), and each emerged at a time when his special skills were exactly those needed, in exactly the right place.

The first of these was John Jervis, born in 1735 and by the start of the war already a vice-admiral. He had fought in the Seven Years' War against France which ended in 1763, and at Quebec had been entrusted with General Wolfe's dying message to his fiancée. By 1795 he was Commander-in-Chief of the Mediterranean fleet and his naval philosophy was beginning to stamp itself on a generation

of commanders. He was severe, demanding and a feared disciplinarian. He loathed corruption, disloyalty and cowardice, and his
strategy for beating the French was to bring overwhelming naval
force to bear against them, not just to keep them at bay but to destroy
France as a sea power. Having lost control of the Mediterranean at
the end of 1796, he defeated a Spanish fleet off Cape St Vincent in
February 1797, then sent Nelson to victory at the battle of the Nile
a year later. In 1799 he briefly retired from active service, once more
assumed command of the Channel fleet, then finally became First
Lord of the Admiralty in Henry Addington's government.

In this post he ruthlessly reformed naval administration and
tackled the corruption then rife in the dockyards, but he was criti-
cised by William Pitt for leaving the navy under-strength when war
resumed in 1803. Nevertheless, he was given another active
command in 1806 before finally retiring a year later at the age of
seventy-one. He died in 1823. As supreme commander at sea, though,
Earl St Vincent, as he then was, had effectively passed his baton to
Nelson in 1798.

This son of a Norfolk parson, forty-one years old and already a
famously wounded war hero, though with a very mixed record, was
no great administrator like Jervis; still less a politician. He was a
battle commander. His first great fleet engagement had been the
battle of Cape St Vincent in 1797 under Jervis. Here, he brilliantly
precipitated the action by plunging his ship *Captain* pell-mell into
the enemy line. A year later he tracked down the French Mediterranean fleet at Aboukir Bay (in what became known as the battle of
the Nile) and destroyed it, stranding Bonaparte and his army in Egypt
and re-establishing British maritime control between Cadiz and
Malta. In 1801 he fought another battle at Copenhagen; less necessary
and less glorious, but equally effective in stamping British naval
supremacy on the Baltic and North Sea which was so vital for trade.

After the illusory Peace of Amiens in 1802, the next three years concentrated the navy's purpose: to prevent, at all costs, invasion by Napoleon's army of England. The trick was at one and the same time to bottle the enemy up in her ports, and tempt her to come out and fight the decisive battle at a time and place of the Royal Navy's choosing. The Long Watch, as it was called, ended in overwhelming victory at Trafalgar. That battle is popularly thought to have destroyed forever the French maritime threat. It did nothing of the sort. But at the precise moment of Nelson's death the mantle of supreme battle commander fell on the shoulders of the fifty-seven- year-old Cuthbert Collingwood.

For the next four and a half years he blockaded, chased, outwitted; took, burnt and attempted to destroy the ships of the French fleet to ensure that Bonaparte did not regain control of the Mediterranean. He supported the Spanish uprising, prevented Sicily from falling into French hands, kept Turkey and Russia neutral, policed the Adriatic (and while he was at it stood by to rescue the Pope from Rome and the Archduke of Austria from Trieste). And all the while he had to deal with the bloody and incestuous politics of North Africa. These tasks required a man with skills that went far beyond those of a battle commander. Collingwood had to be both diplomat and statesman, in effect a viceroy, and it happened that he was the only man in the navy (apart, perhaps, from Saumarez in the Baltic, performing a similar role, though on a smaller scale) who could have carried it off.

At the point of his death, in March 1810, and by one of those ironies with which history is littered, the focus of the war moved from sea to land, from east to west; the Sepoy General Arthur Wellesley emerged as the surgeon who would lance Bonaparte's Spanish ulcer and later, as the Iron Duke, ultimately defeat him on the continent of Europe.

The reputations of Wellington and Nelson speak for themselves. Nelson was a professional hero, Wellington a soldier/statesman in the tradition of Marlborough. St Vincent is not nearly so popularly known as his achievements deserve; but he is at least recognised by serious historians as a major influence on British maritime strategy during the Napoleonic wars. Neglect of Collingwood is harder to fathom, though the historian Piers Mackesy, writing of the war in the Mediterranean at this period, did not underestimate him:

> The splendour of the navy's work in the theatre after Trafalgar has been obscured by the absence of fleet actions; and the name of Lord Collingwood has equally been dimmed by his inability to bring an enemy fleet to battle. The fights were small, fierce encounters of sloops and gunboats, cutting-out expeditions, attacks on batteries. Only once did the enemy come out in force. Yet the scale was heroic; and over the vast canvas towers the figure of Collingwood.[1]

Wellington was the son of an earl, learning his craft on the playing fields of Eton, and in India in the Mahratta wars. But in an era when birth mattered at least as much as talent, it is remarkable that St Vincent, Nelson and Collingwood all came from much more ordinary backgrounds, and all went to sea at the same age. St Vincent was the son of a politically unconnected barrister, who gave the young John Jervis £20 at the age of thirteen – but never a penny more after that – and sent him off to join the navy. His poverty as a midshipman meant that he spent more time on the lower decks than he did with other officers. His education was a practical one: years and years of apprenticeship at sea.

Nelson's family were genteel country folk. They had no wealth, but there were useful connections, through the Suckling family – Nelson's uncle Maurice was a Comptroller of the Navy – and the Walpoles. Without this influence Nelson could not have been made post-captain at the extraordinarily young age of twenty. Even so, he served his time in the midshipman's berth from his early teens, and one of his outstanding traits as a commander was his understanding of both officers and men.

Cuthbert Collingwood's family had no money, but they were from ancient Northumbrian stock. An earlier Sir Cuthbert had been involved in the Reiver wars of the late sixteenth century, at a time when the Anglo-Scottish border was ruled, if that is the right word, by rival warlords and their clans. These were hard people, used to fighting and robbing and sleeping with one eye open. Sir Cuthbert Collingwood was a man of some consequence, able to raise eight hundred or even a thousand men to go raiding against families with whom he was feuding. He was kidnapped on one occasion by a Scots war party after a raid went horribly wrong, but he was not averse to meting out justice to his own: he executed seventeen of his tenants to prevent another feud from starting.[2]

One of his descendants, George Collingwood, was heavily implicated in the Jacobite rebellion of 1715: he was executed at Liverpool and his Eslington estate was forfeited, in a nice irony, to the Greenwich Hospital for Seamen. The Admiral's side of the family had never been anything other than loyal Hanoverians. His father, also Cuthbert, was a Newcastle trader, respectable but not wealthy. He had been apprenticed to a merchant, and then set up in business for himself. When the business went bankrupt, his debtors were distillers, oil-men, soap-boilers and druggists.[3] His wife, Milcah, who hailed from near Appleby in Westmoreland, bore him ten children.[4]

The first seven of these were girls, of whom three survived into adulthood and ripe old age: Mary (1738–1815), Eleanor (1739–1835) and Dorothy (1741–1830). The last three were boys: Cuthbert, born on 26 September 1748; Wilfred, baptised on 11 October 1749, and

John, baptised on 1 June 1750.[5] The choice of the first two boys' names is interesting. Cuthbert was clearly a family name, but it harked back to a very ancient period, when St Cuthbert, the exemplar of the ascetic monk, was a reluctant Bishop of Lindisfarne. St Wilfred was a seventh-century contemporary: Bishop of Hexham, but of an entirely different stamp. While Cuthbert had been brought up in the spiritual, insular Irish tradition of Iona, Wilfred was a Romanist who sought to reflect God's glory in his own earthly splendour. It was Wilfred whose counsel prevailed at the Synod of Whitby in AD 664, spelling the end of the Irish church in Britain. The two naval brothers were, by all accounts,[6] as different as these two in character, but they were held together by the bond of a service which was at least not riven by doctrinal dispute.

Cuthbert Collingwood was born in a house in Newcastle on a street called the Side. It is a steep, narrow street that runs up from the Quayside at Sandhill, past Dog Leap Stairs, up under the shadow of the medieval Black Gate, and towards the fourteenth-century cathedral of St Nicholas, where Cuthbert was baptised. The houses were all torn down in the nineteenth century, at which time the Collingwoods' house belonged to a tobacco manufacturer, but above a doorway of the Victorian redbrick office which stands there now is a bust of Cuthbert, Lord Collingwood, which most natives of the city pass by without noticing. The house lay within a biscuit's toss of city walls which had last been manned against the Scots as recently as 1745. Just two years before Cuthbert was born, the last battle on British soil had been fought at Culloden, and Geordies (a name derived from the army nickname King George's Men) would have been well aware that one of the prime objectives of the Young Pretender's attempted invasion of England was to strangle the coal trade between Newcastle and London by taking that city.

Newcastle in 1748 was still essentially a medieval city. At its heart lay the 'new' castle built by William the Conqueror's son Robert in 1080, after ten years of rebellion and destruction had laid waste most of the northern counties. For the next six hundred years Newcastle was a border town, garrisoned by the King's troops against the threat of invasion from Scotland. In 1644 it held out under siege for three months before being taken by Parliamentary troops, and for two years after that the counties of Northumberland and Durham were occupied by Scottish forces.

In 1748 the city still had walls which entirely enclosed it, from Close Gate and Westgate in the west to Sand Gate in the east, from the River Tyne in the south to Newgate and Pilgrim Street in the north.[7] During Collingwood's lifetime most of the walls would disappear as the town boomed in the early wealth of the industrial revolution. Ancient houses would be torn down to build grand new streets; bridges would span wooded denes; street lights, mains water and sewers would appear. Cuthbert would miss most of it.

In 1748 the castle dungeon was still being used as the county gaol, where prisoners were chained to the walls and exhibited by the gaoler for twopence a piece. The Side, where the Collingwoods lived, was close enough to the Quayside, an infamous haunt of 'coarse and impudent wenches',[8] to be primarily mercantile. It was 'from one end to the other filled with shops of merchants, goldsmiths, milliners, and upholsterers'.[9] The Quayside itself was permanently ranged with vessels of every kind: keels, which carried coal from upriver down to sea-going colliers near the river's mouth at Shields; coasters, barges, sloops, fishing cobles and ferry boats. From the bottom of the Side, beneath the towering walls of the castle, a single bridge spanned the river to Gateshead and the Great North Road. This ancient bridge, like that of medieval London, was still lined with shops and houses. Across it, once a week, the South Mail coach would come, 'guarded by a man before on horseback with a drawn sword and, behind, by another with a charged blunderbuss'.[10]

Since 1711 Newcastle had boasted a newspaper: the *Courant*, joined by the *Journal* in 1739. Newspapers would be read by subscribers, very often shared amongst the patrons of dozens of coffee houses (more numerous even than today), and merchants kept a very close eye on news from across the world. Regional papers of the eighteenth century were necessarily less parochial in outlook than their modern equivalents. Parliamentary debates were frequently reported in great detail. In the week Collingwood was born in 1748 the paper contained dispatches from St Petersburg, Rome, Dresden, Stettin and elsewhere, wherever there were British interests – which indeed spread across the world.[11] There was a report that nineteen privateers had sailed from 'Havannah', and there was anticipation that peace might soon be signed with France and Spain at Aix-la-Chapelle. The paper also contained news that locusts had appeared in Orkney, and that at the Assembly Room in Durham there was to be a concert on the Cymbalum, the only instrument of its kind in England. There were advertisements too: for Daffy's Elixir and Dr Bateman's Pectoral Drops.

Newcastle was on the cusp of great things. Although the town had been shipping coal to London for hundreds of years, the engineering achievements that would liberate the region's latent wealth were in their barest infancy, supporting a population of only twenty thousand people and as yet untarnished by industrial pollution, labour strikes and unemployment. John Wesley, building in Newcastle the second Methodist chapel in England in 1742, liked it very much: 'If I did not believe there was another world I should spend all my summers here.'[12] Coal was plentiful and still easy to win at shallow depths: Daniel Defoe reported his impressions of 'Mountains of Coal' to an ignorant London audience. Getting the coal to the river was another matter: for miles around, the countryside was laced with wooden wagon ways, the coal hauled by horses across the world's first 'railway' bridges and embankments to reach the Tyne and the Wear. The North's first coking plant had just been opened at Chester-le-Street, and where Thomas Newcomen's 'atmospheric' steam engines were in use, they were used for pumping water: either out of mines, or from streams into millponds to keep water-wheels turning.

Coal export from the River Tyne was still primarily aimed at the domestic market in London. Its use as the power to drive the steam age would have to wait for developments in steam engineering and iron-making technology. The lush pastures and easily tilled glacial soils of Northumberland's hills and plains, for so long neglected because of border warfare, had yet to become, as they soon would, the most productive land on the planet. And the region's greatest resource, its engineers, were either infants or had not been born. The main impetus behind these developments would be war.

Apart from twenty years of relative peace during the reigns of George I and George II, the major powers of Europe had been in more or less constant conflict during the eighteenth century. France's chief area of interest was its trading colonies in the West Indies, America and Canada, settlements in India, and the protection of its trade in the Mediterranean. Spain was concerned primarily with South America and the West Indies. The Dutch also had colonies in the West Indies, but more importantly in the East: India and the Spice Islands. Great Britain, reliant even more heavily than its rivals on maritime links, had interests in all those areas. The result was a series of wars, some under the guise of dynastic squabbles, in which these four great powers sought to keep their existing investments, and expand their interests at the inevitable expense of the others. At various times these wars involved all the other powers of Europe:

Denmark, Sweden, Russia, Austria, all linked by complicated familial and political ties, and all seeking to exploit the resources increasingly available through international maritime expansion.

Exploration, colonisation and trade were all primarily naval achievements, and it was through naval power that such trading colonies were protected. North America and Canada offered tobacco and fur and a growing export market; the West Indies were exploited for sugar, and to the south there was gold in seemingly limitless quantities. To the east, from India and beyond, there were spices and silks. Increasingly, too, Africa was being exploited for its minerals and for its supply of slaves, to be employed in America and the West Indies on plantations.

In 1756, when Cuthbert Collingwood was eight, a simmering conflict with France over tensions in Canada and New England was brought to a European boil: by threatening invasion of England, France aimed to tie down a British navy consisting of three hundred ships and seventy thousand fighting men.[13] Although France's plans caused panic in Britain, the attempt was a feint. A more convenient target was selected. In 1756 the French fleet at Toulon carried an invasion army to Menorca and captured the island. What must the eight-year-old Collingwood have thought when it was reported that Admiral John Byng, having failed to prevent the invasion, was to be court-martialled and shot for cowardice? Twenty years later Collingwood would twice be court-martialled himself.

It can hardly have been Byng's fate that decided Collingwood on a naval career. As the oldest son he might be tempted, or expected, to follow his father into business as a trader, except that the business was going bust. He could otherwise have joined the merchant marine, where he might travel the world and where the pay, if one survived, was good. He must have had many opportunities to talk to sailors along the Quayside in Newcastle and it is hard to imagine that exotic items brought from across the world failed to stir his imagination.

There was no great naval connection in the family, although Cuthbert's mother's sister had married Richard Braithwaite, who was a frigate captain. Something, though, must have enthused the three brothers: Wilfred, the second son, was to join the navy too. He served with distinction alongside his older brother and their friend Horatio Nelson in the West Indies, before dying at the age of thirty-eight. John joined the customs service and outlived the rest of his family, dying in 1841 at the age of ninety-one.

Perhaps it was the events of the year 1759 that determined them, the year Collingwood turned eleven. This may have been the year[14] that he attended the Royal Grammar School at Newcastle, along with the two Scott brothers who later became Lords Eldon and Stowell. Known in their day as the Head School, its headmaster was Hugh Moises, a hard but highly capable teacher whose traditional curriculum was classically based: 'Latin was the meat course and salads and desserts were few.'[15] It was drummed into young boys using a combination of authority, passion and flogging. It has been said by all of Collingwood's biographers that his character was formed under this determined administration, but the school's archivist insists that Collingwood did not attend for more than about six months. Unfortunately, all the school's records from that period have been lost during a series of relocations. Certainly Collingwood cannot have attended beyond the age of thirteen, because by then he was at sea with Captain Braithwaite.

The Year of Victories, as 1759 came to be called, was a turning point for the fortunes of the British in the Seven Years' War with France. Its architect was Admiral Lord George Anson, famous for his circumnavigation of the globe in the 1740s and for his naval victories against the French and Spanish, and subsequently First Lord of the Admiralty. By 1759 he had engineered a service that was the largest industrial organisation in the western world and so efficient, despite its many shortcomings, that it could operate in every potential theatre of war simultaneously.[16]

In May it was reported that a British force operating in the West Indies, having failed to take and hold Martinique, had successfully landed on Guadeloupe and captured it from the French. In August the Duke of Brunswick defeated the French army at Minden. That same month, rumours of an invasion fleet had British squadrons patrolling the Channel ports and French Atlantic coast, and the famous Cornishman Admiral Boscawen, reacting to a report that a French squadron had left Toulon and been seen making its way through the Strait of Gibraltar, pursued them into Lagos Bay on the south-west tip of Portugal and defeated them, taking three ships and burning two others.

There was another, less decisive victory in September when Admiral Pocock won a bloody face-off with a French squadron off Pondicherry in south-east India. In October came dramatic news that General Wolfe's expedition up the St Lawrence River had finally come to fruition with the storming of the Heights of Abraham and subsequent capture of Quebec. Wolfe had died heroically.

Finally, in November, Admiral Hawke had come up with his French counterpart Conflans in Quiberon Bay off the west coast of France. In a gale of shocking force, and navigating through treacherous shoals in almost reckless pursuit, Hawke's squadron drove three French ships on shore and two others foundered, while one was captured – her value, in accordance with naval tradition, being divided among the victorious crews as prize money.

One by one, though not necessarily in chronological order, these victories were reported in the *Newcastle Courant*. Eighteenth-century news was always dislocated from events by a combination of tide, weather, distance and a variety of other fates. Nevertheless, the cumulative effect of these victories on the public was electrifying, and it is easy to imagine how the eleven-year-old Cuthbert and his younger brothers might decide they wanted to emulate their heroes.

Hero-worship was not the only reason for a young man to go to war. To begin with, no family with money or land would let the oldest son join the navy: there was too great a risk of him dying and leaving no one to inherit title or business. But Collingwood senior, who let both his oldest sons join, had little in the way of business to pass on, given what in the eighteenth century was the liability of three adult sisters to be provided for. In such impoverished circumstances few other professions were open to them. The law, the army and business all required capital. A career in the navy had its dangers, but it required very little in the way of financial input, and had at least the surety of a career structure. Boys who left home young cost nothing to keep, less to educate.

Apart from the glory that might one day come his way, there is no doubt that a young boy would have heard of prize money: the value of a captured enemy ship shared by the entire victorious crew or crews, but distributed very much in favour of the officers.[17] Collingwood himself would earn little in the way of prize money until Trafalgar, but he died leaving more than £160,000 to his daughters.[18] It may also be that the prospect of a life at sea, full of adventure, seemed more attractive than the favours of his headmaster, just as today the prospect of a career of fame and fortune, however illusory, seduces small boys into believing that a scout from a Premiership football club is watching them practise in the park. Nor should one forget aspects of eighteenth-century culture that seem faintly strange today: duty and service. Collingwood may very well have grown up asking himself how he might best serve his country.

In 1761 Cuthbert's father paid £30 for him to volunteer, probably as a servant, to Captain Braithwaite aboard *Shannon*, a 600-ton 28-gun frigate (very like Jack Aubrey's beloved *Surprise*). This type of ship, known as a 'jackass' frigate, was by this time considered too small to be of much use as a fighting ship. It was a true ship (that is, it had three masts, was square-rigged, and was commanded by a post-captain) and although it might have sailing qualities that could be described as nimble, its armament was too light for it to take on anything much larger than itself. *Shannon* had an internal length of about 110 feet and a beam of just over 30 feet. She carried fourteen nine-pounder guns to a side on a single deck, throwing a broadside weight – the mass of shot she could discharge in one round from one side – of 126lbs. This compared to the broadside of a first-rate line of battle ship, of something over 1,500lbs in a single discharge. *Shannon's* crew numbered about two hundred, of which eighteen were officers, divided into those who held commissions (the captain and two lieutenants) and those who held warrants: master, boatswain, gunner, carpenter, surgeon and so on. Their mates, and the four midshipmen, were ratings, without warrant or commission.

As a volunteer, the thirteen-year-old Collingwood had a theoretical career laid out for him. He was both an apprentice seaman and an apprentice officer. To begin with he would be taught to hand, reef and sail: to learn the ropes (more than thirty miles of them, even in a frigate) and their very technical, sometimes arcane names: shrouds, ratlines, cross catharpins, futtocks, timenoguys and the like. Most future officers would be given into the care of a 'mother' or 'sea-daddy', an old and preferably wise seaman of infinite experience, who would teach them the niceties of knotting and splicing, sewing and shipboard etiquette, and protect them from the worst of any bullying that went on. Forty years later one of Collingwood's own midshipmen, Robert Hay, described the process:

It was my lot to fall into the hands of Jack Gillies, than whom a handier fellow never left the Emerald Isle. The cutting out and making of jackets, shirts and trousers, the washing of them when soiled, and the mending of them neatly when they began to fail, took precedence ... From the knotting of a rope yarn to the steering of a ship under bare poles in a tiffoon, Jack excelled in all.[19]

Collingwood did not instantly become a midshipman the day he arrived in *Shannon*. Midshipman was a rating, not a commission. To become midshipmen (variously known as snotties, monkeys or more significantly young gentlemen) and thus have the right to walk on the holy quarterdeck, wear a dirk and order men to be punished, volunteers had to show that they were capable of bearing the responsibility that went with the rating. A mid' would have to earn respect from men old enough to be his father. Collingwood would be at sea for five years before he was rated midshipman.

His first biographer, and son-in-law, G. L. Newnham-Collingwood, told an old family story of Collingwood's first days after he joined *Shannon*. One of the lieutenants found him crying from homesickness. Although lieutenants were duty-bound to toughen up their recruits, this man comforted Collingwood, and in return was taken to his sea chest and given a large piece of plum cake.[20] It is possible that this lieutenant was William Smith, who until 1758 had been gunner in the *Alcide* before being promoted into *Shannon*.[21] This was an unusual though not a unique move.

A lieutenancy was the first promotional step between midshipman and admiral, the long ladder of an officer's career. A lieutenant's commission could only be awarded as a result of the man passing a stiff examination in seamanship and navigation before the Admiralty Board and on him having served six years at sea, two of them in the navy as midshipman or master's mate. Even then, especially in peacetime, such was the competition for places that many aspiring officers, having passed their exams, remained midshipmen or master's mates for their entire careers. If they were lucky, in the time-honoured and well-understood tradition of the navy, midshipmen became lieutenants, then commanders, then post-captains and finally, if they lived long enough, admirals.

Each step up the ladder called for a number of attributes. One was ability: not just seamanship, but man-management skills which, in a man-of-war where death was a constant prospect, were vital. If men were not prepared to follow an officer's orders because he was stupid or incompetent or tyrannical, they could make his life very difficult indeed. Another was 'interest', or patronage. It was hard to advance solely by merit. Some sort of influence was essential in so competitive a career. The influence might be familial or political or both, or it might radiate from one's own commanding officer. A third requirement was combat. A spectacular wound acquired in action, leading a boarding party, or being given command of a captured enemy ship were persuasive badges of merit. This may well be how William Smith advanced from being gunner – a warrant officer with no commission – to lieutenant, though his promotion would have required him to pass the examination and have his promotion officially endorsed by the Admiralty. Petty officers and warrant officers could be disrated; commissioned lieutenants could not, except by court-martial.

After his lieutenancy, an officer would hope to be made master and commander, probably in charge of a sloop. He was then called captain by courtesy, but did not appear on the holy list of post-captains. Once an officer became a post-captain, his position was almost inviolate. From playing at snakes and ladders, he was now on a conveyor belt which led to the hoisting of an admiral's flag, and which only death or disgrace could rob him of.

Within a year of Collingwood joining *Shannon*, George III had acceded to the throne, and a year after that, in 1763, peace was signed with France. With no prospect of war ahead, and with no influence other than that of a frigate captain, Collingwood's chances of promotion were slim: he would spend fourteen years learning the ropes. He did so in six different ships. Only a few months after joining *Shannon*, during which time he saw service, but no action, in Atlantic and Home waters, escorting convoys to the Baltic, he joined another ship. Braithwaite transferred into *Gibraltar*, an even smaller frigate of 24 guns, and took Collingwood with him as one of his followers. *Gibraltar* must have been known to Collingwood by reputation, because in 1759, during the Year of Victories, she had been the ship which first sighted the enemy squadrons before both Lagos and Quiberon Bay. It gave her a certain cachet.

In *Gibraltar* Collingwood saw service again in Home and Atlantic waters, and also made his first voyage to the Mediterranean. Britain had bases at Gibraltar and Menorca, returned under the terms of the Treaty of Paris which had ended the Seven Years' War and confirmed France's withdrawal from Canada, Nova Scotia, Dominica, Grenada and Tobago.

We know very little of Collingwood's early experiences; his first letter home dates from 1776. It is not even known what leave, if any, he had during that time, or whether he saw his family at all. In all probability he did not, but one experience from this time was recorded. Many years later, when Collingwood was a senior captain, once again serving in the Mediterranean, he was stationed in Corsica. In a letter home he reflected that the last time he had visited that island, serving on board *Gibraltar*, it had left a lasting impression on him:

> A more miserable prospect than that island presents is scarce to be conceived of, the most savage country, barren brown mountains,

rearing their rugged, wrinkled, heads to the skies: the valleys produce a little corn, bad wine and olives, but the barbarians who inhabit there have not industry to cultivate any of them. Their manners are savage, their ignorance is gross, but the part of their character of most consequence to us is the inveterate hatred they on all occasions express to the English. Every man of them travels in the country with a rifle, a gun and a dagger, with which he kills with admirable dexterity such game or Englishmen as he may chance to meet in his way – the ships of war have lost several men stabbed by those fellows – and do it with the same composure that an old butcher kills a pig. The *Gibraltar* had four seamen stabbed the last time they were there, three of them died.[22]

By 1766, still in *Gibraltar*, Collingwood had been rated as a mid-shipman, in his eighteenth year. This reflects the lack of opportunity open to a sailor in peace time rather than a lack of talent. His skills as a seaman were already maturing. There was nothing simple about sailing a square-rigged ship, even one as comparatively small as a jackass frigate. To begin with, knowing a ship's position and how to calculate its course was a hybrid art somewhere between the rarefied mathematics of spherical trigonometry and the finely honed intuition that allowed dead-reckoning to be estimated from a log towed behind the ship every hour, a rough calculation of wind speed and direction, and a guess at leeway, currents and tides. At that very time the voyages of James Cook to the Pacific were just beginning to show that chronometers could give an accurate idea of longitude, but even so reading the positions of sun and moon relied on clear skies. Even the sextant was a relatively recent invention.

All square-rigged vessels, and especially men-of-war, were a compromise design. Frigates, especially, had to be fast and point as close to the wind as possible, though no square-rigged ship could sail closer than sixty-seven degrees to the direction of the wind – regardless of leeway, the tendency for the ship to drift sideways. But to hold enough stores for a long commission a frigate had to be broad in the beam, and to access the smallest harbours she needed a shallow draught. Neither of these factors enhanced her sailing qualities. Nor did the fact that in order to be an effective ship of war she had to function as a mobile battery, mounting as many guns as her frame would take, with as low a centre of gravity as possible.

All competent sailors had a deep knowledge of these factors and how they affected each ship. And each ship, with its particular arrangement of masts, sails and rigging, responded differently. Square-rigged ships generally sailed best with the wind on their quarter, coming from behind midships, but not directly astern. With the wind coming from forward of midships the square rig was a disadvantage: fore-and-aft-rigged ships, like modern racing yachts, are at their best with the wind forward, because their sails act like aerofoils pulling them through the water, and the best fore-and-aft-rigged ships can sail very close to the wind indeed. With a square rig it was necessary to make the sails as stiff as possible to mimic this effect. The leading or weather edge of the sail was pulled as tight as possible with bowlines, while the lee edge of the sail was pulled tight with tacks. The yards from which the sails hung were braced round as close as possible to a fore-and-aft position, and under those conditions the ship could point upwind, tacking or wearing as necessary to gain sea mileage.

The thirty or so miles of rope and cordage that a frigate employed in sailing had two main functions. The standing rigging supported and braced the masts from the front, back and sides. The running rigging was used to manage the sails. Each of the three masts had a possible ten or so sails: on the main mast, for example, the lowest sail was called the main course or main sail. Above that was the main topsail, above that the main topgallant, then the main royal. Extra sails called studding sails might be bent to booms which could be extended on either side of the yards. The foremast was smaller but with a similar arrangement. The mizen mast bore a fore-and-aft sail – the mizen – and above that a topsail and topgallant sail. Forward of the foremast, jibs (hung from stays between the foremast and the bowsprit) were rigged fore and aft, and below the bowsprit extra sails called spritsails could be rigged.

Every combination of these sails, their effects under every type of condition and their relative merits, had to be familiar to any experienced sailor – most able-seamen would be able to sail a frigate with perfect confidence. Collingwood was no exception, and as a midshipman part of his training was learning to manage the two hundred men on the ship as they executed all her possible manoeuvres, each of which required more or less perfect co-ordination to accomplish successfully. Failure to carry out a manoeuvre competently could result in shipwreck or – possibly worse – humiliation. The next, the supreme level of naval competence and skill, Collingwood did not acquire until he was forty-five years of age: the unimaginable, to a modern mind, difficulty of sailing a ship and fighting her at the same time in battle.

The year after he was rated midshipman Collingwood transferred into *Liverpool*, another 28-gun frigate, and by 1770 had been made master's mate, a senior rating for a prospective officer looking towards his lieutenancy. A master's mate was a midshipman with special responsibilities for navigation, assisting the sailing master (the senior warrant officer) with bearings, charts and laying courses. But in addition to these duties he would have responsibilities for a division of the ship's company and would take watches. Fortunately a copy of Collingwood's own log during his time in *Liverpool* remains in the possession of his family. It is the first of his writings that survives. As a narrative it lacks pace, to be sure, but its language, drily understated, and its bare recording of hurricanes and floggings, endless tacking and wearing, taking on stores and mending rigging, preserves an image of eighteenth century naval life that has great vitality.

The first entry is dated Saturday 8 December 1770. *Liverpool* had passed through the Strait of Gibraltar and was heading north-east towards the Balearic Islands. At sea, each day was given a full page of the log, organised into two twelve- hour sections and beginning, in accordance with naval tradition, at noon. Against each hour is a record of the ship's speed, her course, the wind direction, and any remarks. It is laid out with a draughtsman's precision, for Collingwood had an artist's eye as well as a scientific mind. Thus:

> **Saturday 8th December 1770**
> 1 [o'clock] 3 [knots] 4 [fathoms] [course] NE [wind] ENE Fresh gales and cloudy weather.

Later that day:

> Fresh gales and mizzling rain, handed the mizen top sail, and wore ship.

When in port, Collingwood wrote entries in a more diaristic style, recording the mostly administrative events of the ship's life. On 10 December *Liverpool* arrived at Port Mahon, in Menorca. It was probably Collingwood's first visit there. He may have been to Menorca in *Gibraltar*, but on this voyage he recorded pilotage information such as bearings to prominent landmarks, and drew an elegant map of the harbour, with the names of various islands and watering places marked with depth soundings. These suggest it was a new experience for him. On 11 December he recorded that they opened a cask of beef which contained 190 pieces (two short). They hove up the first bower anchor and let go the second bower in its place. The ship's company were employed in watering (filling barrels of fresh water from the nearest springs) and mending the topgallant sails after a recent gale. On the 13th they weighed anchor and set sail for Algier Bay, where they bought bullocks and Collingwood had time to make a careful map of that harbour with soundings.

And so the entries run, day after day. On Christmas Day Cape de Gatte was sighted WNW ten leagues off, and the slings of the cross-jack yard broke and had to be mended. New Year was spent in Gibraltar Bay attending to the rigging and taking in stores and water. Three weeks later they were back in Port Mahon, firing a 28-gun salute for the Queen's birthday. On this visit they careened the ship. This was a major exercise, and Mahon one of the few harbours where it could be carried out. It involved removing everything from the ship: rigging, stores, iron and shingle ballast, guns, top masts, hen coops, the lot. This took twelve days, during which time Alexander Dunn and his mate George (Collingwood does not record their rank, but they were either ordinary or able seamen) absented themselves from duty and were given eighteen and twelve lashes apiece. Careening started on the 31st. To accomplish this, the ship, with only her lower masts left standing, was heeled over by means of cables wound on to capstans mounted on shore, to expose half her bottom. The hull was scraped clean of weed and barnacles, checked for rot, and her copper (if she was coppered) repaired where necessary. Then she was hove upright again, turned round, and the other side would be cleaned. By 5 March she was rerigged, refitted, and with stores taken on ready to sail again.

Britain was not at war, so there are many entries in which foreign ships are encountered and 'spoke to'. Collingwood's remarks are generally confined to the weather, to punishments, and the mostly humdrum business of everyday life aboard a frigate. At Leghorn

(Livorno) he was amused to see a Tuscan man-of-war fire a salute of thirteen guns to a chapel of St Mary as she left port: a 'remarkable instance of blind superstition by which they implore the protection of the Virgin', he wrote in the log.

By now, at the age of twenty-two, Collingwood was a highly experienced seaman. His remarks are intelligent and he takes a keen interest in all aspects of navigation as well as sailing. There are silhouettes of every significant cape or port entrance, and after one entry there is a remarkable drawing of a 'machine' which he had thought up. It seems to be a jury-rigged rudder, to be constructed if the ship lost steerage. It involves an intricate arrangement of ropes, spars and planks, and comes with a detailed description of its practical applications. This was precisely the sort of resourceful, thinking seaman that the navy hoped to bring on.

In March there was a semblance of excitement when *Liverpool* entered Villa Franca (now Villefranche-sur-Mer, near Nice), firing an eleven-gun salute, and one of her men noticed that a Swedish snow (a large unarmed two-masted trading ship) had acquired the barge of an English man-of-war. It had apparently, but suspiciously, been found floating in the Gulf of Lyons. A request for its return was refused, so Braithwaite sent an armed party to retrieve it. This was British naval diplomacy in action: straightforward, effective, and allowing of no compromise.

The lack of real action must have been frustrating. Apart from there being no opportunity for prize money or promotion, this sort of commission involved tedious cruising between the ports of the western Mediterranean with little excitement. Things were enlivened in August 1771 when *Liverpool* visited Lisbon, only to have a gun from Belum Castle on the River Tagus fire two shots at her, one of which passed between the mizen and main masts: 'an insult which the British flag never before received without satisfaction'. Some months later, at Cadiz, they were refused fresh water and stores: 'an absolute infraction of the treaty which at present subsists between His Majesty and the Spanish court'. How much this precocious pomposity was Collingwood's own, and how much was part of the culture of the service is hard to say. It was a trait he carried to his death. The last frisson of this commission was felt when *Liverpool* ran aground in a very severe gale upon Diamond Rock, just outside Cadiz. They managed to 'throw all aback' and get her off. Without a war, this was about as much excitement as a sailor could expect.

CHAPTER TWO

Out of all patience
1772-1777

If Mediterranean cruising had its dull sides, it must have seemed like
heaven compared to Collingwood's next posting. In 1772, under
Captain Roddam (another Northumbrian and friend of the family)
Cuthbert went aboard *Lennox*, the Portsmouth guard ship. *Lennox*
was a 74-gun two-decker whose crew had distinguished themselves
by capturing the Spanish *Princessa* in 1739. In peace time the guard
ship was something of a plum posting. Duties included working on
other ships in harbour, and plying boats from one to another. Benefits
included all the delights of port, regular pay, and not having to keep
watches, which at sea prevented seamen and officers of the watch
from ever having more than four hours' sleep. On top of these advantages, Collingwood had his brother Wilfred with him. But to a pair

of zealous young would-be officers, desperate for active service and the chance of promotion, the guard ship must have seemed a dead end.

In February 1773 Collingwood was sent to Sheerness with a party of eighteen seamen from *Lennox* to join *Portland*, a 50-gun two-decker in the process of being fitted out for a voyage to the West Indies. In the next three weeks he was joined by carpenters, painters, gunners and boatswains as the intricate operation of rigging and arming the ship went on. By the beginning of March *Portland* had anchored off the Downs in East Kent. Sheltered from the worst of the North Sea by the Goodwin Sands, this anchorage provided a rendezvous for hundreds of merchantmen and men-of-war joining convoys for America, the Baltic and the Indies (East and West).

This was Collingwood's first voyage to the Americas; he would not return to the Mediterranean until 1795, more than twenty years later. His log makes it clear that the first part of the passage was swift: three days from the Downs to the Lizard, where he noted passing the Eddystone Lighthouse (rebuilt by John Smeaton in 1759, the Year of Victories). On 13 March, far out in the Atlantic, the captain ordered the ship's company to clear for action so they could conduct a great gun exercise, followed by small arms practice. This is the only entry recording such an exercise in either the *Liverpool* or *Portland* logs. It was not in peace-time conditions that Collingwood developed that passion for gunnery which later earned him the record for broadside firing, and which won the battle of Trafalgar.

On 22 March *Portland* arrived at Madeira where, appropriately, she took on wine, and where Collingwood made a delicate pencil drawing of the island. She sailed again on the 30th, and the next day Mathew Hayes, Thomas Bullard and William Davies were punished with twelve lashes each for the guilty pleasures of their last night ashore in Funchal. Ten days later Collingwood wrote of a tragic accident: for the first time his facility for dry but telling expression springs from the page fully formed:

> Mr Gold, midshipman, fell from the gangway overboard, and every means to save him were abortive, thus died an amiable young man, respected and beloved most by those who best knew him. Fresh breezes and hazy weather.[1]

On 11 April, when the ship's supply of beer ran out, wine was served to the men, as was the navy's custom in tropical waters. These were days of pure blue-water sailing with the ship averaging seven knots and 150 miles a day on the back of the north-east trade winds. On the 17th, forty days out from the Downs, the lookout sighted Domenica, one of the Leeward Islands, and *Portland* anchored in Prince Rupert's Bay. The midshipmen and marines were sent to cut wood, and two days later they sailed again, west and north, across the Caribbean Sea. As they passed each island in turn, Collingwood recorded meticulous observations on pilotage, and drew pencil silhouettes so that he might recognise them again. On 2 May they passed the south-east corner of Jamaica and arrived at Port Royal, where they were piloted into the harbour by 'a negro'. They fired a fifteen-gun salute for the commander of the Windward Islands station, Vice-Admiral Rodney, who responded with his own salute and very decently sent the ship's company a puncheon of rum. Whether or not the officers of the *Portland* drank the traditional West Indies toast, to 'a bloody war and a sickly season' was not recorded by Collingwood. It reflected the high mortality rate among sailors in the West Indies, and the chance of rapid promotion for those who survived.

One of the first and most unpleasant tasks in port was to convene a court-martial, which could only happen when there was a sufficient number of post-captains present. *Portland*'s boatswain, Harris, had been accused of embezzlement, but the court found him innocent of the charge and acquitted him. Not so the boatswain of the sloop *Diligence*. He was found guilty of drunkenness and neglect, and dismissed the service. The same charge against a common seaman would have been dealt with by his captain and the cat o' nine tails in the privacy of his own ship. A popular or useful boatswain might have got away with being temporarily disrated. This man was obviously no great loss to the service.

During the next three weeks in Port Royal, twenty seamen and marines of the *Portland* were punished, each with twelve lashes, for a variety of familiar misdemeanours including theft, drunkenness, disobedience and neglect of duty. What seems unbearably brutal to modern sensibilities must be put into context. Similar offences ashore could attract the death penalty, a sentence prescribed in many of the Articles of War but very rarely meted out; usually for aggravated theft, or for sodomy. Sailors themselves, when they made complaints against authority and 'the system', sometimes cited brutal tyrannising authority, but not what they considered a just punishment, seen as an absolute requirement in a service in which efficiency and obedience were life and death matters. However, Collingwood cannot even then have been overly impressed with his captain's use of the cat for, once in command, he would establish a regime that required very little corporal punishment, and indirectly led to a widespread acceptance that harsh physical punishment reflected a failure of management by officers.

On 26 May *Portland* was still at Port Royal, and now Collingwood's log provides an explanation for the previous acquittal of her boatswain. A second court-martial was held, and this time the defendant was Thomas Bradley, accuser of Harris, the boatswain. He was charged with false accusation, and with endeavouring to suborn witnesses to prove his allegations. The next day, in line with the seriousness with which the service viewed such a crime, he was sentenced to three hundred lashes – little short of a death sentence, and probably thoroughly approved of by all his shipmates. Although Collingwood did not record the aftermath, it was usual to carry out such a sentence in doses, under the eye of the ship's surgeon, so that the offender should survive to see the full sentence out.

On 1 June Collingwood recorded blandly that he was discharged from *Portland* and sent into *Princess Amelia*, under Captain Berkeley, in order to 'navigate her to England'. This sounds rather as if he had been given an acting warrant as master, though there is no available confirmation of this. Although his log states the bare fact of the matter, Collingwood must have left with some regret for his shipmates: he made a full-page drawing in his log showing a melancholy sailor waving sadly at a departing ship.

Before he had a chance to discern the *Princess Amelia*'s sailing qualities, he recorded another death (possibly from fever) of one of the *Portland*'s lieutenants. These are the words of the same man who was to cry openly in front of Lord Chancellor Eldon on the Strand, nearly thirty years later:

> AM. Departed this life Mr. Samuel Price 3rd lieutenant, who for his gentleness of disposition, equanimity, vigilance and unwearied attention to the Service, was universally regretted. Every action of his life was guided by justice, candour and honour; the years of a youth were enriched with knowledge equal to long experience; he discharged his duty to his country like an officer, and to all mankind as their friend; no wonder he lived beloved, and died lamented.[2]

Princess Amelia sailed from Port Royal on 15 June, north-west towards Florida, and then up the east coast of America to Newfoundland, where she arrived off Cape Race at the end of July. This was the normal route home from the West Indies, taking advantage of westerly winds. After an uneventful passage (except for the loss of another man overboard) she arrived back in England in August.

Two other important events occurred in 1773, while Collingwood was ashore. Both would have a profound effect on his career. One was the first meeting (though we do not know when or where it took place) between Collingwood, aged twenty-five, and Horatio Nelson, aged fifteen.[3] In this year Nelson took part in the famous expedition to the North Pole during which he had the mythic encounter with the polar bear, and later went to the East Indies and nearly died on the way home. Despite the difference in years, they immediately struck up a close friendship: Collingwood tall and imposing with a long pigtail tied in a queue behind, a seaman of twelve years' experience, but reserved and shy; Nelson, still little more than a child with just three years at sea, slight in build and sickly, but already having decided he would become a hero and already possessing the magnetic personality that would later prompt so many men to die for him.

The other event was the tipping of a consignment of imported tea into the harbour at Boston on 16 December by a group of young men dressed as Indians: the Sons of Liberty. Boston today, as it always has been, is the most European of American cities, literary, strongly Irish and Italian, but essentially Anglophile. Its Common might be Hyde Park, and its Victorian-looking streets with their elegant cast-iron lamps are reminiscent of Bayswater. Above all though, it was and is a mercantile city, sitting at the head of its grand harbour and best approached from the sea. Unlike Mahon it is physically unrecognisable from the town that Collingwood knew. Two churches, a cemetery, the Old State House and Faneuil Hall are among the few buildings which remain from that period, but they are dwarfed by mirror-glass skyscrapers (a term borrowed from the navy), high-level roads, and even by five-storey redbrick apartment blocks that date from the late nineteenth century. Long Wharf, which in 1773 led from the bottom of Beacon Hill some eight hundred yards out into the harbour, is much stunted, and the vessels which tie up here are more likely to be jet-powered catamarans ferrying trippers to Cape Cod than sailing ships filled with English tea and coal.

At the start of the American Revolutionary War, Boston was a peninsula, indeed all but an island, at the mouth of the Charles River. Across the harbour was Charlestown, these days a very desirable and old-fashioned hill district at the bottom of which is a US Navy dockyard. The oldest floating warship in the world is berthed here: the USS *Constitution*, launched in 1797 to a design which made her the most formidable ship in her class: a 44-gun frigate with an exceptionally strong internal bracing structure which meant she was unsinkable by any British ship of similar size and, in the war of 1812, earned her the nickname Old Ironsides. Once a year on 4 July, to confirm her commission and to remind Britons that she beat them in that war, she is paraded round the harbour.

When Collingwood first went to America she had no navy. She was a colony, or group of colonies, of the British Empire, protected by the ships of the Royal Navy. The reasons behind the Revolutionary War are complex, though they can be summed up as the outcome of a relationship rather like that of a parent to an adolescent child: resentment at the cost of upkeep (an army of ten thousand men) on one side, and on the other, frustration at being asked to pay for that upkeep (the Stamp Duty) without an increased role in family decision-making: no taxation without representation, was the famous cry. One thing is certain. The trigger that started the war was the imposition of a tax on tea imports that led to the infamous Tea Party. Things got out of hand. The Continental Congress was formed to provide a forum for negotiation and protest in response to the Boston Port Bill (known to Americans as the Intolerable Acts), which amounted to a naval blockade. The bloody-minded intransigence of powerful interests on both sides, in the face of large numbers of conciliatory voices, was to lead to armed conflict.

Newspapers of the time, though lacking a sense of historical perspective, reflect the immediacy (and irony) of the events that culminated in all-out war. One of these was the *Boston and Country Gazette and Journal* – a republican organ. The Tea Party was reported defiantly in its pages in December 1773. In January 1774 another consignment of tea was refused entry, but otherwise the paper contained a normal assortment of items: best Newcastle coals were on sale at ten dollars per chaldron. A 'very likely negro man' was to be sold for want of employ,[4] and 'a woman with a good breast of milk wou'd take a child to suckle'.[5] In May the *Gazette* was taking a much more serious tone, when it reported the reaction in London to the publication of the Boston Port Bill and the impending blockade:

> Concerning public matters, I am sorry to say that Things are going from bad to worse, and a Breach between Great Britain and her colonies seems approaching very fast. This accursed tea is the very Match that is appointed to set fire to a Train of gun Powder.[6]

On 23 May the editor of the *Gazette* himself wrote, 'We consider this an attack not just on Boston, but on the whole continent', and on 30 May he called the British measures 'rash, impolitic and vindictive'.

The main loyalist paper, representing both British and American interests in that part of the population (mainly merchants and first-generation immigrants) who deplored the prospect of a breach, was the *Massachusetts and Boston Weekly Gazette: the Newsletter*. It had begun the new year carrying an advertisement that had an air of flippant levity:

JUST ARRIVED FROM THE MOON
In the ship Airy Castle,
One hundred and fifty likely servants of both sexes; among whom
are, lovers, schemers, horse-jockeys, sail-jobbers &c. Enquire of – [7]

And in the same pages was a private advertisement …

MADE THEIR ESCAPE
An husband's affections. They disappeared immediately after seeing
his wife with her hands unwashed at breakfast.

On Thursday 7 July 1774, among announcements of strayed cattle, a burglary, a body found floating in the harbour and notice of a husband wishing to apprehend the wife who had run off with all his money, the paper reported the arrival in Boston harbour of Vice-Admiral Graves in His Majesty's Ship *Preston*, of 50 guns. Cuthbert Collingwood, still a master's mate at the age of twenty-seven, had landed in the New World in a town virtually besieged by the Massachusetts militia. The British army garrison in Boston, under the overall command of General Thomas Gage, also the appointed governor of Massachusetts, was in an invidious position. A drain on the town's resources, and a very obviously resented presence, redcoats were subjected to the sort of harrying that occupying forces habitually suffer: knifings in dark alleys, muggings and thievings, and accusations, false or otherwise, of brutality that had of necessity to be punished for form's sake. Gage's need was for a decisive step by the British government. As he himself suggested, the only way to deal with the colonies was to 'lop them off as a rotten limb from the Empire, and leave them to themselves, or take effectual means to reduce them to lawful authority'.[8] Three thousand miles of ocean and political vacillation at home resulted in that decision, when it was finally made, being made too late.

Gage's temporary solution was to march his regiments off the peninsula along Boston Neck on periodic forays into the hinterland of Massachusetts: to relieve the febrile atmosphere of the town, to reconnoitre the countryside and, acting on intelligence, to look for and seize caches of arms (mostly supplied from France) that were being secreted at strategic locations by the militia. In turn, the republican element in the town reported all the redcoats' movements (and many of Gage's private intentions) back to the Provincial Congress at Concord, twenty miles away.

Vice-Admiral Graves, as senior commander of the naval contingent, had arrived in Boston to ensure the effectiveness of the blockade and support Gage. But the arrival of naval reinforcements in the shape of the two-decker *Boyne* (74 guns) and *Somerset* (64) later that year can only have increased republican resentment. Throughout the late autumn and winter of 1774 Collingwood witnessed the build-up to a war that no one wanted. As if to emphasise that the navy was now a target too, the *Newsletter* of 18 August reported that Nathaniel Corset, a seaman of the sloop *Lively*, had been found floating in the harbour. Out there in the countryside, in a landscape suited to guerrilla warfare rather than the neat manoeuvres of lines of troops, the movement of arms, munitions and militiamen under the noses of the redcoats stopped short of outright conflict, but only just. The Congress had also created a system of 'minute men', a local rapid response force which could put up to twelve thousand men in the field at a few hours' notice. It was useful practice for them.

In November 1774, having long realised that his force of three thousand men was too small, Gage wrote:

> If force is to be used at length, it must be a considerable one, for to begin with small numbers will encourage resistance, and not terrify; and will in the end cost more blood and treasure. A large force will terrify, and engage many to join you, a middling one will encourage resistance, and gain no friends.[9]

This was more or less the conclusion the government was coming to. George III had already decided his own mind, as he wrote to Lord North: 'The New England governments are in a state of rebellion, blows must decide whether they are to be subject to this country or independent.'[10]

In February 1775 Gage decided that staying in Boston would achieve nothing, but without orders he dithered. It was not until April that orders came from London that he should now act decisively: troop reinforcements were on their way. On the 8th prominent opposition leaders left the town. With the Provincial Congress about to adjourn and disperse, Gage finally mobilised his troops, and on 18 April they advanced across Boston Neck and marched north-west. Reconnoitring officers, being spotted by observers, gave the enemy notice and the rebel forces rose in response. The upshot was running battles – skirmishes really – at Lexington and Concord on 19 April, during which the rebels suffered a hundred casualties, the redcoats a humiliating three hundred.[11] These were the opening engagements of a war that would last until 1783 and give birth to the new American nation. Over the next few days twenty thousand militiamen surrounded Boston, completely cutting it off except by sea.

The army's reinforcements arrived in May. By this time disastrous tensions had risen between Gage and Graves. Graves it was whose boats had ferried the dispirited soldiers back across the Charles River from Charlestown on 19 April. Now he realised that Charlestown and the hills behind it (Breed's Hill and Bunker's Hill) offered the enemy too great a strategic advantage. So, he suggested burning Charlestown and fortifying redoubts on the hills, to be covered by the guns of his ships in the harbour. However, quite apart from natural inter-service rivalries, Graves carried with him from England a bitter hatred of Gage's father. Perhaps affected by this as well as a naturally dilatory mind, Gage called the plan 'too rash and sanguinary'[12] and withdrew all British troops from the Charlestown peninsula. What he did allow the admiral to do was construct a battery on Copp's Hill, overlooking the narrows between Boston and Charlestown, and arm it with 24-pounder guns. It was the sort of job the navy relished, perfectly convinced that in the matter of gunnery it knew better than the army. What the dispirited regulars thought is another matter.

The atmosphere inside the town during these few months is hard to imagine. Collingwood's experience of his eighteen-month stint in Boston is confined to three lines of a potted autobiography written after Trafalgar, thirty years later. What is not in doubt is his opinion of the political situation, recorded in the first of his letters that survives. It was an opinion almost universal among the British armed forces and the Tory establishment:

> I am all out of patience with them [Americans], and consider them
> the supporters of a dangerous Rebellion, rather than the assertors
> of the publick liberty; wish from my heart the whole pack were on
> Mount Pisga, then their declamations might get them a dinner.[13]

Since the end of April 1775 thousands of loyalist refugees had been pouring into Boston from many miles around, preferring the fetid certainties of a town under siege to the persecution of rebels. There were still many republicans in the town, and with a worsening food and fuel crisis, and rival mobs roaming the streets at night, the navy must have felt themselves at least relatively well-placed, secure inside their wooden walls anchored in the harbour.

In the second week of June the army's commanders (Gage had been joined by Major-Generals Howe, Clinton and Burgoyne) formed a plan of action, to break out of Boston before their situation became even more critical: to give themselves, in an infamous phrase, 'elbow room'. They would force Boston Neck, take the rebel positions in nearby Dorchester and Roxbury Heights, establish control in Charlestown (as Graves had requested earlier), and advance on Cambridge. They expected the enemy to fall back and disperse, while they re-established control over Massachusetts. Very quickly though, the rebels got wind of their plans, and decided to act first.

Early on the morning of 16 June a council of war was held in Cambridge to formulate a response to the British plans. By that evening Colonel William Prescott had mobilised his militiamen and, joined by others with trenching tools but only emergency rations, they headed across the neck of the Charlestown peninsula, and in the darkness held a heated debate about whether to fortify Bunker's Hill or Breed's Hill. In the end Breed's Hill was chosen, uncomfortably near the batteries across the water, but better placed for an appreciation of the enemy's dispositions. All through the night the Americans dug, throwing up earth and turf ramparts on the edge of the hill. A British officer heard strange noises across the water, but reported nothing.

At four o'clock on the morning of 17 June lookouts on board the *Lively*, anchored in the narrows off Charlestown, saw and heard the Americans digging their redoubt on Breed's Hill, and without waiting for orders *Lively*'s captain ordered her guns to open fire on the rebel positions. The frigate's 9-pounder guns were too small and could not be elevated high enough to damage the earth rampart, however, and all she accomplished was to blow the head off one of the rebels. They were shocked, but they did not run away.

At seven that morning, the British held their own council of war, and their commanders, with Howe to the fore, decided – simply decided – to retake the peninsula by amphibious assault. Graves suggested taking the neck of the peninsula and cutting them off, but the army commanders favoured full frontal assault, grossly underestimating the strength of the enemy's position and their determination. By the time the first troop transports set off from Long Wharf, the Americans had occupied abandoned buildings in Charlestown, and were frantically reinforcing their positions on the hill so that they held, albeit thinly, a line right across the peninsula. Graves's battery on Copp's Hill set to pounding the American positions, but with little effect.

At three o'clock Howe landed with a second wave of troops. His boats were under the command of master's mate Collingwood who, setting the pattern for his later naval engagements, behaved with the utmost coolness and bravery, and spent the rest of that day ferrying wounded men from, and reinforcements and supplies to the army, in an action that, though it lasted no more than two hours, was extremely fierce.[14] There was an additional danger of being hit by fire from British ships and the Copp's Hill battery.

The first British attack, lines of smart redcoats marching up the hill, exposed and unable to penetrate the redoubt, was repulsed at half-past three, with Prescott allegedly ordering his men not to fire till they saw the whites of the enemy's eyes: it led to heavy British casualties. A second wave fared no better, though the Americans were desperately short of ammunition and experienced officers, and were already exhausted from their night's exertions. The British responded by setting light to Charlestown, and all the rest of that day and into the night it burned, watched by the fascinated and horrified population of Boston sitting on the roofs of their houses.

The third British assault succeeded in taking the American redoubts, but with shocking losses: one thousand casualties, as the defenders fell back, then finally panicked and ran. The Americans were driven off the peninsula with honour, and became heroes. The British, failing to exploit their hard-won victory, later abandoned their positions and fell back to Boston. Within months they would evacuate the city. The first great action of the war, which won

Collingwood his promotion to lieutenant, had cost the British army its reputation of infallibility. It would eventually lead to the total loss of the American colonies.

Acting-Lieutenant Collingwood had to return to England to have his promotion confirmed by Their Lordships at the Admiralty. *Preston* was to stay in Boston, so he was sent aboard *Somerset* under Captain Edward le Clas. *Somerset* sailed first to the Royal Naval base at Halifax, Nova Scotia, in December, probably with a number of loyalist Bostonians wishing to be repatriated to England. Her departure for home was delayed by the following order from Graves:

> The present unpromising state of the King's affairs in the province of Canada, the notoriety of the Disaffection of a Number of the inhabitants of Nova Scotia, and the Danger with which His Majesty's Yard and Stores are threatened, will therefore not allow me to let the *Somerset* proceed to England at present.[15]

On 15 January 1776 *Somerset* did finally sail. It was not a propitious time of year for crossing the Atlantic. She arrived in Plymouth in February, 'much shattered in the voyage, by the violence of the weather'.[16] Collingwood might have thought he deserved a spell of leave after the horrors of Boston, and was keen to go north to see his family, especially since his father had died the previous year. But he was even more anxious to capitalise on his new promotion (duly confirmed) by keeping as close to the action, that is, to the Admiralty, as possible. He stayed, probably with aunts, in Castle Street, London. From here he wrote the first of his letters that survive, to his sister Betsy. He thanked her for sending him a warm winter coat, though it seems to have gone missing before it found him, and intimated that the Admiralty had offered him a provisional posting for the spring. The rest of the letter is a mix of family gossip and news from the Admiralty, written in a warm, open and witty style that sets a pattern for the four hundred or so of his private letters that survive.

By April he had indeed been offered a posting, though it was only in a sloop, the 14-gun *Hornet* under Commander Robert Haswell, bound for the West Indies. By chance, an order to Lieutenant Collingwood from the Lords Commissioners of the Admiralty, dated 1 April 1776, has survived: he must have thought it a poor April Fool's joke, for it ordered him to form a press gang:

> Whereas we intend that you shall be employed to raise Volunteer seamen and landsmen in and about London for the service of His Majesty's sloop Hornet at Woolwich, you are hereby required and directed to observe the following instructions ...[17]

These instructions give us a fascinating insight into the celebrated horrors of the press. First, Collingwood was to hire a room for a rendezvous, and cause bills to be printed and stuck up calling for volunteers: seamen aged eighteen to fifty, and landsmen aged eighteen to twenty-five. Then he was to send such volunteers as he had raised, with a list, to *Hornet* at her moorings. Thirdly, he was to send a daily account of his proceedings to the splendidly named Captain James Kirk, regulator for the raising of men in London. Lieutenant Collingwood was to feed and lodge these men, presumably confining them if necessary, until they went on board, at ninepence per man per day. He was to keep the first eight good seamen, the bigger the better, with him on a subsistence of one shilling and threepence per day per man, and to hire a boat for looking among the shipping on the river. He was himself to receive two shillings and ninepence a day for his own subsistence. No mention of cudgels or truncheons; the use of weaponry was implicit.

He was explicitly urged to use all possible frugality and husbandry (something that came very naturally to him, unless it was the press gang itself which taught him these habits) and not to spend more than one shilling and sixpence on lodgings per week, no more than a shilling a head 'entry' money (the King's shilling), and no more than ten shillings for hiring a drummer and fifer and other charges. The cost of handbills was not to exceed £1 10s, and travelling expenses were not to exceed threepence per mile. He was to apply to the Navy Board for a cash float of £20, and deliver an account of his expenditure to Their Lordships. If Collingwood was the most eco-nomical officer of his time, he was wonderfully in accord with the Admiralty Board.

The infamies of the press gang are notorious. Much was written and said about it at the time, especially in parliament, and no civilised person could ever justify it except on grounds of extreme necessity. Many alternatives were proposed, but none whose merits were superior. Collingwood was far from alone in hating its injustices and brutalities, but the fact was that when Britain was at war she had to expand her serving naval personnel by tens of thousands in a very short time. The idea of conscription was universally abhorred in Britain (it was often cited as one of Napoleon Bonaparte's 'crimes'). Regardless of much that was said by politicians unfamiliar with the service, and later written by unscrupulous Victorian historians, it was not common practice to tear working men from their wives and families indiscriminately. The press was only allowed to take men who had been seamen, and very often the presence of a tattoo or give-away rolling gait would serve as ample evidence of saltiness. No doubt there were instances of arbitrary imprisonment and assault, but courts were surprisingly (to modern eyes) responsive to accusations against the press gangs, so most officers in charge of gangs had one eye on their own skins, as well as on their manning problems.

It was in the interests of seamen in time of war to volunteer, because they received a bounty and better treatment. It was equally in the interests of the navy to recruit as many willing men as possible, and only to recruit landsmen when the supply of tars had run out, which happened all too quickly. The worst injustices occurred when merchant seamen were pressed off returning Indiamen, or when men who had been at sea when young, and who had settled to business or a trade at shore and were raising families, were swept up by recruiting officers keen to make up the numbers. Collingwood himself, many years later, deplored such iniquities:

> I have got a nurseryman here from Wrighton [Ryton, in the Tyne Valley west of Newcastle]. It is a great pity that they should press such a man because when he was young he went to sea for a short time. They have broken up his good business at home, distressed his family, and sent him here, where he is of little or no service. I grieve for him poor man.[18]

Hornet sailed for Jamaica to support the expanded Windward Islands station against American privateers and smugglers. Since the start of the war many English supply ships for the army had been captured and, what was worse, France was acquiescing in, if not aiding, the supply of munitions to the Americans. The situation needed very delicate handling if Britain were to avoid a war with France while she was occupied with the rebels.

Hornet had acquired an unenviable reputation under previous commanders during the Seven Years' War. Under four different captains she had rates of desertion that ranged from just over eight per cent to nearly thirty per cent, both in Home waters and in the West Indies.[19] Such a high rate did not speak of a happy ship. Her present commander, Robert Haswell, had held the same rank for eighteen years and it seems to have embittered him, so Collingwood's first commission did not hold great promise.

There were commanders in all wars who were just plain unlucky:

without political influence or interest, and never seeing any meaningful action. Haswell was not one of these. He was simply a rotten officer. A year after joining *Hornet* Collingwood wrote to his brother John, in the second of his letters that survives:

> MY DEAR JOHN, – Every opportunity of writing to you is but too few. The *Lively* brings this. Wou'd to god the *Lively* brought me also for believe me I am heartily tired of my situation, and cou'd a letter contain half the causes of my dissatisfaction you wou'd not wonder at it. What a country is this at present to make a fortune in; all kinds of people wallowing in their wealth acquired by prizes and so extraordinary an exception are we that to be as unfortunate as the *Hornet* is become a proverbial saying, and the Black girls sing our poverty in their ludicrous songs.[20]

Haswell, to begin with, had 'taken all the pains he cou'd to make himself detested, and so far has he succeeded that I am convinced there is not a man or officer in the Ship that wou'd not consider a removal as a kind of promotion.' The treatment he meted out to his new lieutenant, 'a slave wou'd have shown resentment at'. Far worse than his tyranny, however, was his apparent shyness – the cause of the black girls' ludicrous songs:

> After leaving the convoy we passed the very track which the Americans sail in; for 12 days an enemy was in sight each day. We chased but two and always left off the pursuit before we came along side; it was evident he never meant to take them, however he afterwards left off even the ceremony of chasing them and allowed them to pass unmolested sometimes within 1/2 a gun shot. There's a man to support the honours and interests of his country; wou'd to heaven I was clear of him.[21]

Apart from what Collingwood considered a stain upon his own honour and on that of the service, there was also the very important matter of potential prize money to be won on a station where everyone else seemed to be making a fortune from captured American merchant shipping. The lieutenant of the *Glasgow*, Collingwood noted, had already made £500 in prize money in the time that *Hornet* had been on the station. Apart from the hope of promotion, every sailor's dream was to share in prize money. For a sailor a really successful cruise might mean the chance to settle down on shore, perhaps as the owner of a tavern. Rarely, very rarely, there were instances of such glorious prizes (Spanish treasure ships perhaps) that sailors might be seen conspicuously consuming their booty in an orgy of celebration: frying captured gold pocket watches on Portsmouth Hard.[22] For officers, whose share was greater by far than that of a common seaman, it could mean real wealth, and Collingwood watched his chances of both promotion and wealth slipping through his hands day by day.

In the face of such provocation, and having a naturally self-righteous disposition, Collingwood, though 'diffidence, humility and the idea I have of strict subordination caused me to retreat before the face of tyranny', was finally unable to restrain his anger after one outburst of Haswell's 'virulence, rancour and animosity'. He confronted his commander:

> I told him I was determined no longer to bear with his capricious humours, that I was not a mark to shoot his spleen at, and desired him did he disapprove of any part of my conduct to explain himself, nothing wou'd make me more happy than to correct what had given offence to him. Men who act without meaning, or who are ashamed to confess the passion that impels them, are always distressed when explanations are required of them. He had not a word to say and I had a respite from his malign broils, not that they ceased, but he kept out of my way.[23]

Whether Collingwood requested it or whether Haswell thought he could be rid of his turbulent lieutenant is not clear, but in September

1777 Collingwood was court-martialled at Port Royal, Jamaica for disobedience and neglect of orders. If he initiated these proceedings himself, as he had every right to do, he must have been very confident of his case, or of Haswell's reputation on the station. Conviction would have ruined his career. As it was, he was acquitted, though the court admonished him for his apparent want of cheerfulness, and warned him to 'conduct himself for the future with that alacrity which is essentially necessary to His Majesty's Service'.[24]

He may have survived his first court-martial (he faced two in three years), but Collingwood's relationship with Haswell effectively barred further advancement until such time as he could escape his tormentor. Haswell was most unlikely to recommend any promotion for Collingwood; but then, his recommendation would have been worthless. He was a superannuated lieutenant, either very lazy or cowardly or both, prone to tyrannise his officers and men, and almost certainly unable to count on their loyalty. If the local girls were singing songs about him, the gossip of the squadron's wardrooms would have been more damning by far. He would never be made post.

In these circumstances, and with action against the enemy about as likely as it had been on the Portsmouth guard ship, the best Collingwood could hope for was a sickly season to carry Haswell off with the yellow jack (yellow fever). In the end, though he would have to wait another agonising year for it, salvation would eventually arrive in the shape of his old friend Horatio Nelson.

CHAPTER THREE

The bonds of our amity

1777-1786

In the summer of 1777 Horatio Nelson, aged nineteen, was promoted to second lieutenant in the 32-gun frigate *Lowestoffe*,[1] and sailed to the West Indies where he renewed his friendship with Collingwood. He was much luckier with his commander, Captain William Locker, who encouraged zealous, intelligent young officers to develop their skills in the new war against American privateers. A year later, as the progress of the American war looked bleaker by the month, the Admiralty sent the 50-gun flagship *Bristol* and a squadron under Admiral Sir Peter Parker to Jamaica to reinforce the Windward Islands station. Britain's military policies, so successful during the Seven Years' War, were now failing. General Burgoyne, veteran of the ignominy of Bunker's Hill, who at the beginning of

1777 was still confidently predicting victory against General Washington, had been humiliated by defeat at Saratoga. Having lost any remaining loyalist support in the colonies, the army had to be resupplied entirely by sea from Britain. In 1777 alone, American cruisers took 300 British merchantmen. Although between 1775 and 1778 the British in their turn took more than 230 American ships,[2] it was not enough to prevent the Americans from operating out of friendly Caribbean bases belonging to France, Holland and Denmark.

The number of ships available to the commanders in America and the West Indies, specifically frigates and sloops, was limited by Britain's normal peace-time policy of running the navy down, an indication of how unprepared the government was for the American war. This left the Home fleet, now down to something like forty ships of the line, to deal with a worsening situation with France, whose neutrality was strained to breaking point as she offered succour to increasing numbers of American privateers.[3] By February of 1778 Britain had declared war on France. Within two months John Paul Jones, America's first naval hero, was wreaking havoc with raids on the Solway Firth and Belfast Lough. In June Spain, with an eye on the recovery of her lost possessions in Gibraltar and Florida, declared war on Britain just as General Howe's disastrous expedition was withdrawing from Philadelphia, the new American capital.

The situation in the West Indies required officers of enterprise, watchfulness and zeal. Admiral Parker quickly realised that Nelson, young and inexperienced though he was, was of the right sort and, after taking him into *Bristol* as third lieutenant in July 1778, soon promoted him master and commander of *Badger*, a 14-gun brig. Nelson, with his 'interest' at the Admiralty, had gone from master's mate to master and commander in just over a year. This was on 8 December, a day when Parker was required to make no less than fourteen promotions.[4] Losses from capture and disease had left many ships short of their full complement. It was Nelson's influence with Parker that led to Collingwood's rescue from the clutches of Haswell, and promotion: first into *Lowestoffe* under the likeable William Locker and then on the same day that Nelson was made commander, as second lieutenant of the *Bristol*.[5]

As Nelson's luck began to rub off on him, Collingwood followed his friend as if pulled along in his slipstream. Nelson was made post (still just twenty years old: his birthday was three days after Collingwood's) in *Hinchinbroke*, a captured French 28-gun frigate, in June 1779. He was replaced as master and commander in *Badger* by Collingwood, now thirty. Nelson wrote to his brother William explaining why the West Indies was both feared and loved by officers, saying, 'We all rise by deaths. I got my rank by a shot killing a post-captain and I most sincerely hope, I shall, when I go, go out of the world the same way.'[6] When Nelson died at Trafalgar it was Collingwood, once again, who succeeded him.

Within a few months Collingwood succeeded Nelson as post-captain in *Hinchinbroke*, when his friend was invalided home after the first of those rash amphibious expeditions that would blight Nelson's war record for the next twenty years.

In 1779 Britain was under threat of invasion by France. The Channel fleet was in a state of high alert, and that alert extended as far as Jamaica, which was threatened by the presence of a French base at St Domingo. When that immediate danger passed, the governor of Jamaica, Major-General John Dalling, decided, on his own initiative, to attempt a pre-emptive strike on Spanish territories. In the lunatic spirit of Cortez he planned to force a passage to the Pacific Ocean up the San Juan river in Nicaragua, bisecting the possessions of the Spanish New World, and achieving immortality for himself. In April 1780 Nelson was put in charge, in *Hinchinbroke*, of escorting the troop transports to the mouth of the river. Collingwood, in *Badger*, was sent in support. For the first time but not the last, Nelson disobeyed orders and decided to help the expedition along its way, ultimately attempting to storm a Spanish fortress many miles up the river in thick jungle.

The diseases and dangers of the jungle, the snakes, mosquitoes, yellow fever, accounted for a large number of the expeditionary force, and very nearly for Nelson. He had to be sent home to England, and it was feared he would be dead before he got there. Collingwood's ship, waiting week after week off the mouth of the river, fared little better, as he recalled many years later:

> My constitution survived many attacks, and I survived most of my ship's company, having buried in four months 180 of the 200 who composed it. Mine was not a singular case, for every ship that was long there suffered in the same degree. The transports' men all died, and some of the ships, having none left to take care of them, sunk in the harbour: but transport ships were not wanted, for the troops whom they had brought were no more; they had fallen, not by the hand of the enemy, but from the contagion of the climate.[7]

Collingwood replaced Nelson again, this time as post-captain in *Hinchinbroke*. It had taken him nineteen years to get on the 'list', and five since his promotion to lieutenant at Bunker's Hill. From now on, he could comfort himself with the knowledge that if he lived long enough, he would die an admiral. That step would take another nineteen years. In the meantime, he must hope for a bloody war and a sickly season. What he got was a hurricane.

On 18 October 1780, a month before Britain declared war on the Dutch for aiding France, Collingwood was in command of another frigate, the 24-gun *Pelican*, cruising off the south-east corner of Jamaica.[8] With no warning, a hurricane of tremendous force swept through the Windward Islands. Afterwards, Admiral Rodney, seeing the extent of the devastation, wrote that 'nothing but ocular demonstration could have convinced me [of its extent] ... the island [Jamaica] has the appearance of a country laid waste by fire and sword.'[9] *Pelican* was wrecked, thrown on to the Morant Keys where she broke apart:

> The next day, with great difficulty, the ship's company got on shore, on rafts made of the small and broken yards; and upon those sandy islands, with little food, we remained ten days, until a boat went to [Port Royal], and the *Diamond* frigate came and took us off.[10]

This is understatement. It was generally considered that when a ship was wrecked or about to sink, her captain no longer had power of authority over his men. A frequent scenario involved sailors breaking into the spirit room and drowning in as near a state of inebriation as possible. Very few seamen, officers or ratings, could swim, and many understandably panicked in such situations. Collingwood held his nerve, ensured that his officers and men did too, and brought off a remarkable feat of survival, his second in a year. The subsequent court-martial, mandatory for any captain who lost his ship, was a formality. Even so, it was hardly glory.

Back in Port Royal the damage was not confined to the more than one hundred ships that had been lost or driven ashore,[11] or the town's buildings. There was political trouble too. Another gale, this time in the Leeward Islands, had forced Rodney to demand that Parker turn over Port Royal's facilities to repair his ships. Parker, stung by Rodney's tone, and by previous run-ins with him over seniority, pointed out his own priorities and effectively refused assistance. When finally Rodney came to appreciate Parker's situation he did not feel able to back down gracefully. Both of them wrote complaining letters to the Admiralty. It was the sort of bickering among senior commanders abroad that seriously compromised the navy's effectiveness. Such examples determined commanders like Collingwood and St Vincent that the good of the service must always come before personal interests. Rodney, in any case, was an untypical officer. He was a fine and brave seaman and a skilful battle commander, but he was notoriously corrupt, both politically and financially. He made so many enemies, Parker included, that his junior officers' careers were hampered by his recommendation.

Collingwood returned to England early in 1782. It is not clear if he managed to go north this time, but his constant applications to the Admiralty suggest that once more he stayed close to the action in London. Like many an officer ashore, he found the difficulties of command were as nothing to the social complexities that a post-captain, ashore on half-pay, was expected to immerse himself in. In the third of his letters that survive, Collingwood told his brother John that Mrs Massingberd, a 'very comical woman', seemed rather too keen on him. She contrived to write some very warm words about him to her son and asked Collingwood to forward the letter. Mrs Massingberd mixed the covers so that Collingwood found himself (by design, he was certain) reading her glowing praises of him. He does not seem to have taken her very seriously:

> Let a woman alone for a good story. I begin John to think they are more dangerous to encounter than Hurricanes, as they do not give so fair a warning. Would I was abroad again! Better be wrecked a thousand times at sea, than once ashore.[12]

In common with all his letters home, this one was supposed to be circulated among family and friends. Collingwood felt he had an obligation to keep his family up to speed not just with his own affairs, but also the affairs of those with whom he came into contact. He liked to entertain, too, and the sort of throw-away line cast in Mrs Massingberd's direction became a polished trick over the years:

always delivered straight, like the best comedy, and often, especially in later years, casting a dark shadow of gallows humour. In his next letter but one, while he was in Portsmouth, he told his sister:

> Madam the dowager has taken it into her head that after warm summers, follow cold winters, and in fitting her house to resist the inclemencies of the weather, among other things she has provided a husband. Her first was a sailor – chance gave her a sailor – but still doubting to which proffession the preference was due, she now means to give a fair tryal to an old soldier, and matters are pretty near concluded between her and Col Heywood ...[13]

And then ...

> It wou'd be a happy thing if she [Madam Teesdale] was to kick off; she is a withered branch of society and might be lopt off without injury to it, indeed if the whole family was at kingdom come, I think they would be well off.[14]

It would have amazed many of his colleagues, towards whom he maintained a very formal reserve, to discover the mischief and wit that lay behind the straight face; although those who carefully read his piercing blue eyes found hidden depths. Nelson, whose relationships were always intense, was one. Another was Mary Moutray.

After a brief period in command of the 64-gun *Sampson*,[15] Collingwood was given *Mediator*, a fourth-rate, 44-gun two-decker frigate which had captured two French ships bound for the West Indies the previous year. Despite some trouble finding enough men to make up her complement, Collingwood had her ready to sail at the end of September 1783. One of her new midshipmen described a scene that must have been familiar to all sailors:

> As two months advancement of wages were going to be paid to the ship's company before she sailed, the Commissioner's yacht came alongside, and the bumboat people that came off were allowed to

bring their goods on board; the main deck was appropriated for exhibiting their goods, and it became a perfect fair, where the sailors laid their money out long before they got it ...[16]

Bound for the Leeward Islands station at Antigua, *Mediator* carried the new navy commissioner for the dockyard, John Moutray, and his wife Mary. At first, Collingwood was annoyed. He had to give up his own spacious cabin for them, it would cost him money to entertain them in a fitting manner, and he would be ten shillings a day worse off than he had been in *Sampson*. He would not mind too much, he told his sister, if the passengers showed their gratitude once they were there. As it happened, Mary Moutray might have ended her days as Lady Collingwood – or for that matter Lady Nelson.

By a great stroke of fortune, Collingwood was doing someone else a favour, in taking a small boy with him as his servant and apprentice. Baron Raigersfeld, secretary and chargé d'affaires to the Austrian ambassador in London, was sending his thirteen-year-old son Jeffrey to sea. This was a useful political connection for Collingwood, and suggests that he was regarded as a commander with a future. Jeffrey, who himself became a rear-admiral and was a lieutenant in *Speedy* some years before Lord Cochrane had her, wrote an autobiography, *The life of a sea officer*,[17] which describes in riveting detail his experience of serving with Collingwood. Here the Collingwood touch is witnessed at first hand, recalled with some affection:

> During upwards of the three years and a half that I was in this ship,
> I do not remember more than four or five men being punished at
> the gangway, and then so slightly that it scarcely deserved the name,
> for the Captain was a very humane man, and although he made
> great allowances for the uncontrolled eccentricities of the seamen,
> yet he looked after the midshipmen of his ship with the eye of one
> who felt it a duty to keep youth in constant employment ...[18]

Mediator left Spithead and crossed the notorious Bay of Biscay before striking south-west for the Azores. The Moutrays presumably suffered the same fate as the new midshipman:

> I became so very sea sick as to be unable to assist myself in the least ... the waves ran so high, and the sea water out of soundings caused so bad a smell on board, from the rolling of the ship as it washed from side to side in the between decks, that had anyone thrown me overboard as I lay helpless upon the gangway I certainly should not have made the smallest resistance.[19]

Unlike poor Raigersfeld, the Moutrays probably did not recover to find that their sea chests had been emptied by eager hands 'of all superfluities' during their prostration. After Biscay, *Mediator* found herself in the trade winds, and the hands had light work of their passage to Antigua, where she was brought into English Harbour by a pilot with a wooden leg, and:

> No sooner anchored than she was crowded with negro men and women, as well as mulattoes, who brought fruit, bread, milk and other things for sale. The dresses of the women were mostly of light striped cottons, their teeth very white, and from wearing their head dress very high, their *tout ensemble* had rather a coquetish appearance, while their easy manners engaged very sensibly the attention of your young bucks of the navy.[20]

English Harbour, which possesses the only surviving Georgian dockyard in the world, has changed little since 1783. It has a very narrow entrance guarded by forts on either side. The harbour and docks cannot be seen from the open sea, and in periods of war a great iron chain could be hung between the forts to prevent the entry of enemy craft. The hills which surround it on all sides make it one of the best havens for shipping in the Caribbean during the hurricane season, from June to October. From Shirley Heights, nearly five hundred feet above sea level, there is a commanding view of the harbour and approaches. Even now, there are 'hurricane chains' from that time lying on the floor of the shallow basin. These operated rather like the restraining cables on the decks of aircraft carriers: ships entering the harbour flying before the wind would need to stop very quickly to prevent them from running aground, and this they accomplished by seizing cables to the capstans, with grappling hooks at the cables' ends, and towing them astern so that the hooks caught on the chains stretched across the harbour floor and brought the ship to. It sounds like a hazardous operation in any but the most skilful hands.

Antigua was a crucial possession for the British, even though it is a small island, less than twenty miles long. Its highly developed slave plantations produced sugar and rum in great abundance, and its location at the north-east corner of the Leeward Islands made it an ideal base for patrolling the eastern Caribbean. Unlike Menorca, it was easily defended. Only at English Harbour in the south-east, and at the present-day capital St John's in the north-west, were there sufficient gaps between reefs to provide either safe anchorages or landing places for an invasion. At English Harbour the government had invested for many years in the development of docking and careenage facilities, many of which are still in existence. These enabled ship refitting and repair to be carried out without the expense and danger of ships sailing as far as Jamaica or Nova Scotia. In the 1780s a programme of expansion was under way which saw the erection of officers' quarters and water-storage facilities, to add to the sail lofts, mast-houses and slipways. Many of the buildings were constructed in red brick, brought from England as ballast to be replaced by sugar on the return journey. On the hills around English Harbour and at St John's there were army barracks and batteries too, and the remains of military cemeteries testify to the high mortality rates suffered by soldier and sailor alike. Here and there a surviving sugar mill or slave barracks offers a sharp reminder of the economic basis of Britain's Empire.

Collingwood, by the time he arrived here, had decided that the Moutrays were the sort of people he could get along with; so much so, that Mary had managed to penetrate his off-putting professional severity, and come to like him:

> There was a degree of reserve in his manner which prevented the playfulness of his imagination and his powers of adding charm to private society being duly appreciated. But the intimacy of a long voyage gave us the good fortune to know him as he was, so that, after our arrival in Antigua, he was as a beloved brother in our house.[21]

The house in question was called Windsor. It almost certainly stood on the little bluff that overlooks English Harbour from the west, a few hundred yards' walk from the officers' quarters. It had louvred walls and a verandah, and caught the best of the fresh cooling breezes that kept insects at bay. Today, there is very little left of it: traces of a stone foundation and a scattering of domestic debris: china, beer and wine bottles, whelk shells by the hundred. For the most part it has been reclaimed by agave and thorny scrub, Antigua's ubiquitous goats and the odd mongoose (introduced to rid the island of ships' rats, but succeeding only in extinguishing its famous population of racing snakes) its only inhabitants. It is tempting to think that the odd sherd of creamware or pearlware comes from a dinner service used by Collingwood and the Moutrays, and indeed Nelson, who was to arrive here in 1784.

Collingwood became very attached to Mary Moutray, a striking, intelligent and charming woman, twenty-eight years younger than her ailing husband John, who had retired as a post-captain and for whom this posting was a sinecure. She in turn was attracted by the tall naval commander in the prime of life, with his intelligent blue eyes and dry wit. She must have been flattered, too, by his verse:

> To you belongs the wond'rous art
> To shed around you pleasure;
> New worth to best of things impart,
> And make of trifles — treasure.[22]

Evenings with the Moutrays relieved the boredom, discomfort and solitude of the station. Yellow fever was rife in the West Indies, as Collingwood knew only too well from his previous visits. The mosquitoes were another hazard, as poor Raigersfeld was finding to his cost; one bite became an infected ulcer which took fifteen months to heal, and the only partial remedy against them was to be smeared with lime juice:

> By this means I might prevent a repetition of the attacks of this rapacious hoard [sic] of blood suckers, who never fail to make a hearty meal off Johnny Newcome, whilst a beef and plumb pudding flavour is to be extracted from his veins.[23]

There were other hazards for sailors in these parts. One was the temptation for 'Johnny Newcome' – the inexperienced sailor – to shelter from heavy rain under the branches of the manchineal tree, whose poisonous sap raised peculiarly unpleasant boils on the skin; but there were many others:

> In the West Indies, the fuel made use of on board a ship is wood, among which varieties of insects are brought, such as scorpions, centipedes, and tarantulas, with now and then a few snakes; these soon begin to crawl up and down the ship, even into the hammocks, and the men frequently get stung and bit by them.[24]

Anyone on the station who had delicate sensibilities must also have given a thought to the plight of slaves. Raigersfeld could hear the driver's whip 'smacking upon their backs as they laboured in the field, better than a mile off'.[25] Whether he pondered on the morality of the Royal Navy protecting plantation owners, or the government's funding of its navy through the wealth created by slave labour, is doubtful. Similar brutality was casually handed out to many seamen, who had themselves been recruited by the press and were effectively slaves too.

Raigersfeld, when he was not being bullied by his older messmates, was understandably more interested in having fun. He was taught how to swim and even dive by a local, but was banned from attempting the feat of one of his shipmates, whose habit it was to dive from the topgallant yard arm, a height of over one hundred feet, into the shallow waters of the harbour. He was amused, too, with some of the wildlife, including an eel called a torpedo that gave a very sharp electrical shock.[26] One day Collingwood was sent a present of a turtle with ten or twelve of its young. To the amusement of the midshipmen they were kept in a soup plate, where it was 'very pretty to see them blow and swim about'.[27]

In September 1783 Britain signed peace treaties with France and Spain at Versailles, and finally recognised American independence. Shortly afterwards, William Pitt became Britain's youngest prime minister at the age of twenty-four. His younger brother James, who at twenty was made commander of that ill-starred sloop *Hornet*, died in Antigua in 1780, and lies buried in St Paul's church at Falmouth, a mile or so from English Harbour.

By the time Collingwood arrived on the station, Americans were once more trading vigorously with the islands. Collingwood's role in peace time was to show the flag at the various islands owned by Britain, and protect merchant ships from piracy. But it soon occurred to him, as a keen student of politics and the law, that under ancient

Navigation Acts, going back to Cromwell's Protectorate and the Restoration, this trade with America was illegal. The acts stated that only British ships might trade with her colonies. American ships were *de facto* no longer British, and were therefore trading illegally. In 1784 Collingwood decided to deploy *Mediator* in protection of these laws. At least, that was how he saw it. Horatio Nelson, arriving on the station in July 1784 in the frigate *Boreas* (and carrying the new station commander Admiral Hughes), later claimed it was he who started operations against the 'smugglers'. Most historians have accepted Nelson's testimony at face value, but Collingwood was in fact the original instigator of the trouble that followed, even if it was the result of conversations with Nelson at English Harbour that autumn. The reason these actions caused so much trouble was that most of the powerful people in the islands, among them Governor Shirley and Admiral Hughes, were making money from the American trade.

Nelson's influence on the station was immediate; he seemed to invigorate people wherever he went. Within days of his arrival he had established an officers' mess, which he supplied with a hogshead of port and another of white wine, plus twelve dozen bottles of porter, 50lbs of loaf sugar, a firkin of butter, two baskets of salt and 2lbs of black pepper.[28] There were amateur theatricals, and dancing and cudgelling on the decks of the ships. He had also managed to argue with John Moutray. Although senior on the navy list to Nelson by many years, Moutray was now on half-pay, and when he had a commodore's pennant raised on *Latona*, moored at a dockyard wharf, Nelson ordered it struck. Typically, though, Nelson dined with the Moutrays the same night, and very quickly fell in love with Mary.

Collingwood, meanwhile, was at Grenada: 'a great loss to me,' wrote Nelson.[29] He was back at English Harbour by November and Nelson, despite the Moutray's company, was glad to see him. 'What an amiable good man he is! All the rest are geese.'[30] They both spent evenings up at Windsor, where they would frizz Mary's hair for a ball, and she managed to persuade them to draw each other's portrait. These are preserved in the National Maritime Museum at Greenwich, where they make a striking contrast. Collingwood, though a fine draughtsman, never managed to draw faces convincingly, and in this picture Nelson is wearing a wig, having had his head shaved after a bout of yellow fever: it is not flattering. Nelson hated the West Indies climate. He was 'woefully pinched' by mosquitoes[31] on his night-time walks, and the fever never seemed far away. On the other hand, Nelson's silhouette of Collingwood is a naval paradigm – as if Collingwood was not so much an individual, as an embodiment of the right true naval officer: straight, firm, steady. Collingwood had a much stronger constitution and seemed unaffected by bugs or heat.

On 15 December 1784, after the end of the hurricane season, *Mediator* was cruising off Antigua when an American vessel was sighted, making for St John's.[32] By this time Collingwood's brother Wilfred (a year younger than Cuthbert, though apparently he already looked ten years older) had arrived on the station in command of *Rattler*, a 14-gun sloop. All three captains must by this time have discussed the Navigation Acts and decided it was their duty to prevent American trade in the islands. Collingwood sent a lieutenant on board the American, whose master claimed that his mainmast required repair. Collingwood's response is interesting, in the light of Nelson's later comments. He shepherded the American vessel to St John's, had her tie up alongside him, and sent his carpenter aboard to help effect repairs – knowing full well there was nothing wrong with her. In this way, the American was prevented from landing his cargo, but without any grand gesture or threat on the navy's part. It was the sort of subtle tactic that Collingwood later developed into a diplomatic art form on the grandest stage.

The American master immediately complained to Governor Shirley, who referred the matter to the attorney-general, while the merchants of St John's quite understandably railed against this disruption of their trade. The attorney-general's opinion was that Collingwood had no right to interfere with the trade, hoping to end the matter there. Collingwood, though, knew he had the full weight of the law – and, he hoped, the Admiralty – behind him. The following day he wrote:

> For my authority for not suffering her to proceed further, I refer your Excellency to the Statutes (12 Chas: 2 and the 7th and 8th of William and Mary) excluding Aliens from Commerce with the British Colonies, which statutes I am ordered to put in full force and execution.[33]

It must have come as an unpleasant surprise for the attorney-general to confront a post-captain able to quote chapter and verse of the law to him. Collingwood had no intention of backing down. The matter was naturally referred to the senior officer on the station, Admiral Hughes, though none of the captains expected much support from him. Hughes was living in Barbados, having already made an enemy of Nelson on the passage out. He came up with an entirely unsatisfactory compromise, ordering his captains to report the arrival of foreign ships, but to take no action against them unless by the express orders of the governor. There was little or no chance of Shirley acting under his own initiative. Nelson and the Collingwoods were furious with their admiral, though they cannot have been surprised. Collingwood wrote to his sister in January 1785:

> Of this man here [Admiral Hughes] nothing but nonsense can be expected. Because our diligence reflects on his neglect, he dislikes us: we are seldom with him, but often enough. It is by dint of much trouble that I brought about the exclusion of the Americans from

these islands. To my representation from Grenada he made a reply which can never be produced as an instance of his knowledge or zeal for supporting the rights of British ships and seamen. When we all met at Barbadoes, however, the point difficult as it was, was carried, and the Americans are excluded to the great grief of those Governors, collectors, and American merchants who made immense sums by this illicit trade ... The people of this island clamour'd loudly against my conduct, and I was pester'd with letters ...[34]

Thus fortified by the moral superiority of the righteous, the three captains carried on. In February Collingwood seized the *Lovely Ann*, a merchantman flying an Irish harp flag, and in July the *Dolphin*, an American brig. Wilfred and Nelson were at it too. It soon became clear that they were going to be sued for wrongful seizure; indeed they were pursued by lawyers for many years afterwards. Potentially they could be ruined by what they saw as their duty. Nelson took it upon himself to ask the Admiralty for indemnification against litigation, and to his and Collingwood's great relief the Admiralty supported them fully.

Nelson later wrote a very full account of the entire episode. It reveals a pathological trait in his character. Fond as he was of Collingwood, and eager to give him praise, he still could not allow that Collingwood had been the instigator of the policy:

> The Captains Collingwood were the only officers, with myself, who ever attempted to hinder the illicit trade with America; and I stood singly with respect to seizing, for the other officers were fearful of being brought into scrapes.[35]

This is a downright lie. Nelson would never have dared repeat it in public, and yet he seems not to have been able to resist taking for himself any glory that was going. It does not even have the taint of personal rivalry; he seems simply incapable of granting that another officer was as zealous, if not more so, than himself. It would not be the last time that his friend suffered at his hands in this way. Did Collingwood know of this trait? It is hard to believe that he did not. Later, he admitted that Nelson was prone to flattery, and sometimes allowed himself to be surrounded by the wrong people, but he was adamant that Nelson always put the service and his friends before himself. This sounds like loyalty overcoming truth.[36]

Meanwhile, life on the station continued, though not for the Moutrays. John was seriously ill, and early in 1785 they returned to England. 'I shall miss them grievously,' wrote Collingwood, 'she is quite a delight and makes many an hour cheerfull, that without her wou'd be dead weight.'[37] Nelson was even more effusive. 'Her equal I never saw ... I took leave of her with a heavy heart. What a treasure of a woman.'[38] John Moutray died shortly after returning to England. Both Collingwood and Nelson corresponded with Mary for the rest of their lives, often in terms that can only be described as very warm. Had she been a widow earlier, one or other, probably both of them, would surely have proposed marriage to her.

Collingwood, meanwhile, was having trouble with his 'monkeys'. 'The boy Pennyman is quite a plague, a dirty lad without one good quality to set against a great many bad ones.'[39] Raigersfeld and any others who showed promise were allowed into his cabin on a Sunday morning. Here the captain tried to give them a taste for letters, made more palatable by the prospect of sharing his breakfast. Collingwood preferred to see his young gentlemen thrive on the carrot, but he had no hesitation in employing the stick when he thought it necessary, whatever his later reputation for banning the use of the 'cat' might suggest:

> One morning after breakfast ... all the midshipmen were sent
> for into the Captain's cabin, and four of us were tied up one after
> the other to the breech of one of the guns, and flogged upon

our bare bottoms with a cat-'o-nine-tails, by the boatswain of the ship; some received six lashes, some seven, and myself three. No doubt we all deserved it. Some time after this another of the midshipmen and myself were put to mess with the common men, where we lived with them for three months ... At first I was indignant at such treatment, but there was no help for it ... and I am very glad I was so placed, as it gave me a great insight into the character of seamen ...[40]

... precisely Collingwood's intention. This was the same treatment that Patrick O'Brian's Jack Aubrey was so grateful for when, as a mid' in *Surprise*, he was disrated on the same Leeward Islands station – though in his case it was for keeping a trollop in the cable tiers. Collingwood was not only sensible of the effect of his discipline on the midshipmen themselves. He knew its effects on the crew, too, as Raigersfeld and his mates found to their cost on one occasion:

The Captain, a well read man as well as a clever seaman, took it into his head one day that he would like to see the midshipmen work their day's-work from their own observations before him on the quarter deck; they did so, but only three or four out of twelve or thirteen could accomplish this with any degree of exactitude, so calling those to him who were deficient, he observed to them how remiss they were, and suddenly, imputing their remissness to their pigtails, he took his penknife out of his pocket and cut off their pigtails close to their heads above the tie, then presenting them to their owners, desired they would put them into their pockets and keep them until such time as they could work a day's-work, when they might wear them again if they thought proper. This *coup de main* afforded visibly an internal smile upon the countenances of all present.[41]

One of the problems inherent in the West Indies economy was its reliance on monoculture. Almost every square yard of land was turned over to the production of sugar cane, so fresh food for hungry soldiers and sailors was often in short supply, and during the summer months when hurricanes could strike without warning, there was little chance of being resupplied from England:

> So very seldom was it that fresh provisions could be had at this time in the West Indies, that the captain of the hold used to catch rats, (of which there was an abundance in the ship) in the night, and by eight in the morning, generally four or five rats were ready cleaned and spread out as butchers dress sheep for the inspection of amateurs; and those who purchased the rats for a relish, had only to pepper and salt them well, broil them in the galley, and they were found nice and delicate eating; so that this captain of the hold's fishing for them, for he caught them by a hook and line, became a source of profit. As to the rats, they fed off the best of the ship's provisions, such as biscuit, flour, peas, &c. and they were full as good as rabbits, although not so large.[42]

What stores the ships did carry suffered greatly from the effects of a tropical climate:

> The biscuit that was served to the ship's company was so light, that when you tapped it upon the table, it fell almost into dust, and thereout numerous insects, called weevils, crawled; they were bitter to the taste, and a sure indication that the biscuit had lost its nutritious particles; if, instead of these weevils, large white maggots with black heads made their appearance, then the biscuit was considered to be only in its first state of decay; these maggots were fat and cold to the taste, but not bitter.[43]

Towards the end of the hurricane season of 1785 *Mediator* sailed for Barbados. She was becalmed off the island of Deseada (la Désirade, off Guadeloupe) for a night, but at dawn the next day it was obvious a nasty blow was on the way. Reefs were taken in the topsails and the courses were hauled up. At one in the afternoon the sky became black, and the edge of the horizon seemed to be covered with a white foam that advanced with extraordinary rapidity. Before the hands, called from below to shorten sail, could even get up through the hatchways the squall struck, and *Mediator* was instantly on her beam ends. Men were deafened and made stupid by the noise of wind and foam screaming through the rigging, as all hands desperately tried to haul down the yards on to a near vertical deck. And then as suddenly as it had risen the wind fell, the skies opened and torrents of water fell on the ship.

Many of the men involuntarily began to huddle together under the half deck, along with bemused goats and sheep, all with a sense of awe and impending danger, until, at last:

> A terrible crash took place in the fore part of the ship, accompanied by a tremendous explosion and stench of sulphur; deep groans followed, – sixteen men upon the main deck were knocked down, some were apparently dead, and others groaning; relief was instantly afforded, and in about four hours after all were well again. A lightning ball had struck the fore topmast, passed into the pigsty, and through the galley into the waist, where it burst and overthrew seventeen men; eleven pigs in the sty before the mast were killed, belonging to the Captain; the silver buckles in the shoes of the gunner were melted into wire, and himself was knocked out of the roundhouse forward.[44]

Amazingly, no one was killed. By the 1780s the Admiralty was supplying its ships with lightning conductors, but bizarrely they came in a box to be deployed when necessary. *Mediator*'s evidently never saw the light of day. As a reward for the exertions of the ship's company in fishing the foremast (in effect putting huge plank splints on it) and setting the ship to rights, Collingwood had his dead pigs distributed among them. Raigersfeld's mess made a 'very good dinner from it, and considered it a God-send'.

Mediator returned to English Harbour at the beginning of 1786. Here she was hove down and careened, and then sailed for England. Raigersfeld subsequently had a long, though disappointing, career. He served as a lieutenant on the 14-gun sloop *Speedy* a few years before her famous cruise under Lord Cochrane. Refusing promotion to another ship, he was captured in her and spent six months on parole in France where he was nearly executed on a trumped-up charge. He escaped, and later became a post-captain, though he saw no action. He ended his career as a rear-admiral, a 'yellow' admiral, without an active command. Surprisingly, he acquired great skill as an artist, and exhibited paintings four times at the Royal Academy.[45] In 1815 he encountered Napoleon on the deck of *Bellerophon* and made a sketch of the former emperor. He wrote in his autobiography that he spent no more valuable time in his life than when Collingwood disrated him and he learned the ways of the lower deck.

Nelson lamented *Mediator*'s departure, writing that 'had it not been for Collingwood, it would have been the most disagreeable station I ever saw'. Wilfred missed him as well. The two brothers would not see each other again.

CHAPTER FOUR

A comfortable fire and friends
1787-1792

Collingwood arrived in England in July 1786, paid off his ship's company, and went to London to see about getting another command. There was little chance of success. He was still a relatively junior post-captain on a list of four hundred or so.[1] He might justly feel that he had fulfilled his duty in the West Indies, but had his behaviour found favour with the Admiralty? The Royal Navy was, after all, the executive tool of a British mercantile empire. In any case, and whatever the Admiralty's opinion of Collingwood's professional merits and operational judgement, Britain was now at least nominally at peace with the other powers of Europe, and the navy's capability was being reduced. No one was being given a ship.

Collingwood stayed in London that autumn, dealing with the

legal aftermath of his and Nelson's enforcement of the Navigation Acts. William Pitt the Younger was prime minister. The Prince of Wales had scandalously, and in secret, married Maria Fitzherbert. Henry Cort had invented the puddling process for smelting iron with coke that would make iron the engineering material of the industrial revolution, and Edmund Cartwright had developed the power weaving-loom. James Watt's patent rotary steam engine was already replacing Newcomen's old atmospheric engine and was beginning to revolutionise the mining industry. The Marylebone Cricket Club was founded later that year, and Thomas Lord opened his first cricket ground in Dorset Square. The world was changing. As winter came, Collingwood at last went north to see his family.

There is no record of his having been to Newcastle since he left in *Shannon* at the age of thirteen, though he may have been home for short visits during his brief periods ashore. His father was dead. His ailing mother and his sisters Dorothy and Mary were still apparently at Newcastle.

His home town had changed too. The old bridge with its shops and houses had been destroyed by flood in the winter of 1771–2 and its elegant replacement, partly designed by John Smeaton of Eddystone lighthouse fame, had just been finished.[3] The bull-ring and parts of the city walls by the Quayside were gone, and for the first time there were street signs. There was now a theatre and Assembly Rooms, and in the last few months of 1786 a Mr Lunardie had ascended in a hot-air balloon from the Spital, his too-rapid descent proving fatal.[4] A Royal Mail coach had just started a service to London via Leeds at a cost of four guineas, taking more than forty hours to complete the journey.[5]

Some things did not change. Newcastle's newspapers were full of familiar items, such as deserting pitmen and indentured servants, or rumours of counterfeit guineas being circulated, but also the finding of a young woman's body half-buried in a churchyard. One William Smith, a surgeon, was advertising a course in midwifery, and to ensure his students had ample material to practice with, he offered poor women in the town and neighbourhood 'free delivery'. There were also advertisements for a variety of panaceas, guaranteed to cure all sorts of ailments in improbable ways:

MOLINEUX'S SMELLING MEDICINE
For the Scurvy, Itch, Pimpled Faces, Scald heads, Films in children, and all cutaneous eruptions, by *Smelling Only*. 1s 1d per box.

It was specially recommended for all captains of ships. Had he been given a ship, Collingwood might also have tried Dr Pitcairn's eye-water, the Cephalic Snuff, or Dr Bodrum's restorative cordial. The work of Scottish doctor James Lind on the causes of scurvy had been known for a generation and more, and the anti-scorbutic properties of lime juice and sauerkraut had been proved by James Cook in his circumnavigations. However, Collingwood was among many in the navy who clung to the virtues of their own experience. 'I have less alarm about scurvy than most people; clean and dry ship and good air of the poop are my specificks,' he once said.[6] When he wrote that he had been at sea for fifteen months without dropping anchor, and had an empty sick bay, so it is hard to argue with him. But his journals, even as Commander-in-Chief of the Mediterranean fleet, show that he took great pains to ensure his crews got regular supplies of fresh fruit, vegetables and meat. This was a better diet, and a healthier lifestyle, than many enjoyed at home, especially since industrial and agricultural innovations were exacerbating rural unemployment.

Now there was bad news for the Collingwood family. On 23 June 1787 the *Newcastle Courant* carried the following death notice:

On 20th April last, in the West Indies, Captain Wilfred Collingwood, Commander of His Majesty's Ship *Rattler*. By his death his friends have lost a most valuable and affectionate relative, and his country an active and zealous officer.

The news had been received by Cuthbert himself, in a letter from Nelson. It was written on 3 May from *Boreas* at the island of Nevis where Nelson, almost bereaved by the absence of Mary Moutray, had been paying court to the widow Fanny Nisbet, and married her:

MY DEAR COLLINGWOOD,

To be the messenger of bad news is my misfortune, but still it is a tribute which friends owe each other. I have lost my friend, you an affectionate brother; too great a zeal in serving his Country hastened his end. The greatest consolation the survivor can receive, is a thorough knowledge of a life spent with honour to himself, and of service to his Country. If the tribute of tears be valuable, my friend had it. The esteem he stood in with His Royal Highness was great. His letter to me on his death is the strongest testimony of it. I send you an extract from it. 'Collingwood, poor fellow, is no more. I have cried for him; and most sincerely do I condole with you on his loss. In him His Majesty has lost a faithful servant, and the service a most excellent officer.'

A testimony of regard so honorable is more to be coveted than anything this world could have afforded, and must be a balm to his surviving friends. The *Rattler* had been refitting at English Harbour, and, when I arrived there in the middle of April, Wilfred was a little complaining, but I did not think at first any thing dangerous was to be apprehended. But in a few days I perceived he was in a rapid decline. Dr Young told me to send him to sea, as the only chance. He sailed on the Tuesday for Grenada, where I was in hopes, could he have reached Mr Hume's, some fortunate circumstance might turn out; but it pleased God to order it otherwise. On Friday the 21st April, at ten at night, he left this life without a groan or struggle. The ship put into St Vincent's, where he was interred with all military honours; the regiment, president, and council, attending

him to the grave. I mention this circumstance to shew their respect
for his character. It is a credit to the people of St Vincent's, which
I did not think they would have deserved. Adieu, my good friend,
and be assured I am, with the truest regard, your affectionate friend,
    HORATIO NELSON[7]

The Royal Highness referred to by Nelson was the Duke of Clarence,
later William IV, variously known as the Sailor King or Silly Billy. He
had been sent to the West Indies in command of the frigate *Pegasus*
shortly after Collingwood's return to England, and became close to
Nelson. He was a competent sea officer, but no more; a strict disciplinarian, volatile, self-conscious and a hard drinker.[8] Later in life he
wrote admiringly to Collingwood, although they never met. Nelson
himself returned to England in the summer of 1787, having been
so ill before he left that he shipped a puncheon of rum for his body
to be preserved in. He would have to wait even longer than Collingwood for his next command.

For two years Collingwood's correspondence almost dried up.
There were occasional letters to the Admiralty, assuring them of his
continued and immediate readiness to be of service, but they were
written with little hope of fulfilment. The lack of letters means we
do not know where he was living during this time. Judging from his
later life, he spent much of the time walking in the hills and fields
of Northumberland, carrying pocketfuls of acorns to drop into
hedgerows and patches of waste ground so that England's navy
would never, in the future, want for oak to build her ships with. He
read a great deal too, of history and literature, and he kept a weather-
eye on the news. A convict colony had been established at Botany
Bay on the far side of the world, and His Majesty's armed transport
ship *Bounty* had set off for the Pacific Ocean to bring breadfruit plants
back to the West Indies. Here they might be cultivated to reduce the
islands' dependence on imported food.

In 1788 a proposal to abolish the slave trade failed in the House of Commons, and there was a constitutional crisis. The first of the King's apparent attacks of madness occurred, causing a mental collapse towards the end of the year. In February 1789 Pitt introduced a Regency Bill into the Commons in a panicked attempt to limit the potential powers of the Prince of Wales, a Foxite Whig whose politics were inimical both to his own father and to Pitt's conservative government. Shortly afterwards, to widespread relief, the King recovered his health and the bill was dropped. In April the crew of the *Bounty* mutinied in Tahiti, and set their commander, William Bligh, adrift in the ship's launch. Bligh, who had been James Cook's sailing master, navigated this tiny open boat more than three thousand miles to the East Indies and returned to England, like a ghost reborn, in 1790. He later fought in some style at the battle of Camperdown. He was also present at the battle of Copenhagen and in 1805 became governor of New South Wales, where he was overthrown and imprisoned by the army garrison. He died a vice-admiral.

Unexpectedly, in the summer of 1789, there was a prospect of action for Collingwood. The great maritime powers of Europe guarded their territories jealously, no matter how remote they were. Trading companies had for hundreds of years been planting their countries' flags wherever there was the chance of exploiting local and regional resources. When other countries became interested, there was conflict. Such was the case with the eastern Pacific seaboard. Spain had traditionally claimed rights to exploit it from Cape Horn in the south all the way up to Alaska. Whaling, fur-trading and timber were huge potential sources of wealth requiring only the establishment of settlements and infrastructure to profit from them. But, as the world grew smaller, notably after Cook's voyages in the 1770s, Britain extended her maritime interests further, believing she had little naval competition. Cook himself had refitted his expedition at a tiny settlement called Nootka Sound on Vancouver island, and by 1789 the British East India Company had established a fur-trading post there.[9]

In May of that year Spain sent a small squadron from Mexico to seize the company's assets. The crews of the impounded British vessels were treated as prisoners of war and taken to a Spanish port. Strong diplomatic representations were made on both sides. Spain appealed to France for support. Britain prepared to mobilise, spending an astonishing £3 million in funding the navy for a full-scale war. Collingwood, like most of the other post-captains ashore on half-pay, followed these events with interest. Although the word in the service was that Spain could not possibly fight the Royal Navy alone, and would back down, he began to watch developments with an even keener eye than usual. Six years of peace had seen the navy's battle fleet run down to fifty-five ships of the line. The so-called Spanish Armament would come just in time for Britain to prepare for the largest conflict in European history.

In that same year, 1789, there was turmoil in France where, on 14 July, the Bastille was stormed by the Paris mob. France was bankrupt. Autocratic and centralised, with her maritime strategy crippled by the expense of a continental army, her involvement in the American War of Independence had created a financial crisis. The size of the debt itself was somewhat smaller than Britain's. But the British government's debt was founded on economic reality, scrutinised by parliament; and it attracted interest of three per cent. France's debt was founded on and legitimised by the unaccountable fiscal and divine authority of King Louis XVI, and at eight per cent interest it was crippling.[10]

Britain's economy was recovering from the loss of her colonies by finally resuming trade with them, and was boosted by the rapid growth of her unfettered manufacturing revolution at home. France, flooded by cheap mass-produced English goods, was overwhelmingly an inefficient agricultural economy with an overly complex and largely unenforceable tax system. Failure of successive harvests led to riots in 1788 and a demand for the King to summon the Estates-General, which had not convened since 1614. The aim, ironically, was to emulate Britain by forming a constitutional monarchy. Amidst economic collapse the attempt failed, and anarchy ensued.

In such circumstances Spanish appeals for French help in the Nootka Sound affair unsurprisingly fell on deaf ears. Nevertheless, Spain decided to play its hand to the brink of war. The British government, aware that its indecision in American affairs had already led to one disaster, continued to mobilise the navy and prepared to take on a Spanish fleet it was sure of beating. While politicians and economists complacently predicted an accommodation with Spain, Collingwood decided to return to London to pursue his claim for a ship, just in case. From May 1790 his pen was again taken up, this time at 62 Dean Street, in Soho, from where he wrote to the Admiralty:

> SIR, As I understand a naval armament is about to be fitted out and a Number of ships to be commissioned, I beg to offer myself to serve in any ship to which their Lordships may be pleased to appoint me to command, the duty of which appointment their Lordships may be assured I will most faithfully execute to the utmost of my ability and power ...[11]

While he waited, he did not hesitate to pull any strings he could think of. All the plums[12] had been bagged by captains with superior interest: sons of parliamentary members, captains who were themselves members, or those who had influence at the Admiralty. Captain Conway, and Admiral Bowyer, both of whom Collingwood knew, had mentioned his name to Lord Chatham, the First Lord, as had Collingwood's kinsman W. Spencer Stanhope, MP for Hull. There was a vague promise of a 32-gun frigate, which might mean anything and nothing. It was now that he would find out whether his experience and reputation counted for anything.

Nelson, back home in Norfolk, was to have no luck in finding a ship. He was in bad odour with the Admiralty, having turned a blind eye to some of the Duke of Clarence's indiscretions in the West Indies. His infatuation with royalty, like his predilection for amphibious assaults and flirtatious women, was a character trait which nearly cost him his career on more than one occasion.

Just in case he did get a ship, Collingwood wrote to his sister Mary, asking her to get his sea things ready for him. Typically, the letter contains very detailed instructions, leaving absolutely nothing to chance, with the same attention to minutiae with which he would later draft orders for rescuing the Pope or procuring bullocks from Tetuan. He enclosed the key to his bureau ...

> The key to my trunks are in it. Every thing that is in my bureau except the ragged shirts leave in it, fill it with linen from the trunk, so as to prevent its shaking but with such things as are least heavy. All the papers that are in it leave just in the state they are, all the plans and draft books put into the larger chest, with such books of navigation and signals as are on the book shelves and, in the drawers under them, three spy glasses. The shortest night glass not to be packed, it may stay; in a right hand drawer in the top of the bureau is the great object glass of the largest telescope, it must be screwed in its place ...[13]

And so on. Copies of Addison's *Spectator* and Shakespeare were to be included too, along with linen, table cloths, plain spoons, 'fish things' and teaspoons. He still thought it improbable that the Spanish would fight without the French, but in case they did he would not be left behind for the sake of a few necessaries, though he thought his heavy candlesticks were not worth packing for the extra postage they would incur. In a postscript he reminded Mary that she would find the object glass for the telescope rolled in an old glove. Two weeks later, in another letter to Mary that was full of gossip, he reported on his new dog, which he does not name but which may be Bounce, who was to be with him for nineteen years:

> My dog is a charming creature, every body admires him but he is grown as tall as the table I am writing on almost.[14]

By the middle of June he could report that he had at last received a summons from the First Lord, and been offered a ship. The letter is full of nervous excitement at the prospect of going to sea again. He had turned down the chance to command a 64-gun ship, the *Ardent*, because he suspected she would be stuck on boring convoy work. Instead he was appointed to a 32-gun frigate, *Mermaid*, chosen to be part of a squadron under Admiral Cornish bound for the West Indies where Collingwood's experience would be valuable. He was pleased. He had been given an important command more or less solely on his own merits, and he dismissed Mary's unasked question about taking a pay cut:

> As for the difference in emolument; in a frigate the expenses are somewhat less and if I can get her into the W't Indies I will make the Dons [Spaniards] pay me the difference once or twice a month I hope.[15]

The same letter offers an insight into naval recruitment that paints a more civilised picture than the press gang. Captains were, by virtue of their sole authority on board ship, petty warlords whose officers and men were tied to them by mutual bonds of protection, trust and reward. Thus, years later, Lord Cochrane could recruit volunteers with a handbill calling for experienced seamen who could run a mile carrying a barrel of Spanish gold on their shoulders. A disparate crew might, during a long commission of several years, be brought to resemble an extended family, as Collingwood himself achieved. But in a newly commissioned ship, quite apart from the difficulty of making up the numbers, there was a distinct danger that officers and men would not bond quickly enough to make the ship instantly ready for battle or dangerous manoeuvres.

Collingwood's method was to ask selected former shipmates to join him, and to beg that they bring some of their mates along as volunteers. This he did by getting his sister Mary to put the word about that he was recruiting. Many of these followers were from the north-east, and in this way Collingwood was able to nurture his ship's companies from a basis of regional cultural and social ties. Even at Trafalgar he brought with him into *Royal Sovereign* a number of Geordies whom he called his 'Tars of the Tyne'. His reputation as a stern but decent captain went a long way to attract volunteer seamen who might otherwise be pressed into less amenable ships. Such was the way of these things that as *Mermaid* was refitting, Collingwood's 'old man' William (William Ireland, his steward) turned up to join him, having just come from India. One person he would not be taking with him was the son of Mrs Airey, a family acquaintance. 'I am afraid he is doing no good. He is really now come to such a degree of depravity that in consideration to the other young men he cannot be taken into any ship.'[16]

In July Collingwood was in *Mermaid* at Sheerness fitting out. He was still writing to Mary with instructions for sending his things. He reported that the Admiral, Lord Howe, had been very kind and attentive to him, and there was also news of Bounce: 'My dog is a good dog, delights in the ship and swims after me when I go in the boat.'[17] Mrs Airey's son had disappeared.

The stand-off between Britain and Spain continued through

the summer of 1790 and into autumn. By October *Mermaid* was at Portsmouth with the rest of the squadron. In another, uncharacteristically skittish letter to Mary he revealed that he was now reluctant to sail to the West Indies, his supposed destination, because he had reached an understanding with a young woman. He must have been courting her in Newcastle, and finally summoned the courage to propose while he was fitting *Mermaid* out. The young woman in question was Sarah Blackett, daughter of John Erasmus Blackett, the mayor of Newcastle. Collingwood had persuaded his uncle, Edward Collingwood of Chirton near North Shields, to act as his marriage broker, but had not heard the result of the negotiations. But he entreated Mary to get to know Sarah, who appears to have been a diffident young woman:

> And have you been to visit my dear Sarah? She wishes very much to be well acquainted with you but is so shy that you must encourage her. I think if you wou'd let her drink tea with you in my Doll's [Dorothy's] room she would soon lose that reserve ... I am quite distressed that I must leave things as they are.[18]

However, leave things he did, for very soon *Mermaid* sailed on a cruise to the West Indies in Admiral Cornish's squadron. By this time, Spain had backed down over the Nootka Sound incident. Pitt won the November general election with an increased majority. There was nothing to do in the West Indies but show the flag. Collingwood might have enjoyed it, as a pleasant way of spending the winter, but not having heard from Mary or Sarah in six months he was relieved to return to Portsmouth in April 1791.

> MY DEAR MARY, I am sure you will be glad to hear of my arrival. I assure you I am exceedingly happy at my return, and consider I pray you that for six months I have not heard a word of you, until to-day Mrs Hughes shewed me a letter from Sarah wherein she says

she had been visiting you … I have brought nothing from the W't Indies but a bottle of snuff and a roll of tobacco. I had intended some good grog, but was ordered home before I cou'd get it.[19]

Collingwood was not yet able to leave his ship and go north. Persistent rumours of a war with Russia which, like the Spanish Armament, came to nothing, kept the squadron on alert. *Mermaid* also needed urgent repairs, having sprung her masts (i.e. they had cracked) during the stormy Atlantic crossing. But he went home as soon as the ship was paid off. Cuthbert and Sarah were married on 18 June 1791 at St Nicholas' cathedral in Newcastle, no more than fifty yards from the house where he was born.

Collingwood in the bosom of his family was a quite different man from Captain Collingwood. He immediately made friends with Sarah's sister, her uncle Edward Blackett, and another uncle by marriage, Alexander Carlyle. Cuthbert and Sarah visited many of them, and a host of other collateral relations, during 1791 and 1792. When they were away he wrote to Mary, keeping her up to date with all the gossip. From Musselburgh he wrote that Sarah's aunt, Mrs Carlyle, was 'in a very weak state of health but she frets herself on every little trifling occasion and has so many fears and apprehensions about nothing, that I do not think she will ever be much better'. Edinburgh was one long round of social engagements, and they were woken every morning at six with the noise of carriages returning from parties. Used as he was to the hard world of the sea, Collingwood was amazed at what he saw as the dissoluteness of the idle classes:

This has been called the land of cakes; it may well be called the land of pensions. There is hardly a family of note, either famous or infamous, who have not (some one of them) a pension. Even the Lady Augusta Murray who was the other day found in bed with the

village apothecary, has since that by the interest of her friend
Dundas [Viscount Melville, later first Lord of the Admiralty] got a
[pension] of 300£ a year.[20]

During 1792 the Collingwoods rented a house on Oldgate in
Morpeth. It was, and is, a large red-brick townhouse, square and
rather formal, positioned half-way along the town's oldest street and
close to an old bridge across the River Wansbeck. Morpeth, the
county town of Northumberland, was an Anglo-Saxon and medieval
market town some fifteen miles north of Newcastle on the Great
North Road, set in rolling fertile arable and grass lands. Unable to
compete with Newcastle economically, it has stayed much the same
size as it was seven hundred years ago when the local merchants
hired the famous Scottish astrologer and alchemist Michael Scott to
make the Wansbeck tidal as far up as the town. Even his magic failed.
Collingwood liked the house and the town very much. It was close
to the countryside he loved, and blissfully remote from the smoke
and bustle of Newcastle. He took a keen interest in the garden,
planting vegetables, building a summer house and creating what he
called his quarterdeck walk. He established a nursery of oak trees
and formed grand plans for improvements. Between 1792 and
his death eighteen years later he spent a total of less than two
years here.

By September 1792 the Collingwoods had a daughter, Sarah,
who had been born in May. They had had her inoculated against
smallpox, and her face was covered with 'irruptions', but the doctor
was pleased with her, and thought she would do very well. The
second daughter, Mary Patience, arrived in August 1793, by which
time Cuthbert was at sea again.

During the summer of 1792 a close watch was being kept on
events in France as the country descended into chaos. Quite naturally

many British people, especially those who had property to lose, saw the spectre of revolution appearing on their own doorstep. Part of Tom Paine's seditious *Rights of Man* had been published the previous year and was much discussed in England. King Louis XVI and his family had tried to flee France a year earlier and been brought back to Paris, where they were interned in the notorious Temple prison. The new Legislative Assembly was opposed not only by Royalist factions in France, but also by Prussia and Austria who, like Britain, did not want to see revolution becoming an export trade. Paris was in ferment, under the volatile rule of the Commune and its *Sans Culottes*. In April 1792 France declared war on Austria and Prussia, claiming royal collusion in acts of 'foreign aggression'. In September the monarchy was abolished and a General Convention formed, headed by Danton, Marat and Robespierre. Collingwood, as ever, followed events:

> If the French people are not all mad, I pity most sincerely those who have yet retained their senses. The news expected now is of the most important kind; let us see if there is more wisdom in the counsils [sic] of the General Convention than there was in the National Assembly. I doubt it ... I hope the miseries of France will be such a lesson to the Patriots of this country as will teach them the danger of reform and shew them the true value of this form of government, which affords the means of happiness to all who have from nature dispositions to enjoy it.[21]

There is little doubt of Collingwood's political affiliations here (though he had an intense dislike of party politics: his party was Old England, he once said). In a sense he was right. Britain's monarchy was comparatively benign because it was controlled so effectively by commercial interests.[22] One reason why Britain could mobilise for war so quickly and efficiently was that her naval power was the instrument of maritime trade. As 1792 wore on, the threat to that

trade from France's upheaval grew more serious, politically and economically. France invaded the United Provinces (Holland), confis-
cating property and imposing revolutionary economics there. The
Convention also believed that an invasion of Britain would tilt that
country into its own revolution.[23] European political instability was
indeed adding to the internal tensions created by Britain's manufacturing revolution. In November Collingwood admitted as much
in a letter to Nelson, whom he had not seen since he left Antigua
in 1786:

> You must not be displeased that I was so long without writing to
> you. I was very anxiously engaged a great part of the time, and
> perhaps sometimes a little lazy; but my regard for you, my dear
> Nelson, my respect and veneration for your character, I hope and
> believe will never be lessened. God knows when we may meet again,
> unless some chance should draw us to the sea-shore. There are
> great commotions in our neighbourhood at present. The seamen
> at Shields have embarked themselves, to the number of 1200 or
> 1400, with a view to compel the owners of the coal-ships to advance
> their wages; and, as is generally the case when they consider them-
> selves the strongest party, their demand has been exorbitant ... the
> times are turbulent; and the enthusiasm for liberty is raging even
> to madness.[24]

In common with other periods of dramatic technical innovation
there was great strain on social relations. An emerging entrepre-
neurial middle class was prosperous and confident. For those in work
wages were rising, but unemployment had led to riots, rick-burning
and Luddism. In some respects the north-east of England was lucky.
As Scottish millwright Andrew Meickle was introducing the mechanical grain thresher that would turn thousands of peasants off the
land, coal mining and the industries that were to ride on its back
were booming. The big towns could and did soak up much of

Northumberland's migrating rural population. In the 1780s Britain's mercantile tonnage would double.[25] But as her wealth increased so did social and economic inequality, and it was not only the mercantile class who watched developments in France. Workers such as the Shields seamen were curious to see how far they could flex their new-found muscle.

Collingwood's loyalties were now divided between the delights of his wife and daughter, a 'comfortable fire and friends', and the thought of his own possible employment at sea. In January 1793 Louis XVI was executed. In February France declared war on Britain. By the 17th of that month Collingwood was back in London, hoping for a ship.

ABOVE The Side, Newcastle in 1834, looking up from Sandhill and the Quayside towards the cathedral. In Collingwood's day it was 'from one end to the other filled with shops of merchants, goldsmiths, milliners and upholsterers.' *(By kind permission of Newcastle Libraries and Information Service)*

LEFT Collingwood's birthplace, 1855. The Collingwoods had lived in the tall house in the foreground, at the top of the Side, within a biscuit's toss of the Norman 'New' castle. *(Newcastle Libraries and Information Service)*

OPPOSITE ABOVE Newcastle upon Tyne in the early 19th century. The Collingwoods lived between the castle and cathedral, close to the Quayside with its colliers, keels and merchant ships – an infamous haunt of 'coarse and impudent wenches'. (*Newcastle Libraries and Information Service*)

OPPOSITE LEFT The Side today. Above the entrance to Milburn House, a bust of Collingwood on the site of his birthplace is passed unnoticed by most of his fellow townsmen and women. (*Edifice / Eddie Ryle-Hodges*)

ABOVE Collingwood as an admiral, old before his time. Jane Austen wrote of admirals that 'they are all knocked about, and exposed to every climate, and every weather, until they are not fit to be seen. It is a pity they are not knocked on the head at once...' Portrait by Henry Howard, 1769–1847, oil on canvas, 1807. (*National Portrait Gallery, London*)

PORT
MAHON
Minorca

A St. Phillip's Castle and Town.

B The town of Mahon.

C Saffron Island, whereon are six Careening wharfs.

D The yard, where are the several store houses.

E Bloody island whereon is the seaman's hospital.

F Rat island.

G Quarantaine is

H Guard tow

I A magazi

K Watering

ABOVE Master's mate Collingwood's survey of the harbour at Mahon, 1770. His attention to detail was obvious at an early age. (*By kind permission of the Collingwood Family*)

LEFT The title page of Collingwood's log aboard the *Liverpool*, a 28-gun frigate, on which he served in the Mediterranean between 1767 and 1771. (*The Collingwood Family*)

BELOW Englishmen abroad: Port Mahon in the 18th century, looking from the town below Pigtail Steps across to the Royal Naval base. Anon., c1783. (*Museum of Menorca*)

k H Month & Days	Winds	Remarks in Port Royal
1773	S E:	First and latter part fresh breezes a
nday 22	N N W:	fair weather, middle part light air
	S E & E:	the Long boat employed watering
nday 23	S E:	First part light breezes with rain and
	West	ening, latter fresh breezes and fair. A
	E S E:	punished John Shuter, and John Ro
		with 12 lashes each for quarreling
nday 24	S E:	First part fresh breezes, latter light
	N N W:	and fair weather
	E S E:	
sday 25	S E:	First and latter parts fresh breezes,
	N W:	light airs; A M punished Patrick Fe
	E S E:	gass, Dennis Sullivan, and John Ca
		with 12 lashes each for drunkenness
		quarrelling;
nesday 26	East	First part light breezes and fair, la
		fresh breezes and squally with thun
	N N E:	lightening and rain; A M at 8 fire
		gun and made the signal for a cour
		martial to be held on board this ship
	Variable	on Tho: Bradley seaman, for defama
		Harris Boatswain, & accusing
	E N E	of embezlement of stock, and endea
		ing to suborn witness to prove his
		action; at 10 repeated the signal
		light airs and thick hazy weather, wi
		frequent showers of rain lightening
nsday 27	N E:	thunder; P M at 2 the court martial c
		when the charge being fully proved th
	Variable	prisoner was sentenced to receive 30
		lashes; A M his majesty's ship the
		and Ferret sloop sailed hence, pur

A page from Collingwood's log aboard *Portland*, the 50-gun ship on which he sailed to the West Indies for the first time. The lower two entries recount the fate of Thomas Bradley, the man who had falsely accused boatswain Harris of embezzlement and whose punishment was 300 lashes. (*The Collingwood Family*)

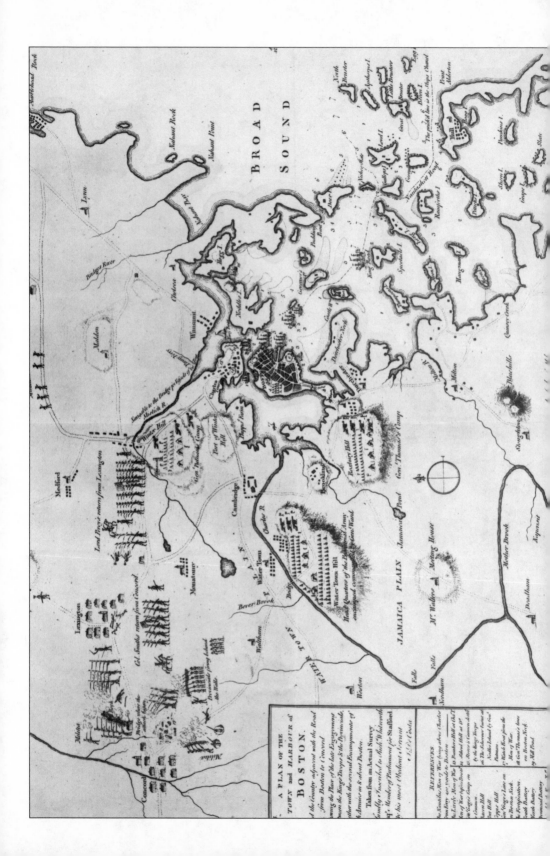

A PLAN OF THE TOWN and HARBOUR of BOSTON.

TOP Bunker's Hill June 1775. Royal Navy warships fire impotently up at the rebel redoubt while boats, under the command of master's mate Collingwood, ferry wounded redcoats and reinforcements across the bay. (*Library of Congress*)

ABOVE Bunker's Hill. Army commanders ordered the hill to be retaken, just as one might order tea and scones. The first two waves of redcoats were mown down by rebels who were ordered not to shoot till they 'saw the whites of their eyes'. 'The Battle of Bunker Hill' by Winthrop Chandler, 1747–1790, oil on panel, c.1776. (© 2005 *Museum of Fine Arts, Boston. Gift of Mr and Mrs Gardner Richardson, 1982. 281*)

OPPOSITE Boston in the age of revolution. When Collingwood arrived here in 1774 the town was virtually under siege following the Tea Party. Charlestown and Bunker's Hill are to the north of the city across the mouth of the Charles river. (*Hulton/Getty*)

LEFT Charlestown today: US naval base and home of USS *Constitution*, 'Old Ironsides'. Behind, the giant obelisk stands on the site of the rebel redoubt on Breed's Hill. (*Topfoto*)

BELOW The gun deck of USS *Constitution*, built in 1797. Technically a heavy frigate, she outgunned any British ship of the same class, humiliating the Royal Navy during the War of 1812–1815. (*Author*)

CHAPTER FIVE

The sharp point of misfortune

1793-1795

A ship of the line was a very different beast from a frigate. When Collingwood was appointed flag captain to Rear-Admiral Sir George Bowyer in 1793, it was a pivotal point in his career. Gone were the easy discipline and independent command that came with a frigate. Collingwood had served in a ship of the line before, but never a second-rate[1] like *Prince*, with ninety-eight guns on three decks. The post of flag captain was difficult, if not impossible, to excel in. Theoretically in control of running the senior ship in a squadron, a flag captain could never quite forget the admiral looking over his shoulder, perhaps waiting for him to make some ghastly mistake. If battle honours were to be won, the admiral was likely to take them for himself. But generally speaking, junior captains of whom great things were expected were appointed to flag ships. So if the post was double-edged, it could at least be interpreted as a compliment and would lead, as Collingwood said himself, to a claim on a line of battle ship in the future.[2] Collingwood and Bowyer had met as long ago as 1782 and Collingwood must have impressed the older man.[3] The patronage system was working for him, but entirely on his own merits.

The sailing qualities of second-rate ships offered little pleasure. They were floating batteries, designed to ride the storms of the Atlantic and wait for a set-piece battle, to slug it out with an enemy of similar size and power. *Prince*, even among second-rates, was a notoriously slow sailer, 'forever in the rear'.[4] Nevertheless, Collingwood was at sea where he wanted to be, and Bowyer at least gave him the freedom to develop his skills further: as a manager of men, and as the supreme exponent of naval gunnery. It is Collingwood on whom Jack Aubrey very explicitly models himself in the O'Brian novels when he aspires to bring the enemy into close action as quickly as possible and fire at them with deadly accuracy and speed.[5]

Gunnery was as different an art in frigates and ships of the line as command was. Three times as many guns to begin with, many of them much larger, with bigger gun crews, and much more dangerous to fire and be on the receiving end of. The lower gun decks of a 98-gun ship carried 32-pounder cannon. They brought to the ship both her stability and her dubious sailing characteristics.

Ships of the Royal Navy, when at full complement, were over-manned from a sailing point of view. Compared to merchantmen there was a positive superfluity of men to lay out along the yards, trim the sails, haul on tacks and braces and complete the never-ending variety of tasks required to keep such a monstrous piece of armament at sea. They were over-manned so that when the ship beat to quarters for action, there were enough crew to sail the ship and man the guns. When the marine beat his drum, a sort of organised pandemonium broke out – baffling to a landsman, but a perfectly synchronised execution of orders long refined and practised – at least, they would be when Collingwood finished with them (it cost him 'some fat', as he admitted to his sister Mary).[6] Every man on the ship, from the cook upwards, had to learn his place and role in any and all situations. For ordinary and able seamen this meant their position on one of the masts during tacking and wearing; their watch; their ancillary jobs and, of course, their place in action.

Except in the most unusual circumstances, a ship of the line was geared to fire from one side at a time. There were enough men to serve all ninety-eight guns with a seven-man crew, but in action each of the forty-nine guns on one side of the ship would be manned by ten or twelve. Extra gunners were needed to fire the carronades and nine-pounders which were mounted on the forecastle, quarterdeck and poop (but which confusingly did not count in the ship's rating).

To take a single deck: the lower deck of HMS *Prince*.[7] Two lieutenants would be in overall charge of the deck. They were like assistant directors in a grand theatrical performance, with an eye on everything at once, deeply sensitive to the performance and morale of their junior officers and men. At the companionways marines were stationed in their bright red uniforms, muskets loaded, in case any man should panic and run. Under the lieutenants were midshipmen, the stage managers, each one caring for a number of gun crews, ensuring they were supplied with powder and shot, helping when guns exploded or were overturned, redistributing crews after injury. The crews and their guns were serviced by powder boys and the gunner and his mates. Powder, especially, had to be managed with extreme care; too much on the decks at one time and the ship might catch fire or explode; too little and there would be hell to pay.

Every gun (they all had names and were regarded with jealous affection by their crews) had a captain. He controlled the firing sequence: a man of great experience and skill, one of the most valued men on the ship. It was a lack of experienced gunners, more than anything else, that led to a sequence of decisive naval defeats for France and Spain in the next twenty-two years. Gunnery could only seriously be practised and perfected at sea in live-firing exercises repeated regularly; ships' crews who spent their lives in port under blockade would prove it, with a firing rate perhaps a quarter or a fifth of the navy's.

There were twelve stages in the firing of a three-ton 32-pounder cannon.[8] When the drum beat, the gun crew would raise the gun port, remove the gun's tompion, cast off the gun- and breeching-tackles that held it tight against the ship's side, and run it inboard with training-tackles. One man would clean out the barrel with a sponge – or a worm (like a corkscrew on a long pole) if a damp or failed charge had to be withdrawn. A cartridge of powder would be passed and rammed down the barrel, followed by the 32-pound ball. This was held in place by a cotton wad, also rammed down the barrel. Then the crew would haul on the gun-tackles to heave the muzzle of the gun out of the port, and the tackles would be carefully laid out on the deck to prevent them tangling during recoil – a potentially deadly error.[9] Now the gun captain took a quill filled with powder and inserted it into the touch-hole. The quill pierced the cartridge, so that when the powder in the quill lit, the flame shot down the quill, into the cartridge, and the charge exploded. In a firing exercise, especially under a captain like Collingwood, the gun captain would train his gun for elevation and bearing, perhaps on a target made of barrels; but at close quarters speed was everything, and when you could see the crews of the enemy's guns grinning from their own gun ports twenty yards away, careful aiming was irrelevant.

This was a period of innovation in gunnery. Slow match (a thin rope-like fuse with a glowing end) was reliable but did not allow for precise timing. The quill was an improvement, but during the wars against France flintlocks gradually superseded other methods, though initially they were unreliable. Both these last improvements were initiated by Sir Charles Douglas, one of Collingwood's few equals in the art.[10]

The naval great gun also plays a curious cameo role in the industrial revolution. In the 1770s ironmaster John Wilkinson of Coalbrookdale (known as 'Iron-mad' Wilkinson, he built the first iron boat and was buried in the first iron coffin), invented a type of lathe that could internally bore a cannon barrel to a smoothness and tolerance that had never been achieved until then.[11] This enabled the manufacture of guns with superior accuracy over longer ranges. Matthew Boulton and James Watt, the steam engineers, realised that Wilkinson's lathe would allow them to make steam cylinders of much greater accuracy than before. This was a prime technological breakthrough in the development of the high-pressure steam engine and, subsequently, the locomotive. It is not just in the twentieth century that martial technology has had a civilian pay-off.

At the point of firing a gun the energy contained in the charge was distributed in three ways. The shot itself was projected from the muzzle, perhaps as far as two thousand yards, or through the two-foot oak sheathing of a ship a dozen yards away. The gun recoiled with tremendous power, brought up with a terrific twang by the gun- and breeching-tackles (if they held), and then kept taut inboard by the crew hauling the training-tackles tight (a ship at sea is always pitching and rolling, an almost incidental hazard). The third recipient of energy was the metal of the gun. It grew very hot after repeated firing, and the structure of the iron altered, eventually becoming honeycombed. A hot gun recoiled with real venom, trying to leap vertically off the deck as well as recoil. In the worst case the shot might be a little too large for the barrel, and a disproportion-ate amount of energy would be transferred to the gun, causing it to explode with consequences that are barely imaginable. Add to these dangers the necessity of crew members getting out of the way of the recoil, and their all-too close neighbours on either side, and it is easier to understand the need for a very high standard of training.

When Collingwood and Bowyer joined *Prince* in the early months of 1793, Britain was in the middle of her largest naval mobilisation for thirty years. There were simply not enough men to go round, as Collingwood was forced to admit to the Admiralty:

> SIR, – I beg to represent to you that there are at present on board H.M. ship *St Albans* 30 or more volunteers who entered for H.M. ship *Prince* and on board the *Royal William* 10 or more. Ever since their Lordships did me the honour to appoint me to the command of this ship, I have exerted all my industry to raise men for her Com-plement and being particularly connected at Newcastle I engaged my friends there to use their influence with the seamen which they did so effectually that near 50 men were entered on the assurance given them by those Gentlemen that they were to serve in the *Prince*. Only three of the Number have yet joined the ship ...[12]

Ties of obligation and patronage went both ways. In the natural sense of justice that prevailed in the navy, those men had just as much right to their captain as he had to them. Collingwood went so far as to copy to the Admiralty a letter written to him by the men themselves, from the *St Albans*:

> SIR, – Have made bold to rite to you to Acquaint you that there is now 30 volunteers or upwards on board of the ship *St Albans* for the *Prince*. From certain appearances it seems as if they mean to put us on board other ships and as we have entered for you, could wish to be there as soon as possible; we have already been

on Board of five Different ships since we came from Newcastle. I am, Sir, your most obedient humble servant, THOS. HUNTLEY.

P.S. Tis by desire of the Rest of the Volunteers I trouble you with these lines.[13]

These two letters alone reveal more about the informal code of naval justice and propriety than a dozen statistical theses could. They show the strength of the bond of trust between a commander and his men, and the desire of that commander not to compromise that bond. Collingwood, it is true, was an exceptional leader of men, but it is hard to see how the Royal Navy could mobilise so effectively in wartime unless those bonds were at least common through the greater part of the fleet. The effect on the Admiralty in this case is not known, but the fact that Collingwood enclosed the men's letter suggests he felt his case was unanswerable. The Admiralty, if it was to rely on the zeal and enterprise of its best captains, could not afford to ignore such niceties. Many of the Board's members probably sympathised from personal experience. At any rate, by August *Prince* had sufficient men to sail. This group of fifty or so Geordie seamen may have formed the core of Collingwood's 'Tars of the Tyne' with whom he stopped to talk at their guns on the morning of Trafalgar, saying, 'Let us do something today which the world will talk of hereafter.'

Manning was not the only problem facing the fleet in 1793. The rapid mobilisation was frustrated by inefficiency, inexperience and all the rustiness that might be expected in a great machine recommissioned. Collingwood mounted one of his favourite hobbyhorses, blaming excesses of political 'interest':

Lord Howe cou'd not get down the Channel in fine weather and the middle of summer without an accident; two ships ran foul of each other and the *Bellerophon* has lost her foremast and bowsprit and gone to Portsmouth a cripple. This was not the fault of the ship nor the weather, but must ever be the case when young men are made officers who have neither skill nor attention, and there is scarce a ship in the Navy that has not an instance that political interest is a better argument for promotion than any skill.[14]

No doubt he was right, but there is also a sense that his pomposity, evident as it was in his days as a midshipman, was magnified by the dignity of being Admiral Bowyer's flag captain. His nerves were also frayed in anticipation of another birth at home. He had sent some 'cyder' by a collier to Sunderland for the expectant mother, and by August had been rewarded with another daughter, Mary Patience. He was delighted. If he was disappointed, as many eighteenth-century men might have been, in not having a son, he never showed it.

In the autumn Lord Howe (nearly seventy years of age), Commander-in-Chief of the Atlantic squadron, took the fleet out on a cruise to look for the French. Lord Howe is recognised as perhaps the finest fleet admiral of his day, a master of manoeuvring large numbers of ships in complicated formation. His bravery was famous: as a captain he had led the line at Quiberon Bay in 1759, and was known to hold his fire until the very last moment, preferably until he was within pistol-shot of the enemy. He was particularly interested in reforming the signalling system, its messages composed using a number of rectangular and triangular flags of distinctive design. These were strung in various combinations from signal halyards, repeated from one ship to the next all along the battle line.

In 1790 Howe had introduced the idea of numerical flags, designed to reduce confusion in passing orders in difficult conditions, and to allow greater subtlety of expression. But the system that allowed a signal such as 'England expects every man will do his D.U.T.Y' to be hoisted (and even that was a compromise: the words

'Nelson' and 'confides', originally intended, not being in the book) was not available until Sir Home Popham invented his telegraphic signal system just in time for the Trafalgar campaign more than ten years later.[15] By 1793 groups of Howe's numerical flags were assigned to messages which the Admiralty considered would be necessary. Signal number one was 'enemy in sight'; there were 260 or so others.

Although Howe's fleet covered as large an area of the Atlantic as possible (a line perhaps one hundred miles long, sailing at an average of seven or eight knots), he did not find the French fleet – the Atlantic is, after all, some 10 million square miles in extent – and on his return to port was vilified (unfairly, Collingwood thought) for having failed to bring news of a decisive victory. The fact that Howe did not know where the French fleet was can be put down to the prevailing strategy of the Atlantic fleet, which was to stay in port until news came (from frigates cruising off the coast of France, or intelligence from smugglers, merchantmen and spies) that they were out. Then the fleet would chase them and hope to catch them. It was a defensive strategy, designed to save wear on ships. Within three years British naval philosophy would radically adopt the tactics developed by Jervis, Nelson and Collingwood, which relied on permanent close blockade and constant battle readiness. The primary impetus for this change came in June 1794, when Howe's fleet did finally catch the French. But before that, the country's attention was drawn to dramatic events in the Mediterranean.

The intellectual reforming zeal which fuelled the revolution in France had mutated into the Terrors of 1793. Suppression of all dissent was swift and brutal. Self-justification became Orwellian self-parody: in the words of Saint-Just, 'What constitutes the Republic is the destruction of everything opposed to it.'[16] Church property was confiscated and conscription introduced, while moderates and royalists either fled or planned counter-revolution. That year the

French harvest failed. War against Austria and the United Provinces combined with blockade by Britain led to riots and insurgency in the Vendée, Brittany, and the mercantile cities of the south-east: Marseille, Lyon, Toulon.

Admiral Hood's Mediterranean fleet of twenty-one ships of the line, including Nelson in *Agamemnon*, arrived off Toulon in July. The harbour (in fact two harbours: the Grande Rade and the Petite Rade) had always been one of France's most important naval bases, as it still is today. It was protected by numerous batteries, and lookout posts on the hills behind allowed its defenders to see a blockading squadron many miles out to sea. In the late summer of 1793 a huge fleet was assembled there: thirty-one ships of the line, thirteen frigates and fourteen corvettes.[17] Of the line ships, seventeen were ready for sea, four were refitting, nine were under repair and one was still being built.[18] The French navy was in a terrible state. It was ill-equipped for war and its officer cadre, by tradition an exclusively aristocratic one, had been devastated by revolutionary purges. It would take many years to rebuild its expertise from scratch.

The city was in turmoil. In August a delegation was sent from Marseille to petition Hood to ask for aid in the uprising against the National Convention. Hood sent to the authorities in Toulon asking them if they wished him to enter the city and aid them in the face of an advancing army. The French Commander-in-Chief refused, and in response the navy's petty officers and seamen deserted en masse, opening the city to British forces. Nelson missed all the action, having been sent to Naples to ask for reinforcements from the King of the Two Sicilies. Here he met the Hamiltons for the first time.

At Toulon the British, reinforced by soldiers from a number of allied states including Spain, garrisoned the city. They hoped, it seems, that the revolt would spread outwards from their one bridge-head on the European continent. But everywhere else the revolts were being put down, with shocking force. In Lyon 1,900 people were executed. A similar fate would befall Toulon if the British abandoned it.

The military key to Toulon was the disposition of guns. As it happened, a young follower of revolutionary principles, a twenty-four-year old Corsican artillery major, had just arrived in Toulon. Napoleon Bonaparte persuaded his senior officers to allow him to conduct the crucial attack on British positions, and in December Toulon fell. It was his first serious action, and it precipitated him on the path to military glory and imperial autocracy. Not only did the British fleet have to withdraw in an embarrassing hurry; they failed to complete the destruction of the French fleet in the harbour. For this folly the officer in charge of the mission, Sir Sidney Smith, was never forgiven by many of his colleagues. Collingwood's fury at the entire debacle was probably typical:

> Our miscarriage at Toulon is truly provoking, the more so as gross mismanagement alone cou'd have prevented [the French fleet] being totally destroyed … No preparation was made either for the destruction of ships or arsenal, and at last perhaps it was put into as bad hands as cou'd be found. Sir Sid. Smith, who arrived there a few days before, and had no public situation, either in fleet or army, but was wandering to gratify his curiosity. You know how it was executed. The ships shou'd have been prepared for sinking as soon as he got possession of them, loading them deep with ballast and stones and making a port hole in them near the edge of the water, and then place the ships in those parts of the harbour which wou'd most effectually injure it. If the necessity of sinking them did not arise, the ships wou'd be uninjured; if it did, they might all have been put under water in half an hour.[19]

As it was, a first-rate, three 80-gun ships and fourteen 74s were left behind, along with fifteen thousand counter-revolutionaries, of whom six thousand were executed. It was not the last time that Sir William Sidney Smith would cut a controversial figure. A man with all Nelson's dash, but even more impetuous and with less of his genius, he had been knighted by the Swedish King Gustavus III. In 1796 he was captured by the French off Le Havre and confined in the Temple prison in Paris. He escaped, and somewhat recovered his reputation by a brilliant defence of the citadel of St Jean d'Acre in Palestine in 1799 against Napoleon's army of Egypt. He later joined Collingwood's Mediterranean squadron and made the Admiral's life a misery.

Collingwood himself was still at Spithead, frustrated by the lack of action and wounded by the ignominy of Toulon, but at least in a better ship. He and Admiral Bowyer had transferred to *Barfleur*, another 98-gun second-rate but a better sailer than *Prince*. He was philosophising on the war:

> This war is certainly unlike any former, both in its object and execution. The object is a great and serious one, to resist the machinations of a mad people who, under the mask of freedom, wou'd stamp their tyranny in every country in Europe, and [to] support and defend the happiest constitution that ever wisdom formed for the preserving of order in civil society. The execution is quite mysterious.[20]

Part of the mystery was that the British knew the Brest fleet, which had suffered a recent mutiny, was in the Atlantic again, in two separate squadrons. They could not be looking for battle. In fact, they had come out to protect a convoy of 127 chartered French and American merchantmen bringing food from America to relieve the famine in France.[21] The other part of the mystery was an aspect of warfare which was being invented by the French, and which – odd though it seems to the cynical modern mind – had not occurred to the British. It was the concept of total warfare, in which the destruction of social resilience by starvation through blockade became regarded as a legitimate weapon, and Napoleon its first great exponent. Strategically, the aim of the British must be to capture or destroy the convoy. Militarily, they thought only of beating her navy.

The Brest squadrons, one of five ships, the other of twenty-one, should not have been difficult to beat. None of the captains had anything like the experience of any of the English captains; some were masters of merchantmen, others were no more than lieutenants. However, the Commander-in-Chief was one of the old cadre, a brilliant tactician and severe disciplinarian, Louis-Thomas Villaret-Joyeuse, whose skill and diplomacy had literally saved him from the chop. Even he did not have a free hand. He was accompanied to sea by a political commissar, Jeanbon, who threatened to have any captain executed for failing his duty – a macabre fulfilment of Voltaire's analysis of the execution of Byng.[22] Villaret-Joyeuse had no thoughts of beating the British, only of getting the convoy through. It was the battle of the Atlantic, fought 120 years before the U-boat.

By the beginning of May Howe had got wind of the convoy, so the fleet set sail from Spithead and stationed itself off Ushant. Reconnaissance showed that the bulk of the Brest fleet was in harbour, but preparing for departure. Howe's fleet sailed west to look for the convoy, and to get far out into the Atlantic to wait for the French fleet. He unsurprisingly neither saw nor heard anything of the convoy, and on 19 May returned to his station off Ushant, only to find that the French were out and had got past him, three days before.

Out into the Atlantic again. This time, fortunately, some merchantmen had intelligence of the French fleet, and on 28 May the British finally came up with them, 350 miles west of Ushant. It was little Sarah's second birthday. It is absolutely clear from Collingwood's accounts of the battle in his letters home that he, at least, was unaware throughout the action of the significance of the convoy. Is it conceivable that Howe, knowing of it, kept that information from Admiral Bowyer, or that Bowyer kept it from Collingwood? We do know that despite his reputation for tactical genius, Howe was an improbably poor communicator, prone to ambiguously worded orders and obfuscating language. He did not do what he should have done: send a detachment off to find the convoy. If he had, he would then have realised that all Villaret-Joyeuse's tactics were designed to draw the British away from it by offering them battle – or the appearance of it. He should then have gone after the convoy. What he actually seems to have thought is that he would defeat the French fleet, and then go after the convoy in the sure knowledge of his complete control of the Atlantic. It is easy to judge. A major factor in what followed was the weather, which after the initial days of contact kept the two fleets shrouded in fog, delaying the final action. Those who fought in the battle, which would become known as the Glorious First of June, thought they had done pretty well, even if history judges the victory to have been pyrrhic.

Villaret-Joyeuse was a clever man. When the two fleets sighted each other he was heading north, with the wind from the south. Howe's fleet were to the east, so the French had the advantage of the wind: they could attack or retreat as they chose. If Villaret-Joyeuse had turned immediately in his tracks, Howe might have guessed that the convoy was ahead and chased it. Too simple. So Villaret-Joyeuse trailed his coat,[23] turning west and allowing the British fleet to close. He waited until they were almost up with him before turning south-east, allowing his rear ships to come under fire, knowing that Howe was hooked. It was late in the day. Somewhere to the north, out of sight, the grain convoy was sailing east. The vanguard of the British fleet got close enough in the failing summer light to catch and cripple the 110-gun *Révolutionnaire*, who struck her colours but later managed to get a tow home. Her principal attacker, *Audacious*, herself limped back to port an almost total wreck.

On the 29th the chase continued, away from the convoy, towards the south-east with the French still to windward. Howe ordered the fleet to tack to the west to intercept the rear of the French line; the French line turned on its heels and followed, keen to ensure that the British remained interested. Traditionally, two parallel lines of battle would then have formed, with each ship firing at medium range against an opponent, and the two lines steadily drawing together. These tactics had been developed over a hundred years, and were essentially defensive: they rarely led to the sort of decisive victory Howe was after. The new thinking in the navy was to break the enemy line, mix it up, and produce a general mêlée. Rodney's battle off the Saintes in 1782 had shown that a better trained force, which the British knew they enjoyed, would very likely win in a mêlée, especially if they had superior gunnery. So Howe, in *Queen Charlotte*, now signalled for the fleet to cut the French line (signal number thirty-four) and engage the enemy from the windward side. In steep seas and a rising wind there was confusion, and part of the British van got too far ahead, but the effect was a close engagement and the British came off best before both fleets retired towards the end of the day. Three French ships had been crippled. Collingwood in *Barfleur* had been at the rear of the British line, but:

> On our closing with one of their ships our fire was such that it is astonishing how she swam after it. They returned very little, and we sustained no injury of consequence.[24]

On the 30th, despite a strong swell, fog shrouded the two fleets for most of the day and it was all they could manage to stay in touch. On the 31st the ships on both sides were so enveloped that the two lines broke up, and were only able to reform towards the end of the day when the fog finally began to disperse. As a result of the action on the 29th, Howe's fleet was now to windward and therefore had the weather-gage: he could bring on an action at the time and place of his choosing. The French could either wait for the attack, or flee downwind. They accepted battle. The two fleets were virtually equal in numbers. The French ships were larger and could bring a greater broadside weight to bear, but the British ships had a superior rate of gunfire, with crews who were sharper and more disciplined. Collingwood, with *Barfleur* near the centre of the line, opposite *Le Juste* of 84 guns, saw it like this:

> After closing our line, and putting in order, between eight and nine the Admiral made the signal for each ship to engage that opposed in the enemy's. Came close, and in an instant all the ships altering their course at the same time, down we went on them. 'Twas a noble sight! Their fire soon began, we reserved ours until we were so near that it was proper to cloud our ships in smoke. However, we were determined not to fire until Lord Howe had, and he is not in the habit of firing soon. In three minutes our whole line was engaged, and a better fire was never. It continued with unabated fury for near two hours, when the French broke. When we had engaged for three-quarters of an hour they called from the forecastle that the ship to leeward of us was sinking. Up started all the Johnnies from their guns and gave three cheers.[25]

By the time both fleets, much shattered by the intensity of the action, withdrew to patch up their wounded, and jury-rig their wrecked masts and spars, the British were in possession of seven enemy ships, including *Le Juste*. One of them, *Vengeur*, sank that evening. The prizes had suffered more casualties (1,270 killed and wounded) than the entire British fleet (1,156).[26] In all, there were nearly four thousand casualties on both sides. Even for a naval encounter these are extremely high figures. *Barfleur* had lost nine men killed, with twenty-two severely wounded, including her admiral.

It is easy to understand that a fleet which captures seven of the enemy without losing one of its own must portray that action as a victory. It was certainly seen as such at home where it brought much relief to the government, and indeed in purely military terms, against a numerically equal or even superior force, it was. Nevertheless, Villaret-Joyeuse had achieved a strategic success over the British: he had ensured the safe passage of the vital convoy, and had got away with the majority of his fleet intact.

Collingwood was in no doubt of the glory which attached to the officers and men of the Royal Navy, and to Howe in particular, whose skill he called 'magic'. But, as was so often the case in action, victory was tinged with sorrow:

> At the time we have so much to rejoice at, I have much to lament in the sufferings of my friends, particularly Admiral Bowyer, whose misfortune has quite checked joy in me. He is a brave and gallant man, and was so raised by the success of the day that he made his own misfortune of little consideration; and I believe he would have done himself material injury by his spirits if I had not at last shut him up and prohibited every body but the surgeon and necessary attendants going near him. We carried him on shore yesterday, and I hope he is in a favourable way. It was early in the action when he was wounded by a great shot [his leg was blown off], and I caught him in my arms before he fell to the deck.[27]

Collingwood, having taken effective command of a flagship after the early loss of his chief, and having been in the thick of the action throughout, might reasonably expect to have found favour with Lord Howe. What happened next left the bitterest taste in his mouth.

Howe's official dispatch to the Admiralty was written the day after the battle. It was rushed to Whitehall by Sir Roger Curtis, his

Chief of Staff, and very quickly published. The King was so pleased that he determined to visit the returning fleet in person. Howe praised the whole fleet, singling out for special mention Curtis himself, and his own flag captain in *Queen Charlotte*, Sir Andrew Douglas. However, he was prevailed upon to compose a second letter giving more details. It seems that Sir Roger Curtis drafted it. It caused outrage in the service.

The second letter began by indemnifying Howe against any possible charges of bias – an odd opening. It says that because the Commander-in-Chief had himself a narrow view of the battle, he had called for reports from his flag officers, 'for supplying the defects of my observance'.[28] He then goes on to list those officers 'who have such particular claim to my attention': Admirals Graves, Hood, Bowyer, Gardner and Pasley. Twelve captains are then mentioned, followed by two flag captains who had taken over command of their ships when their admirals were wounded. Three men were conspicuously left out. One was Captain Molloy of *Caesar*. His gross incompetence or possibly 'shyness' led to a court-martial and dismissal from the service; Admiral Caldwell, whose flagship *Impregnable* had not been among those most closely engaged; and Collingwood, who had taken command of *Barfleur* from very early in the action, and undoubtedly been in the thick of it as his 'butcher's bill' indicated.

Collingwood was mortified, and so were many others on his behalf. Captain Pakenham, of *Invincible*, which had been virtually tethered to *Barfleur* throughout the action, was in a position to offer first-hand support. 'If Collingwood has not deserved a medal, neither have I; for we were together the whole day.'[29] Bowyer, too, gave him a ringing endorsement, but because of his serious injury and worries about his eventual recovery, it came perhaps too late, in a letter to Admiral Roddam:

I do not know a more brave, capable or a better officer, in all respects, than Captain Collingwood. I think him a very fine character; and I told Lord Chatham when he was at Portsmouth, that if ever he had to look for a first Captain to a Commander-in-chief, I hoped he would remember that I pledged myself that he would not find a better than our friend Collingwood.[30]

Collingwood, in one of a number of letters in which he vented his anger, thought he knew the reason for the omission:

The appearance of that letter had nearly broke my heart ... I told Sr Roger that I considered the conduct of the *Barfleur* had merited commendation when commendation was given to zeal and activity and that an insinuation that either had been wanting was injurious and unjust ... Lord Howe is less blamed for his letter than his Captain, who has ever been an artful, sneeking creature, whose fawning, insinuating manners creeps into the confidence of whoever he attacks ... The letter ... may be considered as a libel on the fleet.[31]

Collingwood was in no doubt whose door to lay the blame at. He confronted Curtis and remonstrated with him. Curtis's excuse, that no slight had been intended, and that it was all an unfortunate mistake, Collingwood thought 'an ill-told story'.[32] When, some time later, he also had it out with Lord Howe, he began to believe that Howe heartily regretted the letter. Nevertheless, it rankled, and the pain was about to be made worse.

The medal referred to by Pakenham was an innovation on the King's part. After visiting the fleet at Spithead, he presented Lord Howe with a commemorative sword and was then introduced to all the captains:

The King arrived on Thursday and we all attended in our barges to escort His Majesty, Queen etc. to Lord Howe's ship, in great parade. There, I understand, great ceremonies passed of congratulations ... In the evening we attended him on shore and it was notified that the King wou'd have a levée the following day on shore. The letter, and not being admitted on board His Majesty's ship whilst his flag was flying, to pay our duty to him and witness the honours he was doing the Admiral, had soured the minds of every body, and while the nation were rejoicing in a great victory, those who had won it seemed alone dejected and sad.[33]

Collingwood's temper was a little improved by the King's behaviour:

On Sunday had the honour to dine with the King, which was a much pleasanter day than I expected. His Majesty was gracious to all, and there was less ceremony than I looked for.[34]

He was also promised by the soon-to-retire First Lord of the Admiralty, Lord Chatham, that when *Barfleur*'s new admiral should arrive, Collingwood would be given an 'appropriate' alternative ship. But the fact that a medal had been presented to all those named in Howe's infamous letter, and not to Collingwood, wounded his pride very deeply. It would take three years to wipe the stain, as he saw it, from his character, though when he did, he did so in style. What he later called 'the sharp point of misfortune' [35] could not, he knew, be dealt with by brooding. Action was the thing.

Action he got, but more frustration, too. He decided that while he was waiting for his new ship to be ready, he would fly north to be with Sarah and little Sall, and for the first time see Mary Patience, now almost a year old. Kind letters from friends had, he said, helped him bear the 'exquisite pain'; otherwise he would have 'sunk from grief'.[36] He was delighted with his daughters, predicting they would be a source of inexpressible joy. It was all too brief, but:

Short as my visit was, I was well-rewarded by finding them in great comfort, and my little daughters as fine children as ever the sun shone on. We had scarce time to express our joy at meeting before I received an order from the Admiralty to repair hither and take the command of my ship.[37]

Collingwood's new ship *Hector* was a 74-gun two-decker, but was too short of men to sail with Howe's squadron. In his obsession for fleet perfection Howe kept delaying the squadron's departure, to the frustration of all captains, as news was arriving daily of British merchantmen being captured by the French. *Hector's* manning problems were so acute (by October she only had 130 men) that Collingwood was offered another ship, one with a full complement. He accepted, and shifted his chest once more. But *Alexander* was captured by the French before she could get to Portsmouth. Now unluckily unemployed, Collingwood reverted to family considerations. He had heard that his father-in-law's toe was getting better from some unspecified infection; Mary Patience had grown five inches in the year, and Sall about three and a half. Even though winter was now coming on, Collingwood was sufficiently downbeat about his employment prospects to risk heading north again. This time, he had nine days at home before fresh orders came for him to go to Plymouth (a journey of several days, all of them uncomfortable) to take command of *Excellent*, another 74-gun two-decker in which he was to spend the next four years. He was increasingly worried by the progress of the war (the allied armies were retreating in the Low Countries), and especially by the trajectory of events in France:

> The torrent there seems irresistible, the Republicans, by dint of multitudes, drive all before them and will do so as long as they find means to subsist them. One wou'd think so great an Army wou'd destroy itself by ruining the country, wheresoever they come, but we have long thought so and still they go on. God knows how it will end, but I think if we had peace with them they would do the work themselves, by a civil war in France.[38]

Napoleon Bonaparte's rise had been rapid. He had managed to ride various contradictory political waves as the terror ended and Robespierre and the leading Jacobins themselves fell victim to the guillotine. Napoleon was in Paris at the right time when, in the autumn of 1794, the mob rose against the revolutionary government. Given charge of defending the Tuileries, he ringed the palace with guns and fired grape-shot at the protesters, killing hundreds. He was to be rewarded with military command of the French invasion of Italy.

Back in Spithead Collingwood was also concerned about the state of the navy (as indeed he always was). In a letter to Dr Alexander Carlyle dated March 1795 he summed up his views on the bonds between men and officers, which he felt were under threat from tinkering administrators:

> To make the best use of all the powers of a body of men it is necessary the officers shou'd know the characters and abilities of their people, and that the people shou'd feel an attachment to their officers, which can only exist when they have served some time together.[39]

In the same letter, on a much lighter note, he hoped to find that 'Sall can swim like a frog. Why should a miss be more subject to drown by an accident than a master?' Collingwood was itching to be in the thick of things, wistfully hoping he might be given a couple of frigates so he could harry French trade in the Channel. What he got was a convoy, to be escorted into the Mediterranean. Italy was about to become the centre of military attention on the continent, and Britain had embarked on an experimental union with the island of Corsica. Here, Collingwood was once again reunited with his old mess-mate and comrade, Horatio Nelson. Here too, he came under the command of Sir John Jervis.

CHAPTER SIX

Two thunderbolts of war
1795-1799

Corsica is a dramatically beautiful mountainous island with limited natural resources. It has been invaded countless times: the Roman General Scipio was neither the first nor the last. Like other larger islands of the Mediterranean its culture is fatalistic, and for centuries it has been famous more for its bloody vendettas and primeval economy and religion than its arts and sciences. Nevertheless, its geographical location was of strategic importance to the great maritime powers, as were its forests of high-quality timber. And in the late eighteenth century, in a surge of idealistic and political creativity, it gave birth to a remarkable democratic movement that presaged the revolutions of America and France.

In Collingwood's day, and right up to the beginning of the

twentieth century, the Corsican economy was transhumant:
shepherds took their flocks of sheep and goats up to the high pastures
in spring, and brought them back down to their villages in autumn.
Their bread was made from chestnut flour. At night shamanic dream-
hunters stalked human prey, and in spring the herbaceous scrub of
the maquis draped the island with fragrance. The island's infrastructure was almost non-existent, and although its soils are fertile,
arable farming was underdeveloped. This was Collingwood's ever-
observant opinion:

> The valleys are fertile and the sides of those mountains produce a
> fine grape, and were the natives less savage than they are it might
> abound in corn and wine and oil. But they are a curiosity in Europe.
> Surrounded by civilised nations, there seems to have been no
> improvement in their manners, nor their arts, since the Christian
> era. They plough with a crooked billet and pound their corn in
> a mortar ...[1]

Corsica's maritime economy was almost non-existent. Uniquely for
an island, its people were inward-looking and its fishing harbours
never capitalised on international trade. A succession of powers
possessed the island up to the eighteenth century: France, the Papacy,
Pisa, Genoa. Like Menorca and Sicily it lacked a hierarchy of landed
nobility; when the island rose in revolt in 1729 it was representatives
from village communes who organised a parliamentary assembly.
In the face of a Genoese blockade and military intervention from
Emperor Charles VI the rebellion stuttered, winning a few conces-
sions and with sporadic fighting continuing for years, but lacking
the economic and military resources necessary to achieve independence.

In 1736 a swashbuckling opportunist from Westphalia, Theodore
von Neuhof, arrived with an army of mercenaries financed by
Tunisian merchants. Declared king by a bemused parliament, his

reign lasted eight months. For nearly twenty more years the rebellion simmered, as Genoa, Austria-Sardinia, France, and even Britain sought, in a manner familiar from the South-East Asia of the twentieth century, to dip their toes into Corsica's hot waters.

From this unpromising cauldron an unlikely hero emerged: a statesman fit for the European stage. Pasquale Paoli was the exiled son of a refugee leader of the rebellions. In 1755 he was thirty, a captain in the army of Naples. The charismatic Corsican rebel leader Gian'Pietru Gaffori had just been killed in a vendetta. Paoli was called back to the island and elected General of the Nation. He was given almost autocratic power, but with an ideological zeal tempered by plain sense and political nous, he set about dragging his countrymen into the eighteenth century and beyond. He introduced suffrage for males over twenty-five. He clamped down on the vendetta. He founded the University of Corte in the island's mountain capital, and reformed the Assembly into something recognisable as the forerunner of the American Congress. He established a mint and printing press, and among ideological intellectuals of the enlightenment like Rousseau[2] he was celebrated as a genius.

In 1768 Paoli was visited by James Boswell, Dr Johnson's biographer, who was deeply impressed and sang his praises to London society. Boswell found Paoli reading *Gulliver's Travels* and the *Spectator* and *Tatler*. He had even read John Wilkes' anti-government *North Briton* before it was suppressed. To Paoli's delight Boswell sang him Hearts of Oak and even translated David Garrick's lyrics for him.[3] But for all Paoli's charisma and practical abilities his remarkable fourteen-year rule was about to end. Genoa had finally ceded her claims on the island to France, who sent a large force to take control of it. Paoli organised a campaign of what would later be called guerrilla warfare and held them off for a year. But in 1769 the Corsicans suffered a disastrous reverse at the battle of Ponte-Nuovo.

Paoli left the island and went into more than twenty years of exile in London.

Among the elite Corsican families who decided to assimilate themselves under French rule were the Buonapartes of Ajaccio (pronounced Azhaksio in the Corsican dialect). Carlo Buonaparte was one of Paoli's secretaries, a loyal resistance leader. After Paoli's departure he read law at Pisa and returned to become the legal assessor for his home town. Here, in the year of the rebel defeat at Ponte-Nuovo in 1769, his son Napoleone was born. As a teenager Napoleone took advantage of a French initiative to integrate Corsica with the mainland: he was given a scholarship to study artillery at the École Militaire in Paris. Ironically, his choice to specialise in gunnery was the result of a desire to join the navy. He later tried to shed his provinciality by changing his name to the French: Napoleon Bonaparte.

The revolution of 1789 gave Paoli (now in his sixties) the chance to return to Corsica, where he once more resumed military and political control of the island. But as the ideological fervour of the revolution turned to terror, Paoli again became the enemy of the French. Napoleon, now an ideologically committed revolutionary, also returned to the island, waged his first, unsuccessful military campaign against Sardinia, and tried to heal the rift between Paoli and the Convention. Unsuccessful, he decided to evacuate his family to the mainland. They arrived in Toulon in 1793, just in time for Napoleon to achieve fame in the siege of that city by the British.

It was largely as a result of the failure at Toulon that Admiral Hood, recognising the need for an alternative base in the western Mediterranean, decided to embark on the invasion of Corsica which led to the formation of the Anglo-Corsican kingdom. Who made the first move is not entirely clear. Certainly Paoli sought protection from Hood, who determined to attack and destroy the strong

French garrisons at Bastia, Calvi and St Florent. Various abortive attempts were made to land forces in the north of the island: Paoli's reports of French military weaknesses turned out to be over-optimistic. Paoli was using the British at least as much as they were exploiting him. Of the debacle at Toulon he wrote: 'the capture of Toulon is fortunate. It obliges the English to liberate us.'[4]

The 'liberator' of Corsica was Horatio Nelson who, impatient with Hood's cautious approach, took it upon himself to pound first Bastia and then Calvi (in June 1794) into submission, when perhaps blockade might have been less costly. At Calvi not only did Nelson lose an eye to shrapnel; the amphibious force lost two-thirds of its men to malaria and dysentery. Among Nelson's losses was Lieutenant James Moutray, Mary Moutray's son, to whom Nelson erected a stone at the 'Cathedral of the Nebbio' in St Florent.[5] Nelson, in reporting the boy's death to his friend, wrote to Collingwood that he had hardly ever known so amiable a young man.[6] In the same letter Nelson welcomed Collingwood back to the Mediterranean:

> My dear Coll, I cannot allow a Ship to leave me without a line for my old friend, who I shall rejoice to see; but I am afraid the Admiral will not give me that pleasure at present. You are so old a Mediterranean man, that I can tell you nothing new about the Country. My command here is so far pleasant as it relieves me from the inactivity of our fleet, which is great indeed, as you will soon see.[7]

Nelson was blockading Tuscan ports. The admiral in question, Sir Charles Hotham (Hood having retired), engaged the French in desultory fashion in two inconclusive actions, and was half-sympathetically blamed for them by his colleagues. He was witheringly described by Sir Gilbert Elliot as 'a piece of perfectly inert formality'.[8] By August 1795 Collingwood was in Leghorn (Livorno), having delivered his convoy to St Florent (San Fiorenzo in the Corsican dialect). St Florent is a small fishing port in northern Corsica, separated from its much larger neighbour Bastia by Cap Corse and the high pass at Col de Teghime. Here Collingwood had arrived on the 23rd. He had previously been acquainted with the island in his days as a midshipman in the *Gibraltar*, during Paoli's first period in power. During that visit he seems to have been traumatised by the stabbing of three of his shipmates, for he referred to the episode in a letter to Sir Edward Blackett. He had retained a deep prejudice against the island:[9]

> They have no idea of restraint by laws, or making an appeal to them when injured, the blood of the offender can alone appease them; they are always armed, even when they go to church. Such is our new kingdom.[10]

The Anglo-Corsican kingdom was doomed from the day of its inception. Having lost America to republicanism, Britain had no intention of making what it saw as the same mistake in Corsica. So instead of allowing Paoli to get on with running an island that many, Collingwood prominent among them, thought ungovernable and not worth the effort, they imposed a viceroy on him: Sir Gilbert Elliot. Elliot and Paoli squabbled from the outset. Neither trusted the other, with reason, and there was deep resentment at the British military presence, fomented with relish by large numbers of infiltrators sent from France. As was the case in Menorca, there was enormous local resentment at being controlled by heretics, as the Catholic population saw them.

Britain, suspecting from intelligence sources that Spain would soon enter the war on the side of France, could not afford to lose the island as a source of timber and other supplies, and as a base for its Toulon blockade. To make matters worse, France was about to send its new military hero Bonaparte on a campaign into Italy that would not just alter the balance of power on the continent, but would also revolutionise warfare. He would push his armies farther and faster than any before him since Alexander and Caesar. As Collingwood observed:

> Is it not wonderful that this young man Bonaparte, without that experience which has been thought necessary to the command of great armies, is able to defeat all the schemes and armies that the best Austrian officers can present to him?[11]

No doubt this was partly a comment on the capabilities of the Austrian military machine; but it shows also how closely Collingwood kept in touch with events that others might have thought too remote to be of interest. Meanwhile, Collingwood spent much of the winter of 1795–6 in Corsica, to his dismay. *Excellent*, which otherwise he found true to her name, had been struck by the *Princess Royal* in the middle of a dark and rainy night while on blockade, and been forced into Ajaccio for a new foremast and bowsprit. Collingwood's opinion of Corsicans had not improved (not helped by having been forty-eight hours on deck when he wrote the following):

> This part of Corsica is still more barbarous than San Fiorenzo: the least offence offered to one of the inhabitants is resented by a stab, or a shot from behind a wall. Yesterday one of them stabbed another in the public square, and walked away, wiping his dagger, while no one attempted to stop him, or seemed to think it a violent measure, concluding, I suppose, that he had a good reason for what he did. Some bad carpenters were discharged from the yard on Saturday, because they were not wanted, and on Sunday morning they took a shot at Commissioner Coffin, as he walked in his garden, but missed him.[12]

Paoli he thought something of a fraud. The island was too expensive to maintain, and too much trouble. In any case it soon proved impossible to keep it in the face of French successes. By the end of 1796 the Royal Navy was driven from Corsica and the Mediterranean. Much of this was due to Bonaparte's campaign against the Austrians in Italy. Neither Naples nor Austria could now be counted on for support (and both believed Britain had failed them when they needed her). The Italian peninsula was being devastated, as Collingwood told Sarah's uncle Sir Edward Blackett:

> The French, puffed with the victories of their armies, and having in view some indemnification to their exhausted finances by the plunder of those countries they overrun, shew no disposition to peace. In Italy they have collected immense sums of gold and silver, and do not confine their plunder to specie, but every monument of art and magnificence which has rendered a country respectable and is moveable, they carry off. Their army is a band of robbers, acting under a most horrible tyranny which it is melancholy to see has stretched its injustice over so great a part of Europe. To be their friend or foe is equally ruinous.[13]

This might have been a prophetic warning to Spain. It shows again how closely Collingwood observed events outside his own personal experience. What he could see with his own eyes was that Britain did not have a coherent plan for abandoning Corsica. The French, growing in economic and military confidence, were poised to retake the island. Back in London the government had, during the winter of 1795–6, already formed the view that Britain would be forced out of the Mediterranean.[14] With all continental ports closed to her, and no likelihood of the French fleet being tempted out of Toulon, she had effectively been defeated without being brought to battle. Even so, withdrawal would not be easy. Indeed, such was the depressed view of the situation in London, that in October 1796 Pitt was sending diplomatic signals to Paris with the aim of suing for peace.

In the ports of Corsica the navy at any rate was on the alert.

Paoli had gone into exile in London once more, and the British were regarded with as much animosity as the French.[15] All stores were now kept on board to prevent theft or destruction by the local population and by French infiltrators. Time was running out. Leghorn had been seized by Napoleon. In August 1796 Spain signed a treaty with France. By the autumn Nelson was with a squadron at Bastia, while Collingwood was with the newly arrived Sir John Jervis and his squadron at St Florent. Nelson tried to cross the pass to reach them on foot, but the road was already held by hostile forces. On 19 October Nelson evacuated Bastia in the dead of night but was boxed in by a gale while the garrison tried furiously to un-spike the guns of the citadel.[16] St Florent was under threat too. Jervis warned the town he would destroy it if its guns fired on his ships. Collingwood and others were instructed to blow up the tower called La Mortella that guarded the entrance to the bay: their success can still be seen in the almost exact half of the tower which survives. Oddly, that tower's effectiveness persuaded the Duke of York, some years later, to build the famous string of misnamed 'Martello' Towers along the south coast of England that, perhaps as much as the Channel fleet, dissuaded Napoleon from his long-nurtured plan of invasion.

Eventually both British squadrons got away, narrowly missing a Spanish interception force in the night. A relief squadron under Admiral Man never arrived, his conduct a matter of speculation among his fellow officers, as Nelson noted in a chatty letter to Collingwood sent from Bastia to St Florent by sea:

> My Dear Coll,
>
> Thanks for your newspapers which were a very great treat ...
>
> (P.S.) we have reports that Man is gone through the Gut [Strait of Gibraltar] – not to desert us I hope, but I have my suspicions.[17]

What had happened was that Man had arrived on station with no provisions, and had been sent back to Gibraltar by Jervis. There he had encountered the Spanish fleet, and decided to return to England.[18] How he escaped Byng's fate is a mystery. So Jervis, Collingwood, Nelson and the other captains of the Mediterranean fleet sailed west through the Strait of Gibraltar at the end of 1796, expecting not to return. And there was worse news from home. The French had attempted to invade Ireland. On 16 December fifteen thousand troops and with them the Irish rebel leader Wolfe Tone, set sail from Brest, aiming to land in Bantry Bay. The invasion was foiled by a brilliant spoiling operation on the part of the frigate captain Sir Edward Pellew, ably assisted by terrible winter weather. Pellew had sailed his ship *Indefatigable* among the French fleet at night, firing signal guns, rockets and blue lights. The resulting confusion saw the fleet in hopeless disarray the following morning.[19] Nevertheless, it was a stark warning to Britain, and caused something close to panic. There had already been bread riots in England, and in October the King's carriage was stoned by a crowd demanding peace and food. In Newcastle, two banks closed their doors.

A victory was required. France had not given up her plan of an Irish invasion, hoping that a French-sponsored rebellion there would spread to England, or at least allow the Channel to be blockaded. Orders were issued to bring the French and Spanish fleets together at Brest, take them to Holland, and there embark another invasion force.[20] Jervis, stationed with his depleted fleet at Lisbon, received intelligence of the plan. Collingwood wrote to Sir Edward Blackett in January, believing the navy was in no sort of shape to meet them:

> We have had but a lamentable winter. Political events have gone very much against us ... But the elements, the dreadful and almost constant gales of wind, have done us infinitely more harm, and reduced our little fleet to the strength of a cruizing squadron.[21]

In fact, Jervis' fleet was down to fifteen sail of the line. But Jervis, a massive, hunch-shouldered bullish old man unhindered by self-doubt or intellectual contemplation, hard as nails and spoiling for a fight, was no Byng or Hotham or Man – nor yet Howe. He expected to take on and beat any enemy, regardless of numerical inferiority. He also had an appalling sense of humour, almost cruel. He was cele-brated for having called the fleet's chaplains over to his flagship in the middle of a terrible gale, only to dismiss them again. He did a similar thing to a furious Collingwood for the sake of two bags of onions.[22] His temper was legendary. But under his martial fire, the fleet was transformed.

Since taking command the previous year, Jervis had drilled his fleet to perfection. Their gunnery and manoeuvring in and out of line were practised day after day, to the admiration of Collingwood, Nelson and other enthusiastic captains: Troubridge, Dacres, Foley, Miller, Saumarez and Admirals Waldegrave and Parker. Nelson later called them his Band of Brothers. They were the navy's elite. This was the period when Collingwood trained the crew of the *Excellent* to such a pitch that it was said they could fire an extraordinary three broadsides in three-and-a-half minutes.[23] It would never be bettered; and it would prove devastating to the enemy.

In February 1797 the fleet was cruising off Cape St Vincent, the extreme south-west tip of Portugal, hoping to intercept the Spanish fleet's passage north. Jervis was visiting each ship in turn, scrutinis-ing their preparations. His aide-de-camp was a young midshipman called Parsons, who noted that 'the men and officers seemed to look taller, and the anticipation of victory was legibly written on each brow'.[24] One morning Jervis took Parsons with him on a visit to *Excellent*. Parsons, inured to these visits, was persuaded by one of Collingwood's mid's to join him below for a surreptitious lunch of beef and dumplings:

> When all at once I heard, 'Pass the word for the Vice-Admiral's mid-shipman; his admiral and captain are towing alongside, waiting for him.' This alarming information nearly caused me to choke by endeavouring to swallow a large piece of pudding I had in my mouth, and with my cocked hat placed on my head the wrong way, I crossed the hawse of Captain Collingwood, who, calling me a young scamp, and some other hard names, which I have long since forgiven, assured me, in not a very friendly tone, that if I was his midshipman, he would treat me with a dozen by marrying me to the gunner's daughter.[25]

Collingwood was rather more indulgent towards his men than his (or another captain's) midshipmen. His view was that young gentlemen wishing to be officers must set a higher standard of behaviour than common seamen, and that thrashing them occasionally to remind them of their duty (or disrating them, as he had done to Jeffrey Raigersfeld) would do them no harm. No doubt it also earned him kudos on the lower decks.

On the morning of 14 February, St Valentine's Day, 1797 the first ships of the Spanish fleet were sighted through slowly dispersing fog. Nelson (now flying a commodore's pennant), catching up with the fleet in *Captain* the previous day, had spotted them. As the morning wore on it was obvious that Jervis was heavily outnumbered, by twenty-seven ships to fifteen; the Spanish ships were bigger too. One of them was the vast four-decker flagship *Santissima Trinidada* of 130 guns. Collingwood noted that the Spanish bore nearly twice as many guns as the British fleet. It mattered little to Jervis. He had issued a strict series of orders to his captains and admirals, very much preferring obedience to disobedience. As they bore down on the Spanish they kept as perfect a line as any of them had seen, but it was implicit in Jervis' command that he also preferred enterprise to shyness. Not for him another First of June.

The Spanish fleet was strung out ahead in a straggling line, heading south-east towards Cadiz rather than northwards. The wind was almost directly behind them. Jervis, seeing a gap in their line, immediately steered for it, hoping to cut off a group of enemy ships to leeward in the manner which Nelson would use later at Trafalgar. Don Cordova, the Spanish admiral, issued orders for his ships to wear and head north, so that they might keep to windward of the British and retain the all-important weather-gage. His detached ships would have to catch up as best they could. Now Jervis had to deal with twenty-one enemy ships of the line instead of twenty-seven.

The two fleets began to pass each other on parallel, but opposite courses: Cordova to the north, Jervis to the south. The Spanish line was ill-formed and encumbered by the inexperience of its crews. The British line was like taut elastic. Now Jervis signalled to his van, led by Troubridge in *Culloden*, to tack in succession. This would bring *Culloden* smashing into the rear ships of the Spanish line. But Jervis had given his order some minutes too late. By the time the last ships in the line had tacked in succession, the van of the Spanish fleet would have passed out of range to the north. There they might turn south and envelop the British rear. Seeing this, Nelson, two ships from the rear in *Captain*, decided (if decision is the right word for a man who acted almost before thought in battle) to wear out of line and head straight for the ships of the Spanish van. Collingwood, at the rear in *Excellent*, quickly saw what his friend was about, and followed him close behind.

That evening, talking over the events of that tumultuous day:

Captain Calder hinted that the spontaneous manoeuvre which carried those *duo fulmina belli* [26] Nelson and Collingwood, into the brunt of battle, was an unauthorised departure by the Commodore from the prescribed mode of attack! 'It certainly was so,' replied Sir John Jervis, 'and if ever you commit such a breach of your orders, I will forgive you also.' [27]

Meanwhile Nelson, in his relatively diminutive 74-gun two-decker, was caught in a shattering hail of fire as he engaged *Santissima Trinidada* and her consorts: two 112-gun three-deckers, and an 80-gun two-decker. It was enterprise close to the point of recklessness. Within a short time *Captain* had lost steerage and was a virtual wreck. Jervis on board *Victory*, and Troubridge and the others, were now catching up with the action, which became a general mêlée, as Jervis had intended. But Nelson's situation looked irretrievable.

Collingwood was already in the thick of it, and realised that he was his friend's salvation if he could come up with *Captain* and her enemies quickly enough. First, he had to engage the 112-gun *San Salvador del Mundi*. His first few broadsides against her were of unprecedented speed and accuracy, and had such a stunning effect that she struck her colours within minutes. Or so Collingwood thought. He hailed to ask if she had surrendered. The man who stood beside the colours bowed in submission, and *Excellent* pressed on to relieve Nelson. Shortly afterwards the *San Salvador* raised her colours again and kept up a desultory fire on other British ships as they came within range. Most British captains would have boarded her and taken her as a prize. Collingwood, though, had other things on his mind than glory:

> Our next opponent was *San Ysidore* of 74 guns. We did not fire on her until we were within 5 yards of her, and in less than a quarter of an hour made the Spaniards themselves display the British flag, for I did not stay to take any possession, leaving that to be done by the frigates, but with all my ragged sails set, made my way to the *Sn Nicholas* and *Sn Josef*, which ships had been long engaged with my good Commodore and *Culloden* [Captain Troubridge], and had done them much injury. My arrival up with *Nicholas* gave them breathing time. We went so near that until the smoke clear'd away I did not know whether we were fast to her or

not. In her attempt to sheer from us she clapt alongside *Josef*, which was close to her, so that all my shot went through both ships.[28]

Again Collingwood passed on, believing that both ships had struck to him, for now he aimed to have a go at *Santissima Trinidada* herself, who ended the battle virtually wrecked, but who lived to fight again at Trafalgar. During this, his last engagement of an extraordinary day, Collingwood nearly lost the number of his mess when a 50lb double-headed shot narrowly missed his head and, entirely spent, hit the base of the mainmast and rolled at his feet. He kept it as a souvenir to give to his father-in-law, and until a few years ago it was still at the Blackett's country house, Matfen Hall, in Northumberland, though it has since disappeared. 'These are no jokes,' wrote a typically downbeat Collingwood, 'when they fly about one's head.'[29] Another souvenir was the portrait of San Ysidro from the ship of that name, which Collingwood hoped Sarah would like, but which in the meantime adorned his great cabin in *Excellent*. *Excellent* lost eleven men dead and fourteen wounded.

Nelson, meanwhile, was helping himself to a large portion of that glory which was to make him England's Saviour. Collingwood described the famous scene, for his home audience:

> When I left *San Nicholas* they fell on board the *Captain*, which was very much disabled in the severe service she had had, when the Commodore, whose judgement supported by a most Angelic spirit is equal to all circumstances that arise, boarded the *Sn Nicholas*, and having reduced her to obedience sword in hand marched on to the *Sn Josef*, which was fast on the other side of her; the resistance they made was not great, a sort of scuffle in which a few lives were lost, and there on the quarter deck of a Spanish first rate, he received the submission & swords of the officers of the two ships, one of his seamen standing by him, and making a bundle of them with as much composure as he would tie a bundle of faggots.[30]

Nelson himself called it his 'patent bridge for boarding first-rates'. It was the stuff of penny-plain, twopence-coloured cartoonists, and the episode instantly passed into British military folklore. Though the British had only captured four of the Spanish fleet (all of them victims of Collingwood's gunnery), the victory was overwhelming in its effect both on the British public, still smarting from withdrawal from the Mediterranean, and on the Franco-Spanish alliance, whose Irish plans were for the time being scuppered. The action also made a great deal of money for the captains of the British fleet, in prizes and head-money.

For Collingwood, more importantly, there was immediate and unaffected praise for his gallantry. Dacres, in *Barfleur*, wrote to request that he would accept his congratulations 'upon the immortal honour gained by the *Excellent* yesterday. The Admiral joins very sincerely in my ideas. God bless you, and may we all imitate you.'[31] Admiral Waldegrave added his congratulations: 'May England long possess such men as yourself: – it is saying everything for her glory.'[32] But most importantly, he received the following communication from his friend:

MY DEAREST FRIEND,

'A friend in need is a friend indeed,' was never more truly verified than by your most noble and gallant conduct yesterday in sparing the *Captain* from further loss; and I beg, both as a public officer and a friend, you will accept my most sincere thanks. I have not failed, by letter to the Admiral, to represent the eminent services of the *Excellent* ... We shall meet at Lagos; but I could not come near you without assuring you how sensible I am of your assistance in nearly a critical situation.[33]

Why does the word 'nearly' catch in the throat? Is there just a hint that, for all Collingwood's evident brilliance on the day, Nelson could not accept that he had got himself out of his depth and had been in fact rescued by Collingwood? Is it a trace of guilt, that he attained the glory of the prizes which had been won at least as much by Collingwood as himself? Nelson, in his own account of the battle, noted that Collingwood 'disdained' the parade of taking possession of beaten enemies. Was he perhaps a little jealous of Collingwood's disinterestedness?

Collingwood seems not to have read anything into it at all. He was simply delighted that he had been recognised by his peers. And more than that. Nelson was given the Order of the Bath in recognition of his brilliance; he was now promoted to rear-admiral, having already been at the top of the post-captains' list. Jervis was made Earl St Vincent. Now Collingwood was offered a medal, along with the other captains. He told Jervis that he could not accept it, for if he deserved a medal now he had deserved one for the First of June. Jervis replied that that was precisely the answer he had been expecting; and Collingwood, at last vindicated, duly got both. But it is hard to escape the conclusion, not for the first or last time, that had Nelson not been Nelson, Collingwood might also have been a public hero in this, his forty-ninth year.

The year 1797 had started well, and it would end well with another famous naval victory. But in between, as if to emphasise how high the stakes were in this war of revolution and conservatism, there was trouble at home. On 16 April, Easter Sunday, the fleet at Spithead mutinied. Or to be more accurate, it went on strike. Mutiny is an unfortunate word to use, for there were as many variations on the theme as there were men prepared to disobey orders. Mutiny was naturally punishable by death; and yet, there were perfectly understood mechanisms in the Royal Navy by which a man, or group of men, might refuse to obey orders without being mutinous. A ship's crew might at any time petition their captain over grievances. On rare occasions they might petition an admiral over their captain's head. Frequently their grievances seem entirely reasonable. A good captain would negotiate from a position of strength and ensure that the grievances were addressed without surrendering the principle of authority: it was a nice trick to pull off.

The first demand of the strikers was for more food.[34] They wanted to receive sixteen ounces to the pound instead of fourteen. Traditionally the extra two ounces belonged to the ship's purser (hence, a purser's pound is a short measure), an object of more revulsion even than the enemy to most sailors. They also wanted better quality provisions, and an assurance that in port they would have access to fresh meat and vegetables. The most serious grievance of the Spithead strikers was pay. An able seaman received twenty-two shillings and sixpence a month (£1.13 in modern terms), an ordinary seaman just nineteen shillings, compared to an admiral's pay of £1,000 per annum.[35] The rate had not changed since the days of Oliver Cromwell, nearly 150 years before. What was worse, privates in the army got a shilling a day, a matter of great affront to sailors who considered their service both harder and more important. Not only that, but payment was in arrears, and by ticket, rather than coin. Often, sailors would be turned over to a new ship when theirs was laid off, without receiving even their arrears.

The strike was well organised and represented by delegates from each ship. The demands were presented respectfully, and there was no physical threat to individual officers. It was understood that if the French came out, the ships would sail to meet them; otherwise, the Channel fleet would stay where it was until the grievances had been addressed. It is conspicuous that the navy's notoriously harsh punishment system was not a source of open complaint. Arbitrary and cruel use of punishment was, but sailors accepted hard discipline as a necessary evil to maintain the safety and well-being of ships and their crews. However, the names of 107 officers considered tyrannical by their men were also presented.[36]

The sailors' complaints were badly handled. The fleet was in the process of changing command from Lord Howe to Lord Bridport, and somehow the Admiralty failed to ensure that Bridport knew of the strikers' demands until the fleet for a second time refused to go to sea. There was a brief showdown during which five seamen were shot, and the officers commanding were sent ashore. Howe was briefly recalled, came to terms with the strikers, and peace was restored in the fleet after parliament had officially agreed to their terms and given the delegates a pardon.[37] The 107 named officers did not return to their ships.

However, two days after the fleet finally sailed, on 12 May, a much more serious mutiny, a real mutiny, broke out among the ships stationed off the Nore, and spread to the squadron off Yarmouth. These ships were watching and waiting for the Dutch fleet, close to sailing themselves and hoping to establish control in the North Sea prior to another attempt on Ireland.

In this case sedition was at work. This time there was a leader, Richard Parker. There was also dissension among ships' companies as they tried to enforce a blockade of the Thames. Their supply of victuals was cut off, and forts at Tilbury and elsewhere were put on alert to destroy the fleet. There was violence. Admiral Duncan, a man of huge proportions in every respect, had suppressed mutiny in his fleet at Yarmouth by sheer force of personality. Now the Admiralty sent him to the Nore, but the plan backfired, and when reports came of the Dutch fleet preparing for sea, Duncan was left with just his own flag ship and one other to blockade them in the Texel. Eventually the mutiny was suppressed. Parker and twenty-eight others were hanged, and some of the ships with the most disruptive crews were sent to join St Vincent off Cadiz. But a potentially fatal blow had been dealt to the delicate web of obligation and trust that tied men and officers together. Whether a permanent breach would open, and whether it would compromise the fighting efficiency of the fleet, remained to be seen.

In St Vincent's taut, disciplined fleet captains such as Nelson and Collingwood, each with their own methods, brought a measure of control. Collingwood, only too aware of the sensitivity of the situation, wrote to Alexander Carlyle in June that:

> The state of the fleet in England has given me the most poignant grief. How unwise in the officers, or how impolitic in the administration, that did not attend to, and redress the first complaints of grievance, and not allow the seamen to throw off their obedience and to feel what power there is in so numerous a body.[38]

He thought that by their mishandling of the mutinies, the government had allowed the sailors to extort what they now regarded as rights, instead of privileges granted to them by a just and humane society. It was, in his mind, a dangerous and revolutionary precedent: 'The times are convulsed and full of danger: peace alone can restore us to harmony. Heaven grant it!'[39] St Vincent was confident that he could send Collingwood the most troublesome men. 'Send them to Collingwood,' he is reputed to have said, 'he will bring them to order.'[40] One man sent to him had been a seaman on *Romulus*. He had contrived to load a quarterdeck gun and point it at his officers, threatening to blow their heads off. When the man (who might easily have been hanged) was brought aboard *Excellent*, Collingwood spoke to him in front of the other men:

> I know your character well, but beware how you to attempt to excite insubordination in this ship; for I have such confidence in my men, that I am certain I shall hear in an hour of every thing you are doing. If you behave well in future, I will treat you like the rest, nor notice here what happened in another ship: but if

you endeavour to excite mutiny, mark me well, I will instantly
head you up in a cask, and throw you into the sea.[41]

Dangerous times indeed. Collingwood's personal authority came
not just from his conspicuous bravery, skill and seamanship; it came
also from his famous humanity towards his men. He demanded
obedience and respect for officers, and in return he demanded that
they show respect to their men. He would not countenance swearing
from officers, and was particularly annoyed if he heard them calling
to sailors in what he considered a rude manner: 'If you do not know
a man's name, call him sailor, and not "you-sir", and other such appel-
lations; they are offensive and improper.'[42]

For the time being, the immediate danger for Collingwood was
the boredom of the Cadiz blockade: day after day, week after week
of St Vincent's manoeuvres, tight discipline, and almost no social
contact. There was some solace in correspondence, and in Bounce's
company, but Collingwood had been away from his family since the
beginning of the war, more than four years, and he longed for home.

> God knows when we shall break up this blockade, not while there
> is a chance of the Spaniards coming out, or a peace puts an end to it.
> What pleasure wou'd it give me, could I hope to pass my Christmas
> at home? Remember me kindly to all our friends. My best love to
> all at home …
>
> PS … Nelson is gone on an expedition, I believe, to Teneriffe.[43]

Nelson had, indeed, gone on an expedition to Tenerife. This was
designed to intercept a Spanish treasure ship inbound from the West
Indies. It was an amphibious assault; and like Nelson's other forays on
to land, it ended in disaster, the loss of his right arm, and 250 men
killed and wounded. Nelson was invalided home, and the humiliation
of failure, combined with extreme pain from his wound, brought
on an overwhelming depression.

There was better news from the North Sea in October. Admiral Duncan brilliantly defeated the Dutch component of the French invasion fleet off Camperdown.[44] Duncan had a numerical superiority of sixteen to fifteen and larger ships; the Dutch were aggressive and well-trained. Duncan led his fleet in two columns at right angles to the Dutch fleet in a tactic that presaged Nelson's at Trafalgar: part of a tactical evolution which had begun with Rodney at the battle of the Saintes. It was designed to bring on a mêlée which suited the high level of training and seamanship of the Royal Navy. It would work again and again, and no enemy commander in the age of sail found a strategy to counter it.

Duncan's capture of eight ships of the Dutch line, together with two heavy frigates, was the most convincing victory in the first phase of the war. Not only did it decisively end the threat from the Dutch in the North Sea; it 'clapped a stopper' over all talk of mutiny. It gave Pitt's beleaguered government a crucial breathing space, and determined Bonaparte to look elsewhere for a grand military project. Confounded in the Atlantic and North Sea, he turned his attention to another cherished project: Egypt, and the overland route to the Red Sea. Established there, he would be able to attack Britain's most important mercantile asset: the route to the East Indies, which she had enjoyed more or less unopposed for twenty years.

Once more the war was entering a critical phase. France had control of the Mediterranean. Britain's closest base was Gibraltar, but as an isolated garrison it was vulnerable, both to attack by Spain, and from its own descent into dissoluteness:

> I do not understand ... of what use Gibraltar is to us under these circumstances. It rather serves as a trap to catch Englishmen in, and a grave to bury drunken Soldiers in. There is perhaps more dissipation at Gibraltar than in any other station in the world. One great fee of the Governor arises from wine drunk there, and licenses for

wine houses; therefore drunkenness is not a punishable offence in a Soldier. On the contrary, there is a sort of encouragement given to jolly fellows and I am told at least two thirds of the garrison are drunk every night.[45]

The blockade of Cadiz could not be lifted because of the very obvious activity going on in the Spanish fleet, to all appearances ready to sail at short notice. Collingwood and the other captains, longing for home and not having dropped anchor for many months, had to look to their own resources to relieve the hardship and boredom of a winter at sea, when luxuries like the mail and fresh food were in intermittent supply:

> My wits are ever at work to keep my people employed, both for health's sake, and to save them from mischief. We have lately been making musical instruments, and have now a very good band. Every moonlight night the sailors dance; and there seems as much mirth and festivity as if we were in Wapping itself. One night the rats destroyed the bagpipes we had made, by eating up the bellows; but they suffer for it, for in revenge we have made traps of all constructions, and have declared a war of extermination against them.[46]

Collingwood himself was briefly made a commodore, but it was of little comfort to him, especially when news reached the fleet of the intended French invasion of Egypt, and Collingwood found that he was to be left behind. Nelson had returned, once more in fighting spirits now that he had finally been given the true independent command that he had sought for so long. He was to find Bonaparte's fleet, determine their destination, and bring them to battle. After months of frustration he did so, immortally, at Aboukir Bay near Alexandria, in a brilliant and decisive action known to legend as the Battle of the Nile. Bonaparte and his army of Egypt were trapped. Britain once more had naval control of the Mediterranean, and the pride of the French navy had been humiliated. Like most other captains, Collingwood was torn between admiration for the genius of his friend, and fury that he had been left out of the action, by what he saw as favouritism on the part of St Vincent:

> The only great mortification I suffered was not going with Adm Nelson. He [St Vincent] knew our friendship; for many, many years we had served together, lived together, and all that ever happened to us strengthened the bond of our amity, but my going would have interfered with the aggrandisement of a favourite to whom I was senior, and so he sent me out of the way when the detachment was to be made.[47]

This letter was written in December 1798 at Spithead, where Collingwood was in hopes that he might finally be allowed to go home for a spell of leave. *Excellent*, at sea more or less continuously since 1795, needed urgent repairs, and Collingwood thought he might be paid off. Despite his jealousy of the glory of the Nile, Collingwood had already written to his friend offering him his congratulations, unable, he said, 'to express my joy ... for the complete and glorious victory you have obtained over the French'.[48] Nelson did not return to England, as expected: he had been distracted in Naples. For Collingwood, so near home and yet still unable to leave Portsmouth, the agony grew worse as the days passed. He even declined the offer of another command, the 90-gun *Atlas*. All he could think of was Morpeth, Sarah, and his two girls, whom he had not seen for six years.

Finally, at the beginning of February 1799, he found himself at home again in the bosom of his family; and as if to paint the lily, in a general promotion timed for the anniversary of the battle of Cape St Vincent, Collingwood found himself a rear-admiral of the white.

'Old Jarvie'. Sir John Jervis, Earl St Vincent, Commander-in-Chief of the Mediterranean fleet and later First Lord of the Admiralty. Hard as nails and spoiling for a fight, he trained his fleet to a state of near perfection. Portrait by Domenico Pellegrini, 1759–1840, oil on canvas, 1806. (© *National Maritime Museum, London*)

ABOVE Sarah Collingwood. This small sketch may well have been drawn by Collingwood himself; though a talented draughtsman, he never quite mastered the depiction of the human face. (*The Collingwood Family*)

OPPOSITE PAGE
TOP LEFT Nelson. 'An enemy that commits a false step in his view is ruined, and it comes on him with an impetuosity that allows him no time to recover.' Portrait by Lemuel Francis Abbott, 1760–1803, oil on canvas, 1797. (*National Portrait Gallery, London*)

TOP RIGHT Mary Moutray. Charming, intelligent, with striking good looks: she brought out the best in both Collingwood and Nelson, and they were dazzled by her. (*By kind permission of Clive Richards*)

BELOW LEFT Nelson by Collingwood, drawn at Windsor House in Antigua. Nelson was recovering from yellow fever and wore a wig; even so, it is not a flattering portrait. (© *National Maritime Museum, London*)

BELOW RIGHT Collingwood by Nelson. Collingwood must have seemed the epitome of the English naval captain. (© *National Maritime Museum, London*)

The battle of Cape St Vincent, 14 February 1797. A brilliant naval triumph against a much larger Spanish fleet – not for the last time, Collingwood played a crucial role in a victory attributed to Nelson. "The Captain' capturing the 'San Nicolas' and the 'San José" by Nicholas Pocock, 1741–1821, oil on canvas, 1808. (© *National Maritime Museum, London*)

LEFT A gun crew in the heat of battle. Fast, accurate gunnery was the key to British naval success; Collingwood was its supreme exponent. 'A Gun Crew' by Thomas Stothard, 1755–1834. (*Bridgeman Art Library*)

BELOW Careening. Britain's policy of keeping her fleets constantly at sea took a heavy toll on ships and men. Dockyard facilities like those at Mahon and English Harbour were vital. (© *National Maritime Museum, London*)

OPPOSITE PAGE
TOP English Harbour, Antigua. A safe anchorage in the hurricane season, it allowed Collingwood and Nelson to conduct their anti-smuggling operations, re-victual their ships, and carry out repairs. (*Author*)

BELOW The Copper and Lumber store, English Harbour: the only surviving Georgian dockyard in the world. (*Author*)

LEFT Napoleon's statue in Ajaccio, his birthplace in 1769: 'as much villainy as ever disgraced human nature in the person of one man.' (© *Travel Library*)

BELOW St Florent. Collingwood had a low opinion of Britain's Corsican allies: 'they have no idea of restraint by laws, or making an appeal to them when injured, the blood of the offender can alone appease them; they are always armed, even when they go to church. Such is our new kingdom.' (*Author*)

CHAPTER SEVEN

Hope of peace alone

1799-1802

Spring 1799: Napoleon, stranded with his army in Egypt, was striking north through Palestine, about to be brought up with a round turn by Sir Sidney Smith at Acre. Nelson was in Palermo. He had been seduced by the fabulous dissoluteness of the Neapolitan court and the charms of the British Ambassador's wife, evacuating them from Naples to Sicily. St Vincent was too ill to command at sea and lay at Gibraltar, dispensing orders to the fleet. Collingwood was in the garden at Morpeth, contemplating his long-neglected cabbage patch.

Almost delirious with joy, at the same time he had an eye and half of his soul turned towards the sea. He was delighted with his daughters, with his wife, and with the genuine expressions of pleasure he encountered everywhere at his promotion.

I have spent a month of great happiness. Every body and every object about me contributes to it. My Sarah is all that is excellent in woman, my girls as sweet children as ever were. They are pretty creatures and appear to me to have the greatest affection for each other, and for their mother, and to possess tempers that promise them a fair share of happiness, so that if this great promotion which the King has made in the navy should exclude me from serving at sea, and check my pursuit of professional credit, I have as many comforts, and sources of rational happiness, to resort to as any person. But I shall never lose sight of the duty I owe to my country.[1]

Until such time as his country called on him again, Collingwood kept himself busy making plans for the house and the garden. He had designs for the girls' education, too: French, geometry, history, and serious literature – no frivolities for the Misses Collingwood. But his first duty was to the service, and it was a matter of weeks rather than months before he was itching to be back in action. As always he kept a close eye on political and military developments, via newspapers and letters from fellow officers and friends. He had always had strong views on the enemy; he also had a fair idea of their future strategy for the war, foreshadowing Bonaparte's Continental System:

When I consider the impetuosity of the French armies, the ambition of their government, and the impotence of the nations they are about to attack, I am sick with abhorrence of them. That under the mask of friendship to mankind [they] would subject them to the most degrading slavery that ever the human species groaned under … They have tried us in battle, and have failed … It is only left for them to make war on our finances.[2]

Sarah's mixed feelings at this time cannot be better expressed than by those of Jane Austen's fictional Anne Elliot: 'She gloried in being a sailor's wife, but she must pay the tax of quick alarm for belonging to that profession ...'³ Almost none of Sarah's letters to her husband survive, so we do not know how she expressed her sense of isolation to him. The first of her correspondence that does survive is from the following year, when a series of letters between her and Miss Mary Woodman began. By that time Collingwood was at sea again, and Sarah was once more paying her taxes.

In the meantime the Collingwoods were filling their lives with visits to family and friends; Cuthbert had been to London briefly to discuss the possibility of service, but had been offered nothing. He had met the Queen, though, at one of Their Majesties' famous Drawing Rooms. Unlike Nelson, dazzled by the aura of royalty, Collingwood was amused but unimpressed by the experience:

> It was an entertaining sight, to so new a courtier, to observe the pleasure that sprang into the countenances of all, when Her Majesty was graciously pleased to repeat to them a few words which were not intended to have any meaning; for the great art of the courtly manner seems to be to smile on all, to speak of all, and yet leave no trace of meaning in what is said.⁴

A rear-admiral of the white, whatever his service pedigree, was in his own way an unfortunate junior.⁵ Not only was he most unlikely to be given an independent command, but he must also surrender the sailing of his ship to a flag captain. But the thought of being ashore when there was action afoot was no easier to bear in his fifty-first year than it had been in his twenty-fourth when he and Wilfred had been consigned to the Portsmouth guard ship. One awful possibility was that he might be offered a shore command, the worst of both worlds. 'I have no desire to command in a port,' he wrote, 'except at Morpeth, where I am only second.'⁶ He consoled himself with corresponding on the subject of Frenchmen and domestic bliss:

> I hope ere long [the Arch Duke of Austria] will make them hide
> their heads and make the name of Frenchmen as contemptible to
> all men as it has ever been detestable to me. In their best days they
> were ever a set of fawning, dancing, impious hypocrites. Sarah
> wou'd add a few lines to her aunt but she says her fingers ache with
> her work. She is making a new cover for her sofa against her friends
> come – always industrious.[7]

In May Collingwood's political sensitivities were tested when he and
Sarah dined with some of their Morpeth neighbours, who were very
'gay and good humour'd', but:

> When I tell you the dining room where we dined yesterday was
> ornamented with pictures of Tom Paine and Horn Tooke,[8] you will
> conclude we have strange characters amongst us. It was at young
> Burdon's, the son of him who lives at Newcastle; he was bred at
> Cambridge and is a philosopher.[9]

Collingwood was making light of an extremely tense political
climate. Pitt was about to complete the Second Coalition against
France, comprising Britain, Russia, Austria, Portugal, Turkey and
the Two Sicilies, but it was a fragile alliance, and visibly so. A strong
peace party continued to pressurise the King and his cabinet as the
National Debt rose to dangerous levels, and the failure of the 1799
harvest would create even greater tensions. Parliament was about
to pass the Combination Act, giving magistrates the right to ban
political associations of workers.

Compared to France, Britain still had an extraordinarily free
press. Nevertheless, government was sufficiently concerned to have
its agents monitoring clubs and meeting places. In the event, it was
the Irish Question which would, within two years, see Pitt's administration fall. Ireland could not be treated separately from the war

with France, because it had been and still was French policy to incite uprising there. The failed rebellion and French invasion of 1798 that had led to the suicide of Wolf Tone was followed by an Act of Union with the British crown, its imposition softened with bribes and with Pitt's promise of Catholic emancipation. At this last, religious and moral fence, the ever-conservative George III put his royal foot down, and Pitt was replaced by Henry Addington. The stress precipitated a new outbreak of the King's illness.

This crisis was still in the future when, in June 1799, three months after coming home, Collingwood found himself at sea again, hoisting his admiral's pennant in *Triumph*, an ill-named, old-fashioned 74-gun two-decker[10] that was so slow the rest of the fleet kept having to wait for her to catch up. As before, he found the Channel fleet in a deplorable state. To begin with, St Vincent's absence in Gibraltar meant that his iron hand had loosened its grip on discipline in the fleet. Rapid expansion of the navy had effected a corresponding decline in skill and seamanship. There were so many 'unqualified, ignorant people'[11] in the service that accidents were frequent and inevitable. As for Collingwood's own ship:

> I have a captain here [Stephens], a very novice in the conduct of fleets or ships. When I joined her I found she had been twice ashore, and once on fire, in the three months he had commanded her, and they were then *expecting* that the ships company should mutiny every day. I never saw men more orderly, or who seem better disposed, but I suppose they took liberties when they found they might, and I am afraid there are a great many ships where the reins of discipline are held very loosely, the effect of a long war and an overgrown navy.[12]

Summer was spent vainly chasing after the Brest fleet, which had been allowed to get out by the incompetence of the blockading squadron, and was now at large in the Mediterranean. Collingwood, sailing under Lord Keith's command, nearly caught up with them in Menorca, which Keith thought they were aiming to retake. But they were not there. Nelson, whom Keith had requested to cover the island from Sicily, refused to come out: a direct dereliction of duty somewhat less glorious than his later problem with a telescope.

Nelson has often been held up as a paradigm of the English naval officer's devotion to duty. In fact, his devotion was to an older naval concept: that of honour and royal service. It was, ironically, Collingwood, a man older than Nelson by half a generation, who embodied the concept of selfless duty which was to become so fashionable in the first half of the nineteenth century. Nelson may have become infatuated with Emma Hamilton, but he had been equally seduced by the aura of the Bourbon royal family: King Ferdinand and Queen Maria Carolina (sister of the decapitated Marie Antoinette). Even among eighteenth-century royalty they made a pretty unattractive pair, as Collingwood later observed at first hand: lazy, manipulative, self-obsessed and wallowing in personal wealth. Nevertheless, they allowed or persuaded Nelson at first and second hand to believe that his duty was to protect the Kingdom of the Two Sicilies from invasion by the French. His real duty, clearly, was to obey the orders of his senior officer, in this case Lord Keith. But his sense of honour dictated what he thought was a nobler course of action. So for much of 1799 he stayed in Palermo, his ships idle, while his friends shook their heads at such crapulous indulgence.

By the time Keith's fleet caught up with the French they were back in the safety of Brest harbour, and the fleet returned to Torbay with its tail between its legs. Collingwood blamed Keith for his slowness and indecision. There was worse news waiting. An Anglo-Russian campaign in the Low Countries under Frederick Duke of York, King George's unfairly maligned second son, had failed. Napoleon had defeated a Turkish army at Aboukir, embarked on a ship and, undetected, returned to France to find the French economy and the Directory in a state of collapse. In November, on 18 Brumaire, he staged a *coup d'état* in Paris and was declared First Consul. Collingwood wrote from *Triumph*, in which he was blockading Brest, in December:

> I do not know how to form any judgement of its consequences. It appears to me but as another scene in the tragic farce they have been acting for so many years, where Knave succeeds to Knave … Where is now the August Directory who was to give law to the nations of Europe, and the Ancients, that bright constellation of wisdom? – a set of villains who have halloo'd the poor misled multitude to robbery, plunder and murder, all vanished in a moment, their power sunk into the dust by Gipsey Bonaparte's Hocus Pocus.[13]

On Christmas Eve 1799 Collingwood was back in Plymouth, recovering from the storms and hardship of the Brest blockade. It was the worst station to be posted to: ships constantly battled with westerly gales that forever drove them on to France's dangerous coast; otherwise, easterly winds drove them off station and allowed the French fleet to escape. Fog was an additional menace to be dealt with, but one which was hardly appreciated by a public and a City thirsting for good news. The blockade might win the war, but it made for poor headlines. Collingwood's hopes rested on the First Lord, Lord Bridport, allowing him to come up to Portsmouth so Sarah might join him in the New Year; he thought rumours of peace proposals might soon come to fruition:

> Then I will plant my cabbages again, and prune my goosberry trees, cultivate roses, and twist the woodbine through the hawthorn hedge …[14]

There was no peace yet, though. Collingwood was briefly seduced, like many others, into believing Bonaparte would now take a more conciliatory line and, needing even more than Britain to repair his disastrous finances, sue for peace:

> Bonaparte seems more moderate and reasonable, both in his acts and language, than any of the ruling factions in France hitherto have been. Whenever his powers are generally acknowledged by the French nation monarchy is established in his person with another name, but not less absolute than in the reigns of their former kings, with a more formidable army at his command and the Councils subject to his nod. Will the people (versatile as they are) submit to this usurpation after all the clamour they have been making for so many years about Republicanism and liberty and equality, and wading through such scenes of blood and devastation after a phantom? And if they resist, another week may produce another constitution and a new class to treat with.[15]

At Christmas King George had received a letter from Napoleon: 'Why should the two most enlightened countries in Europe ... go on sacrificing their trade, their prosperity, and their domestic happiness to false ideas of grandeur?' wrote the First Consul.[16] The King had his Foreign Secretary, Grenville, reply not to Napoleon but to Talleyrand, demanding the restoration of the French monarchy.

In fact secret negotiations dragged on through the year, while both England and France sought to make strategic gains to be used as bargaining tools. Both countries were in the grip of a severe winter. In London the first soup kitchens were opened to relieve the hungry poor. Now came intelligence that the French had assembled a large force at Brest and were in contemplation of a major expedition: to Ireland, in Collingwood's view. So Collingwood and the Channel fleet returned to the blockade. British strategy had now changed entirely from Howe's day six years before, when the fleet stayed in port to preserve its ships and stores. An active, total blockade was now recognised as the only bar to French attacks on British convoys from the West Indies and America, and for preventing the arrival of France's own convoys. It was a new type of warfare, as Collingwood had foreseen: a total war in which economic strangulation was the chief weapon on both sides.

There was a high price to pay for this strategy. Ships were being lost, as much through incompetence as through the violence of the weather. There was also a mutiny aboard the *Danae*:

> A shocking thing, but those who knew a good deal about her are not much surprised at it. There may exist a degree of violence when severity is substituted for discipline that is insupportable ... The truth is, in this great extensive navy, we find a great many indolent, half-qualified people.[17]

Collingwood was neither indolent nor ill-qualified. Nor was he a brutal tyrannising commander. His punishment log in *Triumph* (he was one of very few commanders at this time who kept one) for the period May 1799 to January 1800 contains a single entry: twelve lashes to Richard Clay at Port Mahon for 'contemptuous behaviour'.[18]

By now Collingwood (and with him Bounce) had transferred into *Barfleur*, the ship in which he had fought as flag captain at the Glorious First of June. She was much more to his liking: spacious and comfortable; or at least as comfortable as a ship on the Brest blockade could be. Throughout that summer the inglorious job of the fleet continued, and only in the inactivity of the French fleet and the disruption to her trade can its success be measured. More momentous events were taking place elsewhere. In May James Hadfield fired a shot at King George in the Theatre Royal, Drury Lane. In June Napoleon won a crushing victory over Austria at

Marengo, wrecking the hopes of the Second Coalition. At a less momentous level, in Newcastle three prisoners escaped from the gaol by climbing up its chimney flues. A fourth stuck fast and was ignominiously removed by the gaol keeper.[19]

Again, watching European events closely, Collingwood anticipated the future. He believed that, having effectively removed Austria from the military equation, Bonaparte would try to make peace with the Baltic states so he might concentrate his resources against Britain. Within a year France had coerced those powers into the Armed Neutrality which would lead to Nelson's next triumph at Copenhagen. One small victory for Britain was the surrender of the French garrison on Malta, which was to remain from then on a key British possession through two more world wars.

In August, briefly, Collingwood shifted his flag to *Neptune*, another 98-gun second-rate, and only three years old. To his father-in-law he admitted how tired he and the entire fleet were with the war:

> How the times are changed! Once, when officers met, the first question was, – What news of the French? Is there any prospect of their coming to sea? Now there is no solicitude on that subject, and the hope of peace alone engages the attention of every body.[20]

For the whole of that summer the Channel fleet kept up its blockade of Brest and the Atlantic coast of France, wearing ships and men ever thinner. Collingwood was back in *Barfleur*, admitting to himself and his correspondents that even his famously controlled temper had become short and 'impatient of contradiction'.[21]

Nelson, meanwhile, was taking an extended break from the sea, though not from Emma Hamilton or the Neapolitan court. He had gone ashore with them at Leghorn on the day of Napoleon's victory at Marengo in June, and travelled right across the war-torn continent

– via Trieste, Vienna, Prague and Dresden to Hamburg. It is on this tour that the most penetrating portraits of him were made, by Füger and Schmidt. From Hamburg he and the Hamiltons, minus the Queen and her retinue whom they had left at Vienna, took passage to England, where they arrived in December 1800 at Yarmouth. Now Nelson was fêted as a conquering hero, and while he and Emma revelled in it, he had also to manage the introduction of his mistress and her husband to his effectively estranged wife Fanny. The scandal surrounding his time in Naples and Palermo, and the notorious ménage with the Hamiltons, had saddened many of his friends. His insubordination towards Keith had put him in ill-favour with the Admiralty. Two months later he was reunited with Collingwood for the first time in three years:

> Lord Nelson is here: and I think he will probably come and live with me when the weather will allow him: but he does not get in and out of ships well with one arm. He gave me an account of his reception at Court, which was not very flattering, after having been the admiration of that of Naples. His Majesty merely asked him if he had recovered his health: and then, without waiting for an answer, turned to General ———, and talked to him near half an hour in great good humour.[22]

In all Collingwood's letters there is only one indirect mention of Emma Hamilton and even then, frustratingly, it is in a letter the original of which has been torn at the crucial point. There is no doubting that Collingwood did not approve of her. Both he and Sarah were staunch supporters of Lady Nelson, and Sarah later made her acquaintance. The letter in question is, however, of great interest because it contains a consciously well-tuned thumbnail portrait of England's conquering hero, without the slightest trace of reserve on Collingwood's part:

Lord Nelson is an incomparable man, a blessing to any country that is engaged in such a war. His successes in most of his undertakings are the best proofs of his genius and his talents. Without much previous preparation or plan he has the faculty of discovering advantages as they arise, and the good judgement to turn them to his use. An enemy that commits a false step in his view is ruined, and it comes on him with an impetuosity that allows him no time to recover. In his private character he is kind heart[ed] [MS torn] [it is] said his attachments in Italy altered his [...] mending them. I could not discover what [...] any great change in him ...[23]

Nelson was soon able to witness at first hand the strength of Collingwood's bond with his own wife. Throughout January Collingwood had been at Cawsand Bay (near Plymouth), refitting. As usual at this time of year, his thoughts were of Morpeth, of Sarah and the girls and the comforts of a Northumbrian fireside. Sarah had written to him to say that since their lease on the Morpeth house was due to expire in May, she was arranging to buy the freehold. This suited Collingwood, who much preferred Morpeth to the smoke and noise of Newcastle.

During the early part of the month he was suffering from 'a dreadful languor that I cannot shake off'.[24] Even the knowledge that he had been promoted to rear-admiral of the red was not enough to cheer him. But by the 25th his spirits had been restored by a letter from Sarah saying that she was to join him.

I am delighted at the thought of seeing her so soon, and it has cured me of all my complaints; indeed I believe the cause of them was vexation and sorrow at being, as it were, entirely lost to my family.[25]

The journey from Newcastle to Plymouth was extraordinarily long and arduous, especially so in winter. Sarah was to bring little Sal too, leaving Mary Patience behind to stay with relatives. Not for the first time, the nuptial bliss of the Collingwoods was to be short-lived, as Cuthbert reported to his father-in-law shortly afterwards:

I had been reckoning on the possibility of her arrival that Tuesday, when about two o'clock I received an express to go to sea immediately with all the ships that were ready; and had we not then been engaged at a court-martial, I might have got out that day: but this business delayed me until near night, and I determined to wait on shore until eight o'clock for the chance of their arrival. I went to dine with Lord Nelson; and while we were at dinner their arrival was announced to me. I flew to the inn where I had desired my wife to come, and found her and little Sarah as well after their journey as if it had lasted only for the day. No greater happiness is human nature capable of than was mine that evening; but at dawn we parted, and I went to sea.[26]

Nelson, who could be as sensitive to his friends' needs as his own, wished he could have swapped places with Collingwood:

How sorry I am! For Heaven's sake, do not think I had the gift of foresight; but something told me so it would be ... If they had manned me and sent me off, it would have been a real pleasure to me. How cross are the fates![27]

Two weeks later, at sea, Collingwood gave another side of the story in an intimate letter to Mary Moutray. He had heard some unpleasant gossip about Nelson's intemperance since he had been made Duke of Brontë,[28] but he assured her that the Nelson he had seen was the same old Nelson she had known at English Harbour:

He was looking very well. How surprised you would have been to have popped into the Fountain Inn, and seen Lord Nelson, my wife and myself, sitting by the fireside cozing, and little Sarah, teaching Phyllis her dog to dance. Sarah arrived the evening before I sailed, so that I have yet only seen her by the light of a smoky candle, and she really looked very well. Older, indeed, very much older; but she will wear me out.[29]

The same letter contains one of those thumbnail barbs that Collingwood had been cultivating for years, and would live to perfect. Mary, it seems, had recommended a young man to him to train as an officer:

Mr. ——, for whom you are interested, has told me that you were known to his mother and brother; and I should on that account have felt a disposition of kindness toward him. But I will tell you freely my opinion. He is as well-bred, gentlemanly [a] young man as can be, and I dare say an excellent fox-hunter, for he seems skilful in horses, dogs, foxes and such animals. But unluckily he is a lieutenant: and as these are branches of knowledge not very useful at sea, we do not profit by them much off Ushant.[30]

Unsurprisingly, Collingwood found this latest cruise as tedious as any he had experienced, knowing that Sarah and little Sal were waiting for him back in port. And worse, such was the weather that they had no communication at all from shore for three weeks. 'We are immured within the sides of our ships,' he wrote, 'and have no knowledge of the world or its ways.'[31] At the end of March he was able to spend a few days with his loved ones, before rejoining the blockading squadron. St Vincent had come out of retirement to accept the post of First Lord at the Admiralty under Addington, and Collingwood believed rightly that the earl was kindly disposed towards him.

While he was at sea events had again overtaken Nelson's life. At the end of January, Emma Hamilton had been delivered of their daughter Horatia, in absolute secrecy. The pain of being apart from her was made worse when Nelson was summoned to the Baltic to deal with the Armed Neutrality, which Collingwood had predicted and which now threatened crucial British supplies of timber and tar. Nelson was posted as second-in-command to Sir Hyde Parker, whom Collingwood described thus:

> A good tempered man, full of vanity, a great deal of pomp, and a pretty smattering of ignorance – nothing of that natural ability that raises men without the advantages of learned education.[32]

So it proved. At Copenhagen Hyde Parker issued his infamous order to disengage halfway through the battle, and Nelson equally famously declined to notice. It was a victory of sorts. The Danes, who fought furiously and took very heavy casualties, agreed to suspend their co-operation with France. But it need not have been, for the prime mover in the so-called Baltic Convention, Tsar Paul of Russia, had been assassinated just prior to the battle, and with his death the coalition collapsed anyway. But it was a success which not only confirmed Nelson's stratospheric status among the British public and press, but brought joy to his friend off Brest. Collingwood saw the termination of the coalition as the almost inevitable prelude to peace.

The atmosphere in London was not nearly so relaxed. The Habeas Corpus Act, cornerstone of British justice, had been suspended, allowing political suspects to be detained without trial. A huge invasion flotilla was being prepared along the Channel coast of France. Historians will continue to speculate whether this attempt on Napoleon's part was serious or not. It was certainly taken seriously by Addington's government, even as peace negotiations continued. So seriously, that Nelson was given command of anti-invasion operations to still the public frenzy. He planned a series of daring attacks on the ships guarding the flotilla's headquarters at Boulogne. These proved disastrous, but a series of harrying raids along the French coast at least convinced the public that something was being done.

Sarah and Sal stayed in Plymouth during the spring and summer of 1801, where Collingwood saw them for little more than a fortnight between cruises. Even now, though, pressed with his own cares and frustrations, he turned his thoughts homeward, asking his father-in-law to remember the gardener at Morpeth:

> I should be much obliged to you if you would send Scott a guinea for me, for these hard times must pinch the poor old man, and he will miss my wife, who was very kind to him.[33]

At Gibraltar, Sir James Saumarez made an enterprising attack on enemy shipping in Algeciras Bay which won him the admiration of his service colleagues. Otherwise, the constant promise of peace seemed as illusory as ever. There was more good news from the Mediterranean, though, as the French army in Alexandria, the remnants of Napoleon's invasion force of 1798, finally capitulated to the besieging British force there. In the end, it was just as Collingwood was preparing to say goodbye to his wife and daughter in October that news came of a peace treaty finally being agreed:

> I was to take leave of my wife after breakfast, and we were both sad enough, when William came running in with one of his important faces on, and attempted to give his information in a speech; but, after two or three efforts, which were a confused huddle of inarticulate sounds, he managed to bring out Peace! Peace! Which had just as good an effect as the finest oration he could have made on the subject.[34]

It could not come too soon. For the third summer in a row Collingwood had barely seen a green leaf on a tree, except through the eyepiece of his telescope, as he told his friend Dr Alexander Carlyle. Now, as he complained to his sister in November, he found himself still in *Barfleur*, watching Bantry Bay for signs of another Irish uprising:

> We very naturally expected that a short time wou'd have returned us all to our family and friends, but the very reverse is the case, and we are kept as far from home as possible. How long this will last I have no conjecture, but it is a proof with what caution the ministers move ...[35]

Collingwood at least had more time for reflection now. At Bearhaven there was a good, safe anchorage, and with large numbers of ships coming and going there was a resumption of social gatherings which had been suspended during the long months on blockade. Collingwood also found time, as he did on every posting, to consider the fortunes of the indigenous population. He had little time for the Irish, and found they made poor sailors unless taken to sea very young. That did not diminish his sympathy for their plight. Now he wondered at the lack of agricultural improvement in the country; it crossed his mind too, that if the staple crop of potatoes ever failed, there would be famine in Ireland. One of Collingwood's junior lieutenants had fallen deeply in love with a local girl, apparently larger than life in all respects – an attachment that his admiral looked on with avuncular indulgence, noting that such an undertaking 'requires nerves'.[36]

Now that peace seemed finally to be only weeks away, Collingwood could reflect on it philosophically:

> The object for which the war was undertaken is I hope fully obtained; it was to resist principles of revolution which the enemy disseminated in our country, and which threatened our existence as a nation ... Now it remains to be proved whether the French are equally sincere and whether the Republican government is more disposed to live in amity with the world than their monarchs were.

> The experiment is a fair one to make: for my own part, I have been
> in the habit of considering a Frenchman as a restless sort of animal,
> prone to change, ever questing after novelty, and ready to quarrel
> on the smallest interruption to his pursuits. Now was this the con-
> stitution of the animal, or the policy of the Court? We shall see.
> I hope nature had nothing to do with it.[37]

In January *Barfleur* was allowed to return to Portsmouth, but it was
a very glum Collingwood who wrote to his sister-in-law to say that
there had been another mutiny in the fleet. With rising hopes of
being paid off, some of the fleet's ships had been ordered to the West
Indies, and their crews, notably that of the *Téméraire*, had overthrown
their officers. Collingwood, as one of the senior commanders, spent
ten days trying twenty of the worst offenders. It was an ugly business
and Collingwood was saddened and troubled by its inevitable
outcome as the guilty seamen were hanged at the yardarm. But there
was no conflict between his sense of humanity and his duty. Duty
lay in preserving the good order of the service:

> It is a melancholy thing, but there is no possibility of governing
> ships, so as to make them useful to the state, but by making
> examples of those who resist the execution of their orders, and I
> hope this will have such an effect upon the whole fleet that we shall
> have no more commotions among them. God knows there are none
> more desirous than I that they might return to their families.[38]

On a lighter note, Collingwood told his sister-in-law that in anticipation of being liberated soon, he had arranged for his most precious
things to be sent up to Morpeth ahead of him; among them was
Bounce, despatched by collier to Newcastle. As part of St Vincent's
naval reforms the fleet was to be cut down, and *Barfleur*, it seemed,
was to be dismantled. Britain had started the war with 135 ships of
the line and 133 frigates, against 80 line ships and 66 frigates in the

French navy. She would end the war in strength, with 202 line ships and 277 frigates, as opposed to the French fleet of 39 line ships and 35 frigates.[39] Such massive naval and trading superiority might be expected to have resulted in a favourable peace for Britain. But when the treaty was ratified at Amiens in March 1802 it was clear that Addington's desire to end the war, and Talleyrand's negotiating skills, had given France the upper hand. Britain was to return all her colonial conquests apart from Trinidad and Ceylon; she was also to return Alexandria to Turkey and Malta to the Knights of St John. Menorca was to be returned to Spain. Britain also forfeited rights to any possessions in the Low Countries. It seemed a high price to pay for more than eight years of war.

But peace was its own reward, at least temporarily. Both countries had paid for the war by expansion: Britain by trade, France by conquest. Both were carrying vast and unsustainable levels of debt. Britain now sought to reduce her debt by reducing the financial burden of the Royal Navy. France was to use the same time to institute wide-ranging political and economic reform, and prepare for the next phase of the contest. Now that her navy was being cut back, Britain must have looked increasingly like an easy target for Napoleon, but the British economy was about to make an unanticipated sidestep that would ensure her strategic and trading dominance for a century. In December 1801 the Cornish engineer Richard Trevithick had carried passengers in his steam carriage at Camborne, for the first time. In 1802 the world's first steam-powered vessel *Charlotte Dundas* would be seen on the River Clyde. Long before the end of the war with France Collingwood's home town Newcastle would be at the centre of a world industrial revolution built with iron, fuelled by coal, and running on railways powered by steam.

Collingwood was himself to play a small part in that revolution.

But for the time being he was kept on tenterhooks at Portsmouth and then at Torbay as the ships of the Channel fleet, one by one, were paid off, their stores and fittings removed, and their hulks dismembered, or laid up 'in ordinary'. Collingwood took the opportunity to acquire two hogsheads of 'most excellent cyder'[40] which he sent to Sunderland by a brig. With typical attention to detail, he gave instructions that whoever picked them up would vent them for their final journey so they might not explode on the way.

It was not until May 1802 that Collingwood finally struck his flag and headed north:

> I am sure I have had my share of the war. I begun it early and see the last of it, and I hope it is the last we shall ever see.[41]

CHAPTER EIGHT

Exemplary vengeance

1803-1805

Rear-Admiral Cuthbert Collingwood was determined to settle into retirement with the relish of a man who knows he deserves it. In his fifty-fourth year his profession was catching up with him.[1] His hearing was not as it had been. He was long-sighted and needed spectacles for reading. He was periodically laid low with rheumatism. Though quite tall for a naval officer at five feet ten inches, he now stooped slightly, from long practice between decks. He was thin and spare and apart from his eyes, which were 'blue, clear and penetrating', he was unremarkable to look at.[2] His habits were as plain and simple as they had always been, and a neighbour from Morpeth later recounted that he 'often walked down to my grandmother's and stood with his back to the fire for a long gossip'.[3]

Now that he had bought the freehold of the house in Oldgate Collingwood determined to make improvements to it. He arranged for workmen to come and pull down the old walls and 'dog houses' at the back of the garden to open it up; and he had plans to buy the cottages opposite, demolish them, and plant a meadow to open out his view of the River Wansbeck. But when a fellow admiral (probably Roddam or Braithwaite) came calling one day and was sent into the garden to find him, Collingwood was not to be seen for some time. The admiral ...

> at last discovered him with his gardener, Old Scott, to whom he was much attached, in the bottom of a deep trench, which they were busily occupied in digging.[4]

When the weather was hot, the family went to bathe at Newbiggin on the coast north of Newcastle. On those days when low clouds scud across Northumberland from the north-west bringing cool air from the Cheviot hills, Collingwood went for long walks with Bounce and a pocket full of acorns.[5] When it rained, he read history or made drawings: three in his hand survive from this period, of Sarah and the girls – though unfortunately not of Bounce.

Somehow, between these pursuits and an endless round of visits to friends and relatives across the county, he had time to produce a healthy crop of vegetables from the garden, and to write to his sisters and other favourite correspondents. He wrote of marriages, deaths, the children overcoming measles, while in her letters to her sister Sarah revealed that Cuthbert's rheumatism had been much worse than he himself revealed.

As the winter of 1802–3 closed in, so did the Collingwoods' social life. Two hundred years ago Northumbrian winters were extremely harsh. The River Tyne still periodically froze solid, as did the Thames, and everybody seemed to suffer from endless colds. Apart from letters, of which none survive, Collingwood's contact with the outside world was through newspapers. The news was not good. While thousands of curious tourists had been taking advantage of the peace to visit Paris, the British government was covertly plotting to have Napoleon overthrown, while the First Consul himself was building men-of-war as fast as his yards could turn them out, and had sent an army of occupation to Switzerland in direct contravention of the Amiens agreement. Britain was also dragging her heels over the Maltese situation, having begun to believe that if and when she abandoned it to the Knights of St John, a new French tenant would move in without delay.

In February, the *Newcastle Courant* reported that the French Ambassador in London, General Andreossi, was contracting English merchantmen to ferry supplies and French troops to San Domingo in the West Indies.[6] The slaves of San Domingo, now Haiti, had begun the only successful slave revolt in history as far back as 1792, when the revolutionary government in France had declared its intention to outlaw slavery. Napoleon, with an eye to economics, had rescinded the ban and now determined to put the revolt down. British merchant captains were only too happy to work for France so long as she paid. The government, still years away from its own historic ban on slavery, maintained a pragmatic silence.

In the view of the *Newcastle Courant*'s editor, much of the talk about a new war was being invented by speculators keen to cash in on fluctuating stocks. But he also noted that 'France seems determined to exclude the manufactures of Great Britain from every country over which she possesses any influence'. The two protagonists were, it seems, inventing cold war tactics as they went along.

On 21 February the schooner *Pickle*, under the command of Lt John Richards Lapenotiere, later famous as the carrier of Collingwood's Trafalgar dispatches, arrived in London with news from

Malta, where Britain was under strong pressure to withdraw the garrison. In France *Le Moniteur* reported that Bonaparte, responding to a request from the town of Orléans for permission to raise a statue to Jeanne d'Arc, had written:

> United the French nation can never be conquered, but our more calculating and adroit neighbours, abusing the frankness and fidelity of our character, constantly sow amongst us those dissensions from whence resulted the calamities of that epoch, and all the disasters related in our history.[7]

Beneath the rhetoric the First Consul, though himself preparing for war, was concerned that it might break out sooner than he wanted. Ideally, he wished to string the Maltese dispute out until the following year, when his military build-up would be complete. But he was pre-empted. Suddenly, on 9 March 1803, King George announced to a shocked parliament:

> His Majesty thinks it necessary to acquaint the House of Commons that, as very considerable military preparations are carrying on in the ports of France and Holland, he has judged it expedient to adopt additional measures of precaution for the security of his dominions.[8]

Collingwood, at home in Morpeth, must have read that Lord Nelson had been summoned for urgent talks at the house of the First Lord, Earl St Vincent. He would also have seen that orders were being drafted for naval officers to prepare for sea. But he had already been given private warning of these new developments, as he admitted to Dr Alexander Carlyle:

> We are again threatened with war, and all its miseries. I have little hope that it can be avoided and, in that case, I suppose I shall be employed immediately. I received a letter five days since [i.e. on 11 March] from Sir Evan Nepean,[9] to know if I was ready (in the

event of being wanted) to go on service at a very short notice. I answered 'to be sure I was' and packed up my trunk and my signal book and am now waiting for a summons to take my station wherever it might be.[10]

In the same letter he went on to defend his old chief St Vincent who, having come down very hard on corruption and inefficiency in the naval dockyards, was now being blamed (by Nelson among others) for reducing the fleet to dangerously low numbers of ships. Collingwood also included one of those rhetorical cameos that one can almost hear Churchill lisping in a crackling Home Service broadcast 140 years later:

I have only to hope, if we are compelled to resist by arms, the ambition and perfidy of that arch enemy to the peace and happiness of mankind, that all will feel in their hearts that detestation of his character and that zeal for the preservation and honour of our country which fills mine, that when the day of trial comes we may strike hard, and with God's help, punish the injustice that would invade its happiness.[11]

In Paris, nine days later, a similarly rhetorical exchange took place at the Tuileries, where Lord Whitworth, the British Ambassador, was discussing His Majesty's announcement with the First Consul:

Whitworth: It is to be hoped that this storm will be dissipated without any serious consequence.
Bonaparte: It will be dissipated when England shall have evacuated Malta. If not, the cloud will burst, and the bolt must fall.[12]

For a few weeks war fever seemed to cool as hard thinking took the place of public posturing. In April Collingwood wrote to his sister that he had not heard another word from the Admiralty. He hoped there might yet be an accommodation with France, though he was not optimistic. Then suddenly on 17 May Britain imposed an embargo on French and Dutch shipping in British ports, and on the following day she declared war. Eleven days later the *Newcastle Courant* reported:

> On Saturday last, Admiral Collingwood passed through this place on his way to the Admiralty to take a command. The Corporation of this town, in compliment to this gallant officer, have offered an additional bounty of one guinea to each seaman entering to serve in his ship.

The *Courant* might also have mentioned that the Admiral travelled with his old and faithful companion, Bounce. The ship in question was initially a frigate, the *Diamond*, whose earlier namesake had rescued Collingwood and his men from a wrecked *Pelican* on the Morant Keys in Jamaica, more than twenty years previously. In what must have seemed very cramped quarters, he raised his Admiral's flag (a red flag at the mizzen) in her and sailed to join Cornwallis off Brest, while the flag ship which had been earmarked for him, *Venerable*, was made ready in port. His hopes for peace, written less than eighteen months previously, had come back to haunt him. He would never see Morpeth, Sarah, or his daughters again.

Britain's maritime strategy, which had proved so successful in the later years of the first part of the war, would continue: blockade the enemy in port, and hope that when they came out they could be brought to battle. Only one more great battle would be fought in this war, and the navy would have to wait two years for it. In the interim, and not before time, England had finally accepted the urgent need to look to her land defences, for Bonaparte seemed more than ever determined to invade and crush his enemy for once and all.

The unlikely hero of this much neglected theatre of war was Frederick, Duke of York. During the first phase of the war his reputation had been built and had fallen on his record as Commander-in-Chief of British forces during their campaigns in the Low Countries. Here he had been defeated at least as much by the incompetence of his allies as by the French. Now, in charge of defending Britain should the navy be beaten at sea,[13] he embarked on a three-year programme of fortification and defensive planning unrivalled since the ninth century. Against seemingly overwhelming political and military obstructions, he established plans for defending London and the south-east with fieldworks which could be thrown up within the time it would take Napoleon's Army of England to cross the Channel: an estimated three days. He ordered reinforcements to be made to the inadequate defences at Plymouth, Portsmouth, Dover and Chatham. He instituted the Royal Military Canal at Romney Marsh in Sussex. And he set in train the construction of seventy-three Martello towers, based on the Mortella at St Florent which had caused Collingwood and Jervis so much trouble in 1795; these would form a shield along the vulnerable coasts of Sussex and Kent.

However, such a programme of defences, which ought to have been instigated ten years previously, would not be complete until the year after Trafalgar. In the meantime Bonaparte was beginning to mass his troops and invasion barges once more along the Channel coasts of France and Holland, with their main concentration and headquarters at Boulogne. Across England companies of militia and volunteers were being raised in an atmosphere of jingoistic fervour. In Newcastle in June a Loyal Armed Association was sworn in to the number of twelve hundred men. In August they marched in ten companies to the Town Moor, where they received their muskets.[14]

In June British forces captured the Caribbean islands of St Lucia and Tobago. An Irish uprising was put down after failing to receive French support, and Bonaparte had just made the worst land deal in history. In granting America the Louisiana Purchase (800,000 square miles for $27 million) he gave up France's last aspirations in the New World for something like five cents an acre.[15] At the same time in India Bonaparte's nemesis Arthur Wellesley was winning a victory at Assaye in the Second Mahratta War, a victory that would cement his early reputation as the 'Sepoy' general.

In August Collingwood finally shifted his flag to *Venerable*, a 74-gun two-decker, and resumed the blockade of Brest. He was well aware of the difficulties of blockading that port: it had two entrances far apart, protected by powerful tides, westerly winds, and rocks which had seen many a wreck. Often, as he reported to his father-in-law, he spent the entire week on deck without ever shifting his clothes, and often stayed awake all night, catching a little sleep now and then on one of the quarterdeck carronades. It was this period of extraordinary tension that his obituarist wrote of, when he described Collingwood:

> upon deck without his hat, and his grey hair floating to the wind, whilst torrents of rain poured down through the shrouds, and his eye, like an eagle's, on the watch.[16]

It is an evocative image, much more so than the stiff and formal poses of his few portraits. He was now convinced that the time had come for Bonaparte to strike decisively. Collingwood's worry was not that he himself might fail, but that his countrymen might be complacent:

> I think in the course of next month Bonaparte's experiment of the invasion will be made, and I only hope it will not be held too lightly; in that consists the only danger. They should not only be repulsed, but it should be with such exemplary vengeance as may deter them from any future attempt to subjugate our country. We should give an example to all nations how to preserve their independence.[17]

Venerable was sent briefly back to port to replenish towards the end of the summer, and Collingwood shifted his flag to another 74-gun two-decker, *Minotaur*. But he was soon back in *Venerable*, able to report that there was no illness in the ship, but concerned that the oncoming cold weather would soon fill his sick bay again; he himself had left port without an extra coat. The Newcastle volunteers raised on his behalf were coming along very well, he thought. But he was worried by accounts that the Spanish might be entering the war, coerced by France.[18] And soon he would have concerns of his own. He had frequently complained about the state of ships leaving the naval dockyards; the yards' jobbery and incompetence were legendary enough for Jane Austen to have her Captain Wentworth comment:

> The admiralty ... entertain themselves now and then, with sending a few hundred men to sea, in a ship not fit to be employed. But they have a great many to provide for; and among the thousands that may just as well go to the bottom as not, it is impossible for them to distinguish the very set who may be least missed.[19]

At the beginning of December *Venerable* was at Cawsand Bay, initially to have a new foremast fitted after a gale, and to give her hardworked crew a brief rest. But, as Collingwood reported to his father-in-law:

> Poor creatures, they have been almost worked to death ever since. We began by discovering slight defects in the ship; and the farther we went in the examination, the more important they appeared, until at last she was discovered to be so completely rotten as to be unfit for sea. We have been sailing for the last six months with only a sheet of copper between us and eternity.[20]

Venerable, which had done such sterling service in the war, and had been Duncan's flag ship at Camperdown, was literally falling to pieces, suffering one of the most notorious faults that corruption could contrive. Her planking had been held together with what were nicknamed 'devil bolts'.[21] It had been known since the first experiments with copper-sheathing that copper and iron made a poor mix in sea water (though the electrolytic process was poorly understood), so hull planking was held on to a ship's hull with copper bolts. But it had occurred to the most unscrupulous shipbuilders that a treenail (a wooden peg) with a copper fitting at either end would look very convincing to a dockyard inspector, and would save a potential fortune on a contract. When the copper and treenail combination failed, as it eventually must, it might do so spectacularly, and some of the 'forty-thieves' as these unfortunate ships were known, had literally sprung apart at the seams in a gale and gone down in minutes with all men. To that extent Collingwood and his six hundred men had been lucky.

The *Venerable*'s crew and her admiral spent Christmas in Plymouth dock, waiting for an alternative ship to be prepared. This was *Culloden*, another 74 and a veteran of the Glorious First of June and the battle of Cape St Vincent (she was also, under Thomas Troubridge, present at Aboukir Bay, but ran aground and took no part in the battle). Although he was only in *Culloden* for a few months before shifting his flag once again, and hating the constant disruption, Collingwood left a lasting impression on one of her midshipman, the young Scot Robert Hay.

Collingwood joined *Culloden* on 6 February 1804. He first took notice of Hay during a game which he had instigated among the young gentlemen to keep them active, racing each other to the crosstrees and back to the poop. On one such occasion Hay, feeling himself at a disadvantage after a slip from one of the shrouds, took a short cut by sliding down a backstay, and beating his friend Dennis O'Flanagan by six feet. Considering that he had broken the rules, Collingwood ordered Hay to the masthead. In a fit of pique Hay decided to show his new admiral that he was made of the right stuff, and proceeded to swing himself up on to the main truck, the highest point in the ship. It was a dangerous thing to do, and in front of an admiral with Collingwood's reputation it was asking for trouble. Hay recalled:

I then took off my hat and waved it around my head in token of exultation. This drew all the eyes of the forecastle upon me. The Admiral seeing all hands staring aloft looked up too, and saw me in the act of waving my hat. 'Maintop there, Sir, jump up and bring that boy Hay down instantly.'

'Aye, aye, Sir. Come down here my fine little fellow,' said Tom Lennox, 'my eye but you are sure to catch it now; I'll warrant two dozen will be the least of it. You may see by the quickness of the Admiral's step that there is something for you in the wind's eye.' Down I came with a palpitating heart. The galley, the breach of the gun, the master at arms, the spun yarn seizings, and, not least, Grimalkin's namesake with her nine scorpion's tails, were all passing in review before the mind's eye. On reaching the quarter deck I stood trembling with hat in hand at the foot of the Jacob's ladder until the Admiral came forward.

'How high did I order you to go, boy?'

'To the cross-trees, Sir.'

'What business, then, had you at the royal masthead?'

'Dennis was up once, Sir, and often taunts me with my inability; as he and the rest of the boys were looking up, I thought it a good time to shew him that I could go there as easily as himself.'

He paused about half a minute, a partial frown clouded his features, and I thought he was considering in his own mind how many dozen he would offer me; but his countenance soon softened and brightened, indicating that the squall I dreaded was blown over.

'Well,' said he, 'I commend you for endeavouring not to be out-stripped in activity; but activity itself may be a fault if not properly regulated. When duty calls, I love to see a man striving for the point of honour and danger; but I can never approve of anyone throwing his life in jeopardy for the sake of a vain boast. You may go below.'[22]

191

Hay's sketches of Collingwood from the early spring of 1804 reveal all the human subtleties of his command, matured over the decades since his own bitter experience under Haswell. Hay remembered:

> Scarcely could [the ship] be put about at any hour of the night but he would be on deck. There, accompanied by his favourite dog, Bounce, would he stand on the weather gang way snuffing up the midnight air, with his eye either glancing through his long night glass all round the horizon, or fixed on the light carried by Cornwallis in the *Ville de Paris* ...
>
> No swearing, no threatening or bullying, no starting were to be heard or seen. Boatswain's mates, or ship's corporals, dared not to be seen with a rattan, or rope's end in hand; nor do I recollect a single instance of a man being flogged while he remained aboard. Was discipline neglected then? By no means. There was not a better disciplined crew in the fleet.
>
> And then how attentive to the health of his crew? How kind to them when sick or wounded! It would have done your hearts good, as it has often done mine, to see a roasted chicken, a basin of fresh soup, a tumbler of wine, a jug of negus, or some other nice little cordial, wending its way from his table to some poor fellow riding quarantine in the sick bay.

In April 1804 Collingwood was promoted to vice-admiral, with a blue flag flying at *Culloden*'s foremast. By now William Pitt had forced Addington's resignation, and against the background of a constant fear of invasion, Pitt returned to power on a wave of patriotic support much like that which propelled Churchill into Downing Street in 1940. With Addington had departed St Vincent, to be replaced as First Lord by Henry Dundas, Viscount Melville. Bonaparte, who on 16 May had been proclaimed Emperor of the French and now styled himself Napoleon I, was massing another army of England at Boulogne. Sir Sidney Smith had been put in charge of attacking the flotilla there. He was to have no more luck than Nelson had previously, despite the new technologies he had been given to experiment with. Fulton's torpedoes and Congreve's rockets had little effect on a well-organised defence. Collingwood thought the whole show a waste of time, but he approved of the change in administration, even though he himself was not what he called a 'party man':

> Mr Addington was a sensible man, and an honorable man, he was industrious and had the best intentions in the world. But the times require talents, which fall to the lot of few men. Perhaps Pitt is the only man in England who can find resources against all the evils we have to encounter.[23]

Collingwood, briefly flying his flag in the old *Prince*, knew where he wanted to be now that events were coming to a head. Convinced that the Spanish were about to take a more active role in the war against England, he thought the Cadiz station, which he knew well, was the place to employ his own talents against Bonaparte: 'as much villainy as ever disgraced human nature in the person of one man'.[24]

By August he had been transferred yet again, this time to *Dreadnought*, a 98-gun second-rate with few sailing qualities, and he set himself to complaining about his midshipmen: 'In general they are so abominably fine, and in their own conceit so wise, that they think nothing wanting to their perfection but a larger hat and a pair of boots and tassels.'[25] Four men calling themselves deserters from the French fleet had been brought on board the blockading squadron, with intelligence that their ships were in a deplorable condition and ripe for mutiny. Collingwood dismissed them as plants. He would have to wait until the New Year before being rewarded with a posting to Cadiz. After spending almost the entire year on blockade, he was grateful to be back at Cawsand Bay in December, writing to Nelson in concern for his health. There had been rumours that Nelson, whose frail body 'was always a flimsy case for his Herculean soul',[26] might have to return home from the Mediterranean, where he was blockading Toulon. Collingwood brought his friend up to date with political and naval news, and reiterated his view that Napoleon was soon to make his move:

> The time is fast approaching when the Military Despotism which rules France, and awes all the powers on the continent, will be put to the test – whether it can be supported by the Army and insidious arts of Talleyrand against the opinions and interests of all mankind.[27]

Nelson's reply did not reach Collingwood until the spring of 1805. He admitted that his constitution was 'much shook', having been almost continuously at sea himself since the outbreak of war, and echoed Collingwood's views of the next phase of the conflict:

> We have had a very dull war, but I agree with you that it must change for a more active one. I beg, my dear Collingwood, that you will present my most respectful compliments to Mrs Collingwood; and believe me, for ever and as ever, your most sincere and truly attached friend ...[28]

Collingwood himself was pretty nearly worn out, as he admitted to his old friend and patron Admiral Richard Braithwaite, his first commanding officer. He was depressed and languid, having not seen a green leaf all year except those he had drawn himself. 'I think', he wrote, 'some of our ingenious citizens should apply their wits in inventing a sort of patent Admiral, a machine that would rub on a length of time without wearing out.'[29]

The time was now coming when the naval policies of the two great maritime powers would be tested. England's navy was wearing thin in its attempt at total blockade. Her ships, still suffering from St Vincent's cutbacks, were being lost to accident and storm at an alarming rate. Her officers and men were exhausted; and yet, they were hardened and practised and ready for anything. Their gunnery was superb, and they sailed their ships with a skill and efficiency which they did not believe could be matched. Furthermore, in five major fleet actions since the start of the conflict with France, they had not lost once.

The French navy boasted large numbers of fine ships. Her men and officers were fresh, and they were determined and brave. Many of them felt themselves a part of Napoleon's glorious destiny, and they believed England could be beaten. What they and their Spanish allies lacked was the discipline and skill that could only come with active service.

At the beginning of 1805 Napoleon began to implement his master plan, which was based on his belief that he needed only to command the English Channel for the time it would take his flotilla to cross from Boulogne to Kent and Essex. To do this he would combine the French Mediterranean fleet under Villeneuve with the Spanish fleets at Cadiz and Cartagena, and the squadron at Rochefort. They would rendezvous in the West Indies, drawing a substantial part of the Royal Navy with them, then double back to descend upon Ireland and the Channel. Villeneuve, and many of his fellow officers, believed Napoleon's plan relied on a military precision which he had been able to impose on land but which no one could impose on the elements of the Atlantic Ocean.[30]

Nevertheless, with little choice Villeneuve took his squadron out of Toulon, managed to avoid Nelson, and made for Cadiz in April. Here he picked up Admiral Gravina's Spanish squadron, barely worth its name and down to six ill-manned ships. The combined fleet of eighteen sail of the line headed west on 9 April. Nelson, unsure of their destination, had to search for them at Sardinia and in Sicily before he got intelligence that they had passed through the Strait of

Gibraltar. It was not until 11 May, while being resupplied off Cape St Vincent, that he was finally sure of their destination, and followed them to the West Indies with ten sail of the line.

Collingwood, whose superior was now Admiral Gardner, was off Finisterre when he heard that Nelson had taken his squadron off in pursuit of Villeneuve. His Secret Letter book, discovered only in the last few years,[31] makes it clear he was expected to follow Nelson, or at least detach a number of his ships and send them in support. The fact that he appeared to dither until it was too late can now be explained by an entry in this book. It refers to intelligence reports describing one of Villeneuve's ships as containing a cavalry unit. Like most entries in what was effectively a draft book for dispatches and covert communications, this was written in his own neat and most distinctive copperplate. Cavalry, he noted in a dry statement of the situation to be sent to William Marsden, the new Secretary to the Admiralty Board, is 'a species of force not calculated for the West Indies service, and which raises in my mind, a doubt of that being their destination.'[32] He also had intelligence that another twelve Spanish ships were nearly ready for sea at Cadiz and Cartagena. 'From these circumstances I judge it is expedient to proceed to Cadiz, with all possible dispatch.' Collingwood had correctly inferred that Napoleon was creating a diversion, as he wrote in the last letter to his friend Alexander Carlyle, who died a month later:

> I think it is not improbable that I shall have all those fellows coming from the West Indies again, before the Hurricane months, unless they sail from thence directly for Ireland, which I have always had an idea was their plan, for this Bonaparte has as many tricks as a monkey. I believe their object in the West Indies to be less conquest, than to draw our force from home.[33]

Villeneuve and Nelson missed each other in the West Indies by a combination of chance and poor intelligence. Villeneuve managed to capture a small merchant convoy out of English Harbour, but then received news that Nelson was after him. Believing the two forces to be equal, and unsure of receiving reinforcements in time, he decided to follow his contingency orders and head for Ferrol to pick up a second Spanish squadron. Nelson, on 12 June, heard that the French fleet had left the West Indies, so he sailed for Gibraltar in the belief that Villeneuve would return to Cadiz. The two fleets missed each other. From Cadiz Nelson headed north to return to England while Villeneuve, receiving new orders, sailed south for Cadiz. In passing, Nelson and Collingwood brought each other up to date with developments. Collingwood left his friend with these words:

> This summer is big with events: we may all perhaps have an active share in them; and I sincerely wish your Lordship strength of body to go through it, and to all others your strength of mind.[34]

Nelson warmed his friend's heart with words of support in exchange:

> Your judgement on these points, and zeal for the Service, promise everything that can be expected, and no one more highly estimates both, than he who has the honour to be, Sir etc, Nelson and Bronte.[35]

Before they met again on the eve of Trafalgar, Collingwood pulled off one of the most extraordinary tactical victories of the war. It is barely mentioned by the majority of historians, perhaps because no ship was damaged or captured, perhaps because it complicates the Nelsonian narrative. Without it, the battle of Trafalgar might not have happened. On 20 August Collingwood was keeping watch off Cadiz. With his flag ship, *Dreadnought* (a slow sailer but a deadly floating battery), he had *Colossus* and *Achille*, both 74s, and the *Niger* frigate. A bomb ship, *Thunder*, lay to the north almost out of sight. Inside the harbour were eight Spanish ships of the line.

At six o'clock in the morning *Dreadnought* was close to the Cadiz lighthouse when, through the haze in the west, came Villeneuve's combined fleet of twenty-six sail of the line. Collingwood's immediate reaction, founded on thirty-odd years of sea experience, was to avoid any sign of panic. He was hopelessly outnumbered and his ships, from being at sea so long, were encumbered with weed (except the very swift *Colossus*), so there was no chance of winning a straight chase. His main concern was not that the enemy should be allowed into Cadiz – that was exactly where he wanted them. His fear was that they should pass the Strait and enter the Mediterranean, either to make an attempt on Sicily with no fleet to oppose them, or simply to pick up the ships remaining at Cartagena. So to begin with, he did what Villaret-Joyeuse had done on the Glorious First of June, and trailed his coat, sailing slowly to the east towards Gibraltar. It is hard to imagine ships of the line displaying body language, but they did; commanders on both sides would be watching intently to read the enemy's intentions: a subtle shift of the helm to gain the weather-gage, an appearance of flight masking slack sheets; Collingwood's body language on 20 August gave the distinct impression of indifference.

After two hours of chasing, Villeneuve detached sixteen of his fastest ships in pursuit of Collingwood's tiny squadron. They were approaching Gibraltar now, and this was the moment when Collingwood was forced to play his unsupported trump card: 'put an impudent face on our shabby weak state', as he himself termed it in a letter to his sister.[36] He ordered the squadron to shorten sail and tack, and stood towards the combined fleet. *Colossus* he sent off to get as close to them as possible, as if to reconnoitre for an action ('which she did most masterly'); and meanwhile, he threw out a series of signals to the east. False signalling to a non-existent relief force was the oldest trick in the book; by itself it would not have

fooled an adolescent midshipman. But reinforcing as it did Collingwood's insouciance and the master-stroke of detaching the *Colossus*,
it raised sufficient doubt in his pursuers' minds. They retired to Cadiz
where Collingwood found them later, resuming his blockade with
grim satisfaction. *Thunder* had escaped too, running so close to the
shoals off Cape Trafalgar that the fleet could not follow her. Collingwood's seamanship and battle skills had been tested at the highest
possible level. With four ships, he had seen off a combined fleet of
twenty-six, condemning Villeneuve and Gravina to the showdown at
Trafalgar, just two months away. The *Naval Chronicle* called the action
'an instance of genius and address that is scarcely to be paralleled in
the pages of our naval history.'[37] If he did not possess Nelson's
impetuous genius in attack, he had proved himself a defensive
virtuoso.

Within days Collingwood's news reached the Admiralty, where
Lord Barham, the new First Lord (Melville having been impeached
on a technical charge of embezzlement) was now able to draw up
his strategy for bringing the enemy out so they could be annihilated.
Nelson prepared to leave England for the last time. Collingwood,
gradually joined by other ships to reinforce the blockade, was worn
to a thread by the tension and the huge weight of responsibility. He
had had no leave in two years, and was beginning to rely very heavily
on two men (neither of them his captain) to support him:

> I have a diligent young man for my secretary[38] and Clavell, my lieu-
> tenant, is the spirit of the ship; but such a captain [Edward
> Rotheram], such a stick, I wonder very much how such people get
> forward. I should (I firmly believe) with his nautical ability and
> knowledge and exertion, have been a bad lieutenant at this day. Was
> he brought up in the navy? For he has very much the stile [sic] of
> the Coal trade about him, except that they are good seamen.[39]

Collingwood was being disingenuous about his relations with Rotheram, a Hexham man. One of his more celebrated midshipmen, Hercules Robinson, remembered vividly in later life:

> Collingwood's dry, caustic mind lives before me in the recollection of his calling across the deck his fat, stupid captain – long since dead – when he had seen him commit some monstrous blunder, and after the usual bowing and formality – which the excellent old chief never omitted – he said: 'Captain, I have been thinking, whilst I looked at you, how strange it is that a man should grow so big and know so little. That's all, Sir, that's all!' Hats off ; low bows.[40]

Apart from Clavell and Cosway, Collingwood's only consolation was Bounce:

> How happy I should be, could I but hear from home, and how my dear girls are going on! Bounce is my only pet now, and he is indeed a good fellow: he sleeps by the side of my cot, whenever I lie in one, until near the time of tacking, and then marches off, to be out of the hearing of the guns, for he is not reconciled to them yet. I am fully determined, if I can get home and manage it properly, to go on shore next spring for the rest of my life; for I am very weary.[41]

By the end of September Collingwood had at last been reinforced by the addition of ships which brought his strength up to twenty-six. The enemy had thirty-four. Nelson was due to resume command of the fleet, and then both he and Collingwood believed they could force Villeneuve out, by starvation if nothing else. What they did not know was that Napoleon, having lost all patience with Villeneuve, had sent a replacement to supersede him; that Villeneuve had heard of this development; and that he was now determined to come out – either to fight the English in pitched battle, or escape into the Mediterranean. Napoleon, having abandoned his invasion plans for the year, was now planning to strike a massive blow against

Austria. The combined fleet would be more useful to him if they were to attack Sicily.

On 7 September Collingwood received a note from Nelson with news that he would be arriving shortly to take command of the squadron. It has often been stated that Nelson, when asked by Lord Barham who should command the fleet, had suggested Collingwood as the right man, and that Barham had refused, saying only Nelson would do. This sounds suspiciously like apocrypha. Nelson had no intention of letting anyone rob him of his destiny. In his note to Collingwood, Nelson said he hoped his friend would remain second-in-command of the fleet. He added, 'You will change the *Dreadnought* for the *Royal Sovereign*, which I hope you will like.' Nelson was having a little joke at his friend's expense. Collingwood's first reaction to this news must have been something like horror. He had with great pains worked *Dreadnought*'s crew to a state of near perfection in seamanship and gunnery. No other ship afloat could match her in a fight; now he was to be removed into a ship whose company were strangers to him. And worse, much worse, was the thought of having to sail and fight *Royal Sovereign*.

Royal Sovereign was a 100-gun first-rate, built at Plymouth in 1786. She was such a slow sailer that she had acquired the nickname 'The West-Country Waggon'. What Collingwood did not know, and what Nelson had chosen not to tell him, was that she had recently been recoppered, and was now the fastest ship in the fleet. It was just such tokens of friendship that men adored him for.

By 25 September *Victory* was approaching the fleet, and Nelson sent another note to ask that no signals be raised or salute be fired on his arrival. On the 28th Nelson joined the fleet, and there was a flurry of social activity welcomed by everyone. A week later Nelson sent Collingwood another note, this time enclosed in a box with a lock and key. This was to be their own private dispatch box, but he urged

Collingwood to telegraph him at any time. 'We are one, and I hope ever shall be,' he wrote. Collingwood replied that he believed the combined fleet must come out soon, as their supply of provisions from France had been completely cut off by Collingwood's blockade of Cadiz. He believed the Mediterranean was now their destination, an opinion which Nelson shared.

On 9 October Nelson sent Collingwood his plan of attack: the so-called Nelson touch. 'When I explained to them the Nelson touch,' he wrote to Emma Hamilton, 'it was like an electric shock; some shed tears, all approved, it was new, it was singular ...'[42] This is perhaps the ultimate example of Nelson creating his own myth. The plan was hardly new. It involved forming two lines of ships at right angles to the enemy fleet, with the aim of splitting their line into three equal parts. In this way, the enemy's van would be cut off and by the time they rejoined the main body of the fleet Nelson's ships would have defeated them in detail in a grand mêlée. Cutting the line was no novel tactic: Howe had tried it at the Glorious First of June, as had Jervis at Cape St Vincent. Cutting the line with two columns was no innovation either: it was precisely the tactic that Duncan had employed with such devastating effect at Camperdown. The unique character of Nelson's battle plan was that it was Nelsonian. He was able to instil in his commanders a total belief in their invincibility which transmitted itself right down to the humblest loblolly boy in the sick bay of the smallest frigate. The Nelson touch was not so much tactical as personal.

When he sent his plan of attack to Collingwood, he accompanied it with what was probably the most significant letter he ever sent to his friend. It cannot have failed to achieve its desired effect:

> They surely cannot escape us. I wish we could get a fine day. I send you my plan of attack, as far as a man dare venture to guess at the very uncertain position the enemy may be found in: but, my dear

friend, it is to place you perfectly at ease respecting my intentions, and to give full scope to your judgement for carrying them into effect. We can, my dear Coll, have no little jealousies: we have only one great object in view, – that of annihilating our enemies, and getting a glorious peace for our countries. No man has more confidence in another than I have in you; and no man will render your services more justice than your very old friend,

NELSON AND BRONTE[43]

Quite why Nelson felt he had to refer to 'little jealousies' is difficult to judge. Nothing in Collingwood's correspondence suggests that he ever allowed himself to display jealousy, if indeed he ever felt it. Collingwood was just as proud a man as Nelson, and quite as sensitive of his reputation among his peers. But he was not jealous of Nelson's public fame, nor of his foreign honours – both of these he found intensely embarrassing. Was this an instance of Nelson's over-sensitivity? Or had there been gossiping tongues in the fleet? Collingwood had his admirers: Duff of the *Mars*, who was to die at Trafalgar, thought him the pleasantest admiral he had met with.[44] But Thomas Fremantle, in *Neptune*, could not abide his apparent severity and reserve, and Edward Codrington, captain of the *Orion*, considered that his attention to detail demeaned him and compromised his dignity. Such prejudices may have found their way to Nelson's ears. But Nelson, who surely knew Collingwood better than anyone, must have known that rank snobbery lay behind those opinions. Collingwood's reply to Nelson on the 9th showed no sign of any tension between the two men:

My Dear Lord,
I have a just sense of your Lordship's kindness to me, and the full confidence you have reposed in me inspires me with the most lively gratitude. I hope it will not be long before there is an opportunity of showing your Lordship that it has not been misplaced.[45]

During the twelve days left to them before the battle Nelson and Collingwood saw each other as often as the weather would allow; their correspondence mostly confined to the business of victualling and preparing the fleet for battle. One of the more difficult items Nelson had to deal with was sending Sir Robert Calder home to face an inquiry into his conduct. Calder's squadron had encountered Villeneuve and the Combined Fleet in July, shortly before Collingwood's brilliant defensive action. Calder had taken two Spanish prizes, but failed to press his advantage: he would go home in disgrace and miss Trafalgar. Few of his fellow commanders felt sorry for him – his aristocratic hauteur had won him few friends. Now, in a typical gesture, Nelson allowed Calder the dignity of returning in his own flagship, *Prince of Wales*, even though he could ill-afford the loss of a ship of the line.[46]

On 19 October, with signs that the Combined Fleet were close to sailing, Nelson wrote to Collingwood, 'What a beautiful day! Will you be tempted out of your ship? If you will, hoist the Assent and Victory's pendants.'[47] On the original of this letter, the last to pass between the two, Collingwood added a note which said, 'Before the answer to this letter had got to the *Victory*, the signal was made that the enemy's fleet was coming out of Cadiz, and we chased immediately.'[48]

On the morning of 20 October 1805 the Franco-Spanish fleet sailed from Cadiz with thirty-three sail to meet the English fleet of twenty-seven. It had taken a whole day, in light winds, for all Villeneuve and Gravina's ships to leave the port. On the afternoon of the 20th, the wind shifted into the west and the Combined Fleet headed south-east, hoping to get to the Strait of Gibraltar before the English could come up with them. Neither fleet could see the other (Nelson was fifty miles west of Cadiz, hoping Villeneuve would make a run for it) but English frigates were reporting every enemy move, night and day. The English fleet headed south-east too, aiming to cut them off. But it became clear that Villeneuve would not make the Strait that night. He decided to head back to Cadiz, but Nelson had anticipated him, and at dawn on the 21st the two fleets sighted each other a few miles off Cape Trafalgar, on parallel courses heading north-west.

As the sun rose, Midshipman Hercules Robinson, aboard Captain Henry Blackwood's crack frigate *Euryalus*, looked out on a sea ...

> like a millpond, but with an ominous swell rolling in from the Atlantic. The delight of us all at the idea of a wearisome blockade, about to terminate with a fair stand up fight, of which we well knew the result ...[49]

On board *Royal Sovereign* Collingwood's new servant, Smith, entered the admiral's cabin at daybreak:

> and found him already up and dressing. He asked if I had seen the French fleet; and on my replying that I had not, he told me to look out at them, adding that, in a very short time, we should see a great deal more of them. I then observed a great cloud of ships to leeward; but I could not help looking with still greater interest at the Admiral, who, during all this time, was shaving himself with a composure that quite astonished me.[50]

This was the man who had seen action at Bunker's Hill, on the Glorious First of June, and at Cape St Vincent. If Nelson inspired his men with passion, Collingwood inspired his with a coolness that was deeply impressive. Still early in the morning, the English fleet began to form into two columns: Nelson in *Victory* taking the weather station with twelve sail of the line astern and a small cloud of frigates about him, Collingwood heading the leeward column of fifteen ships, mostly the smaller and faster two-decker 74s.

On board *Euryalus* Hercules Robinson watched with amusement the crew of Lapenotiere's *Pickle* remove the tompions from her four guns: 'about as large and formidable as two pairs of Wellington boots'. Since Nelson had joined the fleet, almost all the captains had had their ships repainted in the Nelson chequer: a band of yellow paint along the lines of the gun decks, so that when the gun ports were open it gave a chequered effect. Nelson had also ordered the lower masts of the ships to be painted yellow as a form of recognition. Now, as the tension and excitement grew, Robinson took in the whole scene: 'Bands playing, officers in full dress, and the ships covered with ensigns, hanging in various places where they never could be struck.'[51] Many of the fleet's lieutenants had begged their captains and admirals to dress less conspicuously – in such an action they were very exposed and made irresistible targets for enemy sharpshooters. Not one took the advice. The symbolic nailing of colours to the masts was a universal indication of disdain for any thought of shyness or surrender. Losing was inconceivable.

On *Royal Sovereign* Collingwood went to talk to the men on the gun decks. His Newcastle volunteers had been sent over with him from *Dreadnought*, and he stopped to give his 'Tars of the Tyne' a word of encouragement. He addressed his officers, too. Clavell he sent below, advising him to change into silk stockings, as these were much easier for the surgeons to handle when operating on wounds (silk was easier to remove, and thought to be less likely to infect an open wound). To all of them he said, 'Now gentlemen, let us do something today which the world will talk of hereafter.'[52] Down below, a young midshipman by the name of Aikenhead was writing his last letter home. In four hours he would be dead.

> We have just piped to breakfast. Thirty-five sail, besides smaller vessels, are now on our beam about three miles off. Should I, my dear parents, fall in defence of my king, let that thought console you. I feel not the least dread on my spirits. Oh my parents, sisters,

brothers, dear grandfather, grandmother, and aunt, believe me ever yours. Accept perhaps for the last time your brothers' love, be assured I feel for my friends should I die in this glorious action – glorious, no doubt, it will be. Every British heart pants for glory. Our old Admiral is quite young with the thoughts of it. If I survive, nothing will give me greater pleasure than embracing my dear relations. Do not, in case I fall, grieve – it will be to no purpose. Many brave fellows will no doubt fall with me, on both sides.[53]

The Combined Fleet lay in a great arc to the east, heading north-west across the swell, all sails set, with just enough breeze to give steerage way. Resigned to a battle none of them believed they could win despite their numerical advantage, and seeing from the navy's disposition that Nelson intended to cut their line, they were given orders to close up. Now they formed almost a double line, like a trail of tottering footsteps in sand.

At 11 a.m. Nelson hoisted a signal ordering all the ships in his fleet to anchor after the action. It was premature, perhaps unneces-sary, and significant only in the context of the opprobrium heaped on Collingwood by some commentators after the battle. Much more famous was Nelson's signal some forty minutes later. He asked his signal lieutenant to hoist the telegraph 'Nelson confides that every man will do his duty'. The words 'Nelson', 'confides' and 'duty' would all have to be spelt, having no prearranged combination of flags. The lieutenant asked if he might, since time was short, sub-stitute England for Nelson, and 'expects' for 'confides'. Nelson agreed, and the signal was raised. It is often thought that this had an inspirational effect on the fleet. According to Robinson no one knew of the signal's meaning until after the battle. On board *Royal Sovereign* Collingwood's response was, 'I wish Nelson would stop signalling. We all know what we have to do.'[54] By this time all her crew had been at their battle stations for an hour and more. Galley fires had been doused, cabins and their furniture removed and struck down into the hold, along with poor Bounce. The decks had been wetted and sprinkled with sand to mop up blood. Boarding and splinter netting and fearnought screens (canvas sheets covering the entrance to the magazines, kept damp to prevent sparks) had been rigged. The ship's band played patriotic tunes, and her officers stood on the quarterdeck, waiting.

By this time the two British columns were heading directly for the enemy's line, pressing on sail. *Royal Sovereign*, with her newly coppered bottom, raced ahead, not just of *Victory*, a quarter of a mile to the north, but of all the other ships in the squadron. So far ahead that Collingwood forbade Clavell from setting studding-sails, for what must have seemed an age to his first lieutenant. When he finally gave the nod, the studding-sails were instantly sheeted home and *Royal Sovereign* sprang forward until she was several hundred yards ahead of *Bellisle*, her next in line. Strung out over a mile of sea astern of *Bellisle* came the other ships of Collingwood's leeward division: *Mars,* whose Captain George Duff would die before the day was out; *Tonnant, Bellerophon* (Captain John Cooke: another fatality); *Colossus, Achilles, Revenge, Polyphemus, Swiftsure* and then Collingwood's own *Dreadnought; Defiance, Thunderer, Defence,* and last in line the venerable but sluggish *Prince.* For the first twenty minutes, only *Royal Sovereign* was exposed to a deadly broadside which she could not return: it was the price to be paid for Nelson's tactical gamble.

At a thousand yards, six enemy ships opened fire on her. Many commanders would have had their men discharge a broadside of their own to calm their nerves. Collingwood ordered his men to lie down on the decks as the first shots whistled through the rigging and began to tear sails to shreds. The moral effect on the enemy of this slow, deliberate and apparently unconcerned advance was shattering. Collingwood was aiming for the gap between *Fougeux* and the vast three-decker *Santa Anna*, the flag ship of Admiral Don Ignatius d'Alava. Seeing his intent, *Fougeux* closed up tight under *Santa Anna's* stern. *Royal Sovereign* sailed on under an increasingly deadly fire, with the eyes of all the English fleet on her. 'See how that noble fellow Collingwood takes his ship into action. How I envy him!' cried Nelson. And at the same time Collingwood was saying to his fat, stupid, but undeniably brave captain, Edward Rotheram, 'What would Nelson give to be here!'[55] Hercules Robinson was also watching from the deck of *Euryalus* as she scurried around the fleet like a sheepdog, with last minute instructions:

> How I see at this moment glorious old Collingwood, a quarter of a mile ahead of his second astern, and opening the battle with the magnificent black *Santa Anna*, cutting the tacks and shrouds and halyards of his studding sails as he reached her, and letting them drop in the water (grieving, I have no doubt, at the loss of so much beautiful canvas) and as his main yard caught the mizen vangs[56] of his opponent, discharging his double-shotted broadside into her stern.[57]

This first broadside killed and wounded more than a hundred of *Santa Anna's* men and dismounted or destroyed so many of her guns that, in the first instant of the action, she was effectively finished as a battle unit. The two ships now became locked together, and although *Santa Anna's* gunners fought on, Captain Rotheram offered Collingwood his congratulations, believing *Royal Sovereign* had made a capture of an enemy flagship before any other ship in the British fleet had engaged. Even so, d'Alava refused to strike, and soon *Royal Sovereign* was surrounded by enemy ships before she could be supported herself. Two Spanish ships, the *San Justo* and *San Leandro*, and the French *Neptune* and *Fougeux* joined in, firing broadside after broadside into *Royal Sovereign* so that within half an hour of the first engagement she was dismasted and could no longer be manoeuvred. She and the *Santa Anna* were now as it were locked in an embrace. It was as if two punch-drunk heavyweights were trading blows to the end, still somehow standing, but barely conscious – and with the loser's seconds joining in. Cannon balls from the *Royal Sovereign* and *Santa Anna* were seen striking each other in mid-air and falling, deformed and flattened, into the water.[58] It was as hard an action as there had ever been, and it was to the finish. Even so, Collingwood appeared unconcerned. Robinson caught sight of him again:

> Walking the break of the poop with his little triangular gold-laced cocked hat, tights, silk stockings, and buckles, musing over the progress of the fight, munching an apple.[59]

Calm he may have been, but by the end of the day Collingwood was one of only three officers (Rotheram included) left alive on his own quarterdeck. His Master, William Chalmers, had been blown almost in two by a cannon ball, and Collingwood caught him as he fell:

> He laid his head upon my shoulder, and told me he was slain. I supported him till two men carried him off. He could say nothing to me, but bless me; but as they carried him down, he wished he could but live to read the account of the action in a newspaper. He lay in the cockpit, among the wounded, until the *Santa Anna* Struck; and, joining in the cheer which they gave her, expired with it on his lips.[60]

Collingwood himself had been wounded: a great splinter gashed his leg (he was the only injured officer in the fleet who failed to report to a surgeon), and he had been knocked down and winded by a cannon ball which had passed by within a hair's breadth of his old-fashioned tailcoat. Clavell was seriously injured and had been taken below to the surgeons in the cockpit below the water line. *Royal Sovereign* was so exposed that Collingwood ordered the marine commander, Captain Vallack, to take his men from the poop deck. At half-past two in the afternoon, *Santa Anna* finally struck her colours, surrendering to a *Royal Sovereign* who was herself a dismasted near wreck.

It was at this point that Collingwood was told Nelson had been wounded, shot by a marine from the fighting tops of Capitaine Lucas' *Redoutable*. *Victory* had been under deadly fire herself as she approached the enemy line, and would suffer the heaviest casualties in the British fleet: 57 dead and 102 wounded, compared to *Royal Sovereign's* 47 dead and 100 wounded. No one could have known that in ranging alongside the *Redoutable*, *Victory* had engaged a ship whose captain had trained many of his men to leave their great guns and take their muskets into the rigging, to play hell with the enemy's quarterdeck. When Nelson fell it was immediately obvious that it was no mere wound. Collingwood later wrote to their old friend Mary Moutray:

> An officer came from the *Victory*, to tell me he was wounded. He sent his love to me, and desired me to conduct the fleet. I asked the officer if the wound was dangerous, and he by his look told what he could not speak, nor I reflect upon now, without suffering again the anguish of that moment.[61]

This account somewhat contradicts that of Captain Hardy, Nelson's flag captain, who recalled that Nelson had refused to give up command to Collingwood until the actual moment of his death. From now on Collingwood commanded the battle and its aftermath. Victory in every sense was his as much as it was Nelson's. But the reality of command in such a situation was that there were sixty effectively independent commanders in the battle. Each ship was involved in its own private war, and no signals would make much difference now.

Collingwood's leeward division formed a cluster to the south of *Royal Sovereign*, some still engaging the enemy, some already in possession of prizes, others coming to the help of beleaguered comrades as far as the light winds and the condition of their shattered rigging would allow. To the north-east a number of enemy ships had disengaged and were making for Cadiz. Now just a couple of hundred yards away to the north of *Royal Sovereign*, *Victory* lay wallowing on the swell. The ships which had done her so much damage, *Redoutable*, *Bucentaure* and *Santissima Trinidad*, had been surrounded by British ships and one by one were surrendering, themselves mere wrecks. Further north again several British ships were in pursuit of the vanguard of the enemy fleet which had been so suspiciously slow in turning that only now, when it was too late, did they half-heartedly join the fray. Many French and Spanish ships had surrendered (the total would be nineteen, but see Chapter 11), and not a single British ship had struck, though many were mere floating hulks with no steerage or masts to rig a sail on.

By extraordinary chance, out of the forty thousand or so men (and one or two women) who took part in that battle, an account from an ordinary seaman, known only as Sam, survives as a witness to a unique moment. In a letter to his father written after the battle he wrote:

> Our dear Admiral Nelson is killed! So we have paid pretty dearly for licking 'em. I never sat [sic] eyes on him, for which I am both sorry and glad; for, to be sure, I should like to have seen him – but then, all the men in our ship who have seen him are such soft toads, they have done nothing but blast their eyes, and cry, ever since he was killed. God bless you! Chaps that fought like the devil, sit down and cry like a wench. I am still in the *Royal Sovereign*, but the Admiral has left her, for she is like a horse without a bridle, so he is in a frigate that he might be here and there and everywhere, for he's as

cute as here and there … and as bold as a lion, for all he can cry! –
I saw his tears with my own eyes, when the boat hailed and said my
lord was dead …[62]

Collingwood had indeed transferred to a frigate, *Euryalus*, whose
captain, Henry Blackwood, took *Royal Sovereign* in tow late in the
afternoon, with the wind rising and no cables to anchor her. Now
Collingwood, having stood in the shadow of his friend and hero for
thirty years, found himself shouldering a huge burden. His first
concern was for his own ships. Nelson's order to anchor could not be
carried out (few ships had anchors or cables left), and in any case
had Nelson been present he would probably have made the same
decision as Collingwood under the same conditions. There is no
doubting Collingwood's seamanship. No doubting either the perilous
state of the fleet: within a few miles of the treacherous shoals of
Cape Trafalgar, and in a westerly wind that rose by the hour until it
became a full-blown gale, and worse, lasting several days: some of
the worst weather that many of the veteran captains of the battle
had ever experienced. In the circumstances, it is amazing that not a
single English ship was lost.

A ship of the line, at its best, behaved like a well-balanced upside-
down pendulum, its slow corkscrew motion dampened below decks
and exaggerated at the top of its masts. With the loss of topgallants,
topmasts and in some cases lower masts themselves, that balance
was destroyed. Even in a moderate swell the pitch and roll became
violently uncomfortable, and in really bad weather the ship was in
great danger of sinking – broaching-to and capsizing as she was
turned broadside on to the Atlantic swell. Throughout the fleet those
who were not severely wounded or dumbfounded with noise and
shock worked through the evening and on into the night, jury-rigging
topmasts, mending and splicing miles of cordage, bending what

canvas they could spread in order to give their ships some steerage as the wind rose and the horrors of a leeward shore loomed a few miles to the east; carpenters plugged shot holes as well as they could; rudders were operated by steering ropes; dead and dying men were heaved overboard. Several ships were either taken in tow by others, or were themselves towing prizes.

Collingwood's next task was to ensure that, if he could not hold on to the enemy prizes, then at least they should not be allowed to return to Cadiz, or escape into the Mediterranean. So he ordered their destruction, an act that won him few friends among his fellow commanders, whose potentially vast share of prize-money he was casting to the wind. Those with a broader strategic outlook approved, however. Lord Eldon later remembered Earl St Vincent's reaction: 'Collingwood's conduct after the Battle of Trafalgar in destroying, under difficult circumstances, the defeated fleet, was above all praise.'[63] It is easy for historians to judge and criticise. Collingwood's own terse account delivered to William Marsden, the Secretary to the Admiralty Board, gives an idea of what the new Commander-in-Chief had to face. He was constantly receiving reports from ships on their condition, their appalling casualty figures, and of course news of the deaths of friends and officers and men with whom he had served for thirty years. Frigates and smaller boats plied to and fro passing information, rumours, messages between friends, cousins, brothers. Since the end of the battle, wrote Collingwood:

> I have had a continued series of misfortunes; but they are of a kind that human prudence could not possibly provide against, or my skill prevent. On the 22nd, in the morning, a strong southerly wind blew, with squally weather, which, however, did not prevent the activity of the officers and seamen of such ships as were manageable from getting hold of many of the prizes, (thirteen or fourteen) and towing them off to the westward, where I ordered them to

rendezvous around *Royal Sovereign*, [then] in tow by the *Neptune*. But on the 23rd the gale increased, and the sea ran so high that many of them broke the tow rope, and drifted far to leeward before they were got hold of again; and some of them, taking advantage of the dark and boisterous night, got before the wind, and have perhaps drifted on the shore and sunk. On the afternoon of that day, the remnant of the combined fleet, ten sail of ships, which had not been much engaged, stood up to leeward of my shattered and straggling charge, as if meaning to attack them, which obliged me to collect a force out of the least injured ships, and to form to leeward for their defence. All this retarded the progress of the hulks; and the bad weather continuing, determined me to destroy all the lee-wardmost that could be cleared of the men, considering that keeping possession of the ships was a matter of little consequence, compared with the chance of their falling again into the hands of the enemy; but even this was an arduous charge in the high sea which was running. I hope, however, it has been accomplished to a considerable extent.[64]

There was a third task. Despite the terrible conditions, Collingwood ordered that as many enemy sailors as possible should be rescued from ships which were sinking, or in danger of running aground, or which were to be destroyed. It was this act of humanity which won Collingwood, that day, as much admiration among his enemies as he had earned respect from his own officers and men. Henry Blackwood, who came to know Collingwood over the next weeks, wrote to his wife:

> Could you witness the grief and anxiety of Admiral Collingwood (who has done all that an admiral can do) you would be very deeply affected … [he is] a very reserved, though a very pleasing good man; and as he fought like an angel I take the more to him.[65]

Two weeks after the battle, Collingwood's dispatch, having been brought by Lt Lapenotiere of the *Pickle* to the Admiralty the previous night after a dramatic journey of its own, was published on the front page of *The Times*. It was made up of two letters, written on 22 and 24 of October in *Euryalus*'s cramped cabin. The defeated Admiral Villeneuve was there: 'a tallish thin man, a very tranquil, placid, English-looking Frenchman', according to Hercules Robinson.[66] The original drafts of those two letters have recently been discovered in Collingwood's Secret Letter book covering the period 1805–1808.[67] Both are written in his own hand, very fine and legible, despite the awful gale that was threatening to dash the British fleet on the shoals of Trafalgar. They contain several paragraphs which were excised from the published version, and which underline the extreme precariousness of the fleet's position. A full transcription of the draft dispatches is published for the first time in Appendix 1.[68]

The Trafalgar dispatch describes the battle, its aftermath, and the death of Nelson with all Collingwood's cultivated delicacy and elegance of phrase: it is a masterpiece of understated concision. King George wept when he read it.[69] On its publication the country was in uproar, torn between grief and joy. When the mail arrived in Newcastle the following day Sarah Collingwood was in a shop. The coachman, wearing a black hat band, shouted that there had been a great victory, but that all the English admirals were dead. Sarah fainted.[70]

TOP After Trafalgar, Collingwood wrote in his famous dispatch: 'The Enemy's ships were fought with a gallantry highly honourable to their officers, but the attack on them was irresistible.' The Royal Navy suffered seventeen hundred killed and wounded; the French and Spanish more than seven thousand. 'The Battle of Trafalgar: End of the Action' by Nicholas Pocock, oil on canvas, c.1808. (© *National Maritime Museum, London*)

ABOVE Nelson is shot on the quarterdeck of *Victory* by a marksman from Captain Lucas' *Redoubtable*. 'My heart is rent with the most poignant grief,' wrote Collingwood, 'a grief to which even the glorious occasion on which he fell, does not bring the consolation which perhaps it ought.' 'The Fall of Nelson, Battle of Trafalgar' by Denis Dighton, 1792–1827, oil on canvas, c.1825. (© *National Maritime Museum, London*)

ABOVE The storm after Trafalgar. It was one of the worst storms that many commanders had experienced. At its height Collingwood ordered the enemy prizes to be destroyed; but not a single British ship was lost. Painting attributed to John Wilson Carmichael, 1800–1868. (*The Collingwood Family*)

BELOW Collingwood's telescope, its lenses crusted with sea salt. The admiral, typically, had it repaired with an oilcloth and tar bandage. Night after night he scanned the horizon with it: an 'eagle on the watch'. (*The Collingwood Family*)

OPPOSITE PAGE

TOP *Dreadnought*, Collingwood's 98-gun flagship in 1804. He trained his crew to fire an astonishing three broadsides in three-and-a-half minutes. (© *National Maritime Museum, London*)

BELOW Port Mahon. After the Spanish uprising of May 1808 Collingwood was able to base the Mediterranean fleet here once again. His life had more or less come full circle. 'Port Mahon' by Anton Schranz, 1769–1839, oil on canvas. (*Museum of Menorca*)

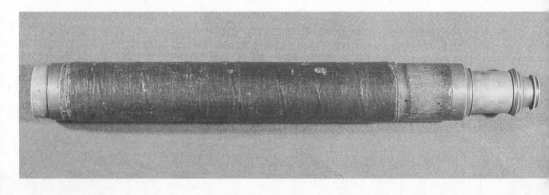

The Dreadnought. Off Greenwich.

Collingwood's last flagship, the 110-gun *Ville de Paris*. He finally left Port
Mahon for England in March 1810, but died at sea the day after she sailed.
'The Ship 'Ville de Paris' under Full Sail' by Thomas Buttersworth,
1768–1828, oil on canvas, c.1803 (© *National Maritime Museum, London*)

LEFT The Fontana Arethusa in Syracuse. Nelson watered his ships at this ancient natural spring before the battle of the Nile. Collingwood based his fleet here during the defence of Sicily. (*Author*)

BELOW Collingwood dined here at La Palazzina Cinese, near Palermo, with the King of Sicily – a reluctant and lazy king but, like Collingwood, a keen gardener. (© *Massimo Listri/Corbis*)

OPPOSITE PAGE
TOP Collingwood House is now a hotel where, every Thursday during the season, its owner gives guided tours. Collingwood's ghost is said to be heard sometimes, fingering odd notes on the piano. (*Author*)

BELOW Pigtail Steps, Port Mahon. It was from here that the fictional Jack Aubrey looked out in vain for a glimpse of *Sophie*, his first command. (*Author*)

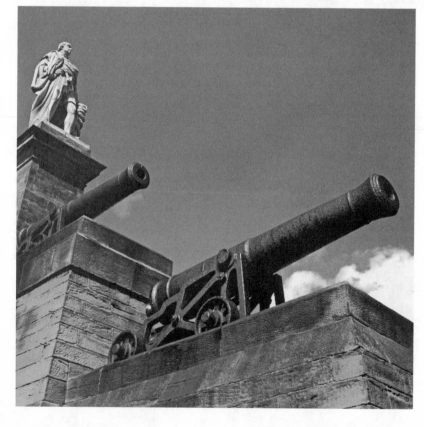

ABOVE Chirton House. Collingwood inherited the house, between Newcastle and North Shields, from his uncle Edward. He thought he might make something of the mine that came with it, but had no desire to live among the filth and noise of steam engines and coal wagons *(By kind permission of North Tyneside Libraries, Museums and Information Service)*

LEFT Collingwood's towering monument at Tynemouth looks appropriately out to sea. The four cannon mounted at its foot came from *Royal Sovereign*: the first guns to fire at Trafalgar. *(Malcolm Sewell/Alamy)*

CHAPTER NINE

Giddy with the multiplicities
1806-1808

Collingwood's head was spinning too, and with good reason. In October 1805 he had been second-in-command to Nelson at a victory which was (and still is) seen as delivering the *coup de grâce* to Napoleon's overseas ambitions. But it did not, and five short months later everything had changed. Trafalgar may have been morally decisive, but it left Britain tactically weaker than she had been before: her Mediterranean fleet was shattered; the enemy still had squadrons at Cadiz, Cartagena, Rochefort, Brest and Toulon. And even as news of an English naval victory filtered through the courts of Europe, so did word of Napoleon's crushing defeat of the Russian-Austrian army at Austerlitz in December. Then in January 1806 William Pitt died, leaving a vacuum at the heart of Britain's wartime strategy that the so-called 'Ministry of all the Talents' (an ineffective coalition) could not fill. With Pitt and Nelson gone, and Napoleon the master of Europe, who would be England's saviour now?

By the spring of 1806, not yet half-way through a staggering seven-year unbroken tour of duty that would kill him, Cuthbert Collingwood had become Commander-in-Chief of the Mediterranean fleet, and effective viceroy at sea from Cadiz to Constantinople. He had been promoted to vice-admiral of the red. He had been created Baron Collingwood of Caldburne and Hethpool.[1] He had been granted a pension for life and given any number of patriotic awards by his fellow countrymen, including the freedom of many cities and towns. He had even inherited a coal mine. And, because it now adorned his arms, he had been reminded of his family's ancient motto, which might have been chosen personally, so apt was it: *Ferar unus et idem* ... Always one and the same.[2]

Collingwood was delighted with the professional praise given him by service colleagues (especially his old patrons Admirals Parker and Roddam). He can only have been amazed to receive a warm, even overly warm, letter of congratulations from his former antagonist Sir Roger Curtis, who addressed him as 'my Dear Cuddy'.[3] He was delighted too that Sarah was enjoying her new-found fame and social popularity. He was gratified by the kind words of the King, and at the Admiralty's faith in his capabilities. His title amused him:

> And so I have a great Barony – it may be called a Barreny to me – value 30s. a year, or thereabouts. But if I live long enough I will make it a place of consideration.[4]

This apparent indifference was not universal, though, as he admitted in a letter to Sarah:

> I am out of all patience with Bounce. The consequential airs he gives himself since he became a right honourable dog are insuffer-

able. He considers it beneath his dignity to play with commoners' dogs, and truly thinks that he does them grace when he condescends to lift up his leg against them. This, I think, is carrying the insolence of rank to the extreme, but he is a dog that does it.[5]

Collingwood wrote to many of his acquaintances about the battle, and in particular about his grief at the death of Nelson. None understood their relationship better than Mary Moutray, to whom Collingwood wrote in December, saying:

> You, my dear Madam, who know what our friendship was, can judge what I have felt. All the praise and acclamations of joy for our victory only bring to my mind what it cost.[6]

In a valediction to Nelson addressed to Sir Thomas Pasley, with whom he had fought in 1794, he wrote:

> He possessed the zeal of an enthusiast, directed by talents which nature had very bountifully bestowed upon him – and everything seemed as if by enchantment, to prosper under his direction – but it was the effect of system – and nice combination, not of chance – We must endeavour to follow his example, but it is the lot of very few to attain to his perfection …[7]

To add to his grief, and his anxiety for the fleet, the military situation was grim. Between Gibraltar and Constantinople, where Russian and French diplomats were vying for political and military influence over the 'Sublime Porte',[8] Britain had just one small base, at Malta, and one dubious ally, in the Neapolitan court. Malta at least was in good hands, having been recaptured by Captain Alexander Ball in 1800. Ball, highly esteemed by both Nelson and Collingwood, was now governor of the island, protecting the crucial Levant trade route to the east, and providing a well-defended base for the navy. He had been a midshipman with Collingwood as long ago as the battle at Bunker's Hill in 1775. Naples had changed little. Queen Maria

Carolina intrigued with diplomats in secret and in the open; her husband the King played the part of a country gentleman.

As Napoleon's eye shifted away from Britain to the south and east, his ambitions once more began to revolve around the overland route to the Indian Ocean, and to domination of the Mediterranean. He could not hope to take Malta without a large-scale amphibious assault. So he turned his attention to Sicily, the largest island in the Mediterranean and the most vulnerable to attack from the Italian mainland. Like the English Channel, the Strait of Messina only needed to be held for a day to effect an invasion. Unlike the Channel, the Strait is a mere two miles wide.

Collingwood's immediate task, after sending his unserviceable ships home (*Victory*, carrying Nelson's pickled body; *Royal Sovereign*, *Bellisle*, *Tonnant* and *Téméraire* were the worst, and could not hope to be repaired outside their home ports) was to blockade the remains of the Combined Fleet in Cadiz, and prevent squadrons at Rochefort, Toulon and Cartagena from getting to sea. That he succeeded seems almost miraculous, especially since his obsession with detail and his inability to delegate were wearing him to a thread. The capture by Sir Richard Strachan's squadron of four of the enemy ships which had escaped from Trafalgar was only a partial relief.

One of the many distractions faced by Collingwood is revealed in his correspondence with Vice-Admiral Don Ignatius Maria d'Alava, who had been critically injured during *Royal Sovereign*'s battle with *Santa Anna*.[9] Although Collingwood had received his sword (or what he thought was his sword) in surrender, he had allowed d'Alava to remain in his ship, as he was not expected to live. *Santa Anna* was driven by the storms into Cadiz, where d'Alava slowly recovered. On 30 October Collingwood wrote to him:

> It is with great pleasure I have heard that the wound which you received in the action is in a hopeful way of recovery, and that your

Country may still have the benefit of your services. But, Sir, you surrendered yourself to me ... and I expect that you consider yourself a prisoner of war ...[10]

D'Alava replied that he was sorry Collingwood had been labouring under the misapprehension that he had surrendered himself. He still had his sabre, and it must have been another officer's sword that had inadvertently been offered as his. It was a disingenuous response, and Collingwood thought it shabby. But he continued to correspond politely with d'Alava over the next months. Relations with the Marquis de la Solana, Captain-General of Andalucia, were more cordial. On 27 October Collingwood had opened a correspondence with him:

Humanity, and my desire to alleviate the sufferings of these wounded men, dictate to me to offer to your excellency their Enlargement, that they may be taken proper care of in the hospitals on shore.[11]

The marquis responded with thanks and an assurance that English prisoners would be treated as courteously as their Spanish counterparts. He sent Collingwood a cask of wine as a token of esteem, and perhaps as proof that in an age when the rules of war were being reinvented, officers in England and Spain, at any rate, still thought of themselves as gentlemen. Collingwood responded as well as his meagre stores would allow:

I wish I had any thing half so good to send your Excellency: but, perhaps, an English cheese may be a rarity at Cadiz; and I accordingly take the liberty of begging your Lordship's acceptance of one, and of a cask of porter.[12]

Collingwood's gifts were apparently consumed at a single party. In return, the marquis sent by fishing boat 'sixty melons, and some baskets of grapes, of figs, and of pomegranates'. The melons were especially for Richard Thomas (Collingwood's captain in his new flag ship *Queen*, a 98-gun second-rate) whom Solana had heard was particularly fond of them. Thomas was the only one of his flag captains that Collingwood either liked or thought up to the job. He had been his signal lieutenant in *Excellent* many years before, and stayed with the Admiral until his death. Fat, stupid but brave Captain Rotheram had, luckily for Collingwood, returned to England in the shattered *Royal Sovereign*. Of him, in the aftermath of battle, Collingwood had written to William Marsden, the Admiralty Secretary, a thinly disguised damnation: 'I cannot sufficiently recommend Captain Rotheram ...'[13] – so at least Collingwood's wit was still intact.

Queen, and the five ships Collingwood could spare from other duties, spent the winter watching, in turn, Cadiz and Cartagena. The Rochefort squadron had got out into the Atlantic but been intercepted by a squadron Collingwood had sent under Sir John Duckworth. At San Domingo he destroyed them. It was one less worry, but still the rump of the navy's Mediterranean fleet was wearing out fast at sea, while the Spaniards sheltered in their harbours and France continued to build new ships at Toulon. The Spaniards carried on their maritime trade under neutral flags, so unless they came out, which seemed most unlikely, there was little Collingwood could do against them. To make matters worse, the 'neutrals' were being insured by English underwriters, as Collingwood pointed out to Sarah's uncle:

> It is a most nefarious practice, which has put me out of conceit with mercantile patriotism. They may give me fine vases and high praises, but they must shew the same regard for their Country which I feel, before they can gain my esteem.[14]

In the same letter Collingwood vented his spleen on another matter to which he had always been peculiarly sensitive: money. He did not dislike it, and frequently mentioned the possibility of its acquisition in his letters, but he abhorred the thought that he might appear to desire it. It looked as if the pension he had been granted by parliament had been supplemented by one for his wife and daughters, pleaded for by a kinsman, William Spencer-Stanhope. When he found out, Collingwood was furious, imagining that the King must think him very ill-bred to have his relatives plead his family's poverty. He wrote, with leaden irony:

> Let others plead for pensions; I can be rich without money, by endeavouring to be superior to everything poor. I would have my services to my Country unstained by any interested motive; and old Scott and I can go on in our cabbage patch without much greater expense than formerly. But I have had a great destruction of my furniture and stock; I have hardly a chair that has not a shot in it, and many have lost both legs and arms, without hope of pension. My wine broke in moving, and my pigs were slain in battle; and these are heavy losses where they cannot be replaced.[15]

Such was his mood during this winter of unremitting effort, when the Admiralty seemed to have forgotten his convenient existence, that Collingwood's pen lashed out in several directions. One target was Nelson's morally bankrupt, hearse-chasing brother William, who had inherited his earldom, to Collingwood's and others' disgust:

> I suppose all the public reward of money will go to the parson, the present Earl Nelson, who of all the stupid dull fellows you ever saw, perhaps he is the most so. Nothing in him like a gentleman ...[16]

He was equally infuriated with Sir Robert Calder, who had written to him after Trafalgar asserting his claim to a share of the head-money, despite having been sent home in disgrace before the battle. But his musings were cut short by news that the Brest fleet was out, and expected to head south. So from Cartagena he once more sailed west to cover Cadiz. His brief departure from the Mediterranean helped precipitate events coming to their head in Naples. The Queen had been stringing the British along while she secretly, but indiscreetly, negotiated with Napoleon to retain Naples. An Anglo-Russian force in the Bay of Naples appeared to strengthen her position. But after the disaster at Austerlitz Russian intervention became impossible. Russia withdrew her forces to Corfu, from where she controlled the Ionian Islands and the entrance to the Adriatic. The commander of the British force, General Sir James Craig, withdrew his five thousand-strong army from Naples to Messina to prevent a French invasion of Sicily, and the Neapolitan court once more retired to Palermo, as they had done in 1799. They were carried in Collingwood's old *Excellent*, veteran of the battle of Cape St Vincent in which he had first exercised his record broadside with such deadly effect.

Sicily is the largest Mediterranean island, its culture a suitably extreme manifestation of the fatalistic resentment and apathy expressed in Giuseppe Lampedusa's masterpiece *The Leopard*.[17] Expropriated by the Neapolitan Bourbons, it lay under twin shadows cast by centuries of foreign domination, and impending natural disaster. Almost as close to Africa as it is to Europe, its volcanic soils are fertile but drought-ridden. It was coveted more for its strategic location: for two thousand years and more it has held the key to domination of the Mediterranean. At its south-east corner the ancient Graeco-Roman city of Syracuse provided a sheltered base and watering facilities for naval squadrons. In the north-east was Messina, the crucial harbour and garrison that controlled movement along the Strait and held the key to invasion from the mainland.[18] Not for nothing were its mythical goddesses Scylla, the sea monster and Charybdis, the whirlpool, still held in awe by sailors. On the north coast lay the capital Palermo, a city of extraordinarily sordid and magnificent contrasts, more African and Byzantine than Italian, militarily indefensible but at the hub of political and court intrigue.

It was from here that Collingwood began to receive letters of supplication in February 1806. 'Our situation is very, very painful and critical,' Queen Maria Carolina had written from Naples in January, even before Joseph Bonaparte had arrived at the head of a conquering army and forced them to flee. 'I count on you to be, as the respectable Lord Nelson was for us, our friend, protector and defender.'[19]

Later in the same month she wrote him another letter, followed by one from her husband. This time her 'entire hope is in the brave and loyal British nation.'[20] She implored Collingwood to send her a division of warships to protect Sicily and recover her kingdom. The King followed with a description of their 'fatal' position, ripe for invasion despite his own 'vigorous efforts' at defending the island.[21]

That sort of moral blackmail might have worked with Nelson, as it seemed to work with Sir Gilbert Elliot, the British minister at the court. Collingwood's sense of duty to the service and to his own ministers in Whitehall allowed him to take a much more dispassionate view of Their Majesties' discomfort. He knew perfectly well their devotion to the British crown was all expediency. He did not feel the natural awe of royalty for its own sake that had so turned his friend's head. He was, however, concerned for the military security of the island, and began to conceive a plan for its naval defence.

First, he had to mitigate the British government's inept handling of what he regarded as crucial allies in North Africa. He had already warned the new First Lord, Lord Barham, of the importance of keeping Morocco and Algiers friendly. The British fleet was heavily dependent on them for supplies of water and fresh food, particularly beef; and their attitude towards French privateers using their ports had to be handled more delicately than the current crop of consuls could manage.

Apart from six months under Moises at the Royal Grammar School, and a lifetime at sea, what had prepared Collingwood for a career as a diplomat? His interest in history and politics, his geographical curiosity, and his natural wisdom; perhaps also the ingenuous honesty and directness of the naval officer. Combining these with his felicity of expression, he now showed that there was more than one weapon available to the navy in its dealings with foreign powers. Where Nelson had threatened, Collingwood deployed enlightened self-interest and flattery:

> To His Highness the most renowned MOHAMED, Pacha of Algiers, the Admiral of His Britannic Majesty's fleet wishes health, peace and the blessing of God.
>
> Your letter, most renowned Pacha, which expressed your satisfaction in our conduct … gave me pleasure …
>
> I am sorry that any misunderstanding should have caused a suspicion in His Majesty's Consul that you were not kindly disposed towards British subjects. As I am not fully informed of the matters which made him doubt the friendship of your Highness, I cannot say any thing about it at present; but I can confidently assure you of the friendly disposition of His Majesty towards your Highness, and trust that the same sentiments on your part will insure to the English that conduct from you which is due to a sincere friendship.
>
> For my own part, when I consider how much it is in the interest of Algiers at this time to be in perfect amity with England, I cannot persuade myself that you would weaken it by any act of yours.
>
> Your Highness cannot shut your eyes to the constant encroachments of an ambitious power, which, setting justice and the happiness of mankind at defiance, would possess itself of all countries – a power whose object is to govern the whole Mediterranean. Establishments in Africa are necessary to the attainment

of that purpose; and what prevents it but the British Navy?

    When Your Highness revolves this subject in your wise mind, you will perceive that the interest of the Regency[22] requires that sincere friendship with England to which you profess to be so much disposed.

    Trust, most renowned Pacha, that in all things in my power you will find me desirous to be your friend ...[23]

Collingwood's good work was being undermined not just by insensitive consuls, but by the actions of his own officers. Gunboats which he had deployed in the defence of Gibraltar, and which he expressly forbade from entering African ports, had been cruising along the Barbary coast, picking up neutral vessels belonging, among others, to Portugal.[24] Collingwood wrote to the new Foreign Secretary, his fellow Northumbrian Charles Grey, to warn him of an impending rift with Morocco:

> Our affairs with the Barbary States, which are now become very important, should only be intrusted to persons who are sufficiently dextrous to conform to manners so perfectly different from those of Europeans.[25]

If the government in London had not previously appreciated the stature of their new Commander-in-Chief, they were in the process of being educated. The few communications he had received from the Admiralty since Trafalgar seemed more concerned with promotions than with the grand strategic picture. But just as his long experience with seafaring matters had taught him everything from the necessity of examining pursers' accounts, to sweeping the night horizon with his own telescope, Collingwood now found he had to take a more personal hand in political matters. From now on, he dealt increasingly not just with senior diplomats, but also directly with deys and beys, with pashas, sultans, kings, queens, emperors and Sublime Portes.

Collingwood's first letter to King Ferdinand at Palermo was written in March 1806. He had sent a small squadron to patrol the Strait of Messina, and hoped that His Majesty would be reassured by their presence. He also made it quite clear that he was looking at a bigger picture. Insofar as a British admiral may patronise the King of a foreign power, Collingwood managed it:

> Most gladly would I repair with my whole force to the coasts of your Majesty's dominions for their protection, were I not well assured that the station which I hold here, by preventing the French squadrons from getting into the Mediterranean, will more effectually answer that purpose than any other position I could take.[26]

Collingwood's problem, as it had been every naval commander's in the Mediterranean, was a lack of frigates: the eyes and ears of the fleet. Nelson had said that when he died they would find 'want of frigates' stamped on his heart. As a theatre of operations, the Mediterranean was simply too big and its politics too complicated to patrol with a cumbersome fleet of battle ships. And with the stifling of French trade there was little other intelligence available. Like Nelson, Collingwood did not want the Toulon fleet to be blockaded too closely; he wanted them to come out so that he could fight them. But he needed frigates to watch them and follow them and report back to him. The Admiralty seemed to have forgotten his existence.

As ever, his mind wandered to domestic events, especially on those rare occasions when a ship brought letters from home. Mary Moutray wrote to tell him that her daughter Kate was engaged, and that she had heard her friend Cuthbert's orders for the fleet after Trafalgar had been used as a sermon. Cuthbert was amused. Two things, he admitted to Mary, did not amuse him. One was that his title had been carelessly drafted so that the barony would only pass through the male line. He was naturally concerned to ensure that, since he was unlikely to have a son, it should pass to his elder daughter Sarah. He had petitioned Whitehall on several occasions, and been promised that the matter was being attended to. Another matter that began to rankle was that Collingwood's recommendations for promotions after Trafalgar seemed to have been ignored, apart from Clavell, whom he had made commander of the *Weazel* sloop on his own authority. He began to wonder if the Admiralty held him in disfavour.

To Sarah he wrote on 21 March, knowing he might have to wait weeks for the letter to be sent. As always, he wished for the French to come out one last time so that he could beat them and go home. In the meantime he asked Sarah to arrange for some of the barer parts of the Hethpool estate to be planted with larch, oak and beech. 'You will say', he wrote, 'that I have mounted my hobby; but I consider it as enriching and fertilising that which would otherwise be barren.' He also urged Sarah to take great care with the girls' education, 'not throwing away their precious time on novels and nonsense'.

He was recalled from these musings by the arrival from England of *Pompée*, an 80-gun third-rate commanded by Sir William Sidney Smith. Collingwood knew all about Smith, the 'Swedish knight'. He was unlikely to forget his role in the ignominious retreat from Toulon in 1793. He gave him credit, rightly, for the heroic defence of Acre in 1799. But he distrusted him, as an officer incapable of obeying orders. This was no time for dash, or for the rockets and torpedoes that Smith had tried at Boulogne.[27] He gave him very strict instructions to defend Sicily against French attack but warned Elliot, the minister at Palermo, to keep an eye on him. His main concern was that the King and Queen would make some disastrous bargain with Joseph Bonaparte to recover Naples. He was also worried that between them Smith and the new commander of the British army in

Sicily, Sir John Stuart, would be persuaded or encouraged to undertake a military offensive on the mainland. He was right to be worried.

Smith began a harrying operation against coastal forts along the Italian peninsula. They were undoubtedly effective as a nuisance, and delighted the King and Queen, for whose tastes Collingwood did not appear sufficiently active. Smith reinforced Gaeta, the coastal fort south of Naples which still held out against the French, and then carried out an ambitious assault on the island of Capri, in the Bay of Naples. In June he persuaded Stuart to attempt a similar assault on Calabria from Messina, both to disrupt the French commander Reynier's invasion plans, and to gain a foothold on the mainland. The result was a stunning success at the battle of Maida. But it could not be followed up; the force retreated across the Strait to Messina, and Smith's failure to protect Gaeta led to its loss too. Nevertheless, and to Collingwood's intense annoyance, Smith was created 'Viceroy of Calabria' by King Ferdinand. That September Collingwood wrote to his brother John:

> I am sadly off with this Sir S. Smith at Sicily; the man's head is full
> of strange vapours and I am convinced Lord Barham sent him here
> to be clear of a tormentor, but he annoys me more than French or
> Spanish fleet and the squadron he has is going to ruin.[28]

In April 1806 Collingwood's own circumstances changed once again. He transferred into *Ocean*, a new 80-gun flag ship: 'without exception, the finest-looking one I ever saw; but, like all new ships, she wants every thing to be done to her, to fit her for war.'[29] News came from England in the same month that Collingwood's cousin Edward had died, leaving the bulk of his estate to Cuthbert. The property consisted of a large house at Chirton near North Shields, together with its coal mine. The mine had not been run with a view to a profit, but now Collingwood was its owner, and he determined to master yet another discipline, albeit from more than two thousand miles away. He hoped he might make enough money from the colliery to ensure the financial security of his sisters and daughters, though he was adamant he would not put up the rents of his tenants if it caused them hardship, and would have none of them turned out of their houses on any account.[30]

Some of the material possessions in the house had been independently left to another cousin, Stanhope, presumably the same Stanhope who had interfered in Collingwood's business before. Now, what he heard of Stanhope's conduct at Chirton enraged him even more:

> The shabby creature wanted the old cask in which the wine was. I wonder he did not claim the bottles too. Really such meanness in people who call themselves, of condition, quite astonishes me. It is very bad condition ... take away the old casks! Did you ever hear anything like it? But I hear he found money in the house, perhaps [in] aunty Lawson's snug corner.[31]

The main impediment to increasing production at the mine seemed to be an argument over a way-leave for a wagon way. In effect this meant that horse-drawn coal wagons running from the mine on wooden rails had to pass over someone else's land to get to the staithes on the River Tyne (Thomas Hedley's *Puffing Billy*, the first working locomotive at a coal mine, would not be built until a year or so after Collingwood's death, just a few miles upstream at Wylam). At the staithes the coal would be transferred into keels or colliers, and then shipped to London to supply the capital's insatiable need for fuel. As it happened, the land in question was owned by the Duke of Northumberland. The difficulties which a series of agents and lawyers made in arranging the way-leave rights ensured that

Collingwood and the duke, a veteran of the Seven Years' War and the American War of Independence, kept up a lively correspondence until Collingwood's death. These letters are of great interest, not just to students of the Industrial Revolution. The duke soon realised that Collingwood's rank as a mere admiral belied his political and diplomatic skills, and so the two men began a frank and mutually interesting exchange of views on political and military developments in Europe. Of more social interest is the fact that the duke treated Collingwood as a social equal in his correspondence, and referred to her grace the duchess's looking forward to getting to know Sarah, now Lady Collingwood. In an age when birth was so much a superior gift to merit, this is extraordinary; it reflects very much on the stature Collingwood had acquired, not just through his career achievements, but through his intellectual and social development as a gentleman.

The cares and worries of a man playing for high stakes on the world stage, which he confessed made him 'giddy with the multiplicities',[32] still gave Collingwood time to muse on one of his favourite subjects: junior officers. One young man, a Mr Haultaine, sent to him by his old patron and friend Admiral Roddam:

> is so entirely useless that [Captain Lechmere] is afraid he must try him by a court-martial to get rid of him. It is this kind of people that cause all the accidents, the loss of ships, the dreadful expense of them, mutinies, insubordination and everything bad. They must produce a certificate that they are 21 years of age, which they generally write themselves, so that they begin with forgery, proceed with knavery, and end with perjury ...[33]

To others, especially if they had some life about them, he was indulgent, as Hercules Robinson recalled many years later, perhaps with a tint of rose in his eye:

Nelson and Collingwood, who were about as yielding as their respective anchor stocks, and who regarded a shower of shot as much as a shower of snowflakes, were as tender-hearted as two schoolgirls. When Collingwood promoted me from his own ship to be lieutenant of the *Glory*, he sent a commendation with me, which, when my new Captain Otway read it to me, made my cheek tingle, knowing how undeserved it was, and feeling that my having been discovered playing with Bounce, the Admiral's dog, 'Poor Bouncey, good dog, dear Bouncey' & c., and feeding 'Nanny', his goat, with biscuit, when she butted her head at me, had effected more than I cared to acknowledge in my promotion.[34]

There were yet more distractions at home. Sarah was busy introducing the girls to society and travelling with them, outspending Collingwood's income in the process. He would rather they were learning geometry and astronomy. Sarah, he was convinced, had determined to move from Morpeth and take up residence at Chirton. While he realised the Morpeth house must now seem small and provincial to the lady of a baron, he regretted that she never mentioned his garden. Chirton, he wrote to his brother John:

is a place I should dislike exceedingly as a residence. I could never bring my mind to be at home there. Yet it has conveniences that Morpeth has not, and is more like a gentleman's house. Had I been fortunate in prizes I would have bought a suitable residence, but as it is I fancy I must make Chirton my home, in a neighbourhood very disagreeable and in the smoke of the coal engines and every kind of filth.[35]

He was still making applications, all in vain, to have his title descend to the girls, while the Herald's Court were recommending (for a suitably outrageous fee) an augmentation to his arms which gave him a wry smile when he thought of it:

I think there are to be more lions added to it, and for an additional
crest a young lady in the character of victory gathering branches
of palm upon the sea, so like the nymphs of Newbiggen gathering
kelp, that I dare say I shall be able to pass it off as a compliment to
them.[36]

For the whole of 1806 Collingwood kept up his blockade of Cadiz,
under constant pressure to reduce the strength of his squadron for
pressing operations elsewhere, and risking allowing the enemy's fleet
of ten or so ships of the line to escape. His meagre forces were now
hopelessly overstretched, and he himself was stationed too far from
the focus of new developments. One of these was at the head of the
Adriatic. Trieste and Venice were now both under French control
after the defeat of Austria at Austerlitz. Collingwood received orders
to blockade the two ports, so he sent *Unité*, a 40-gun heavy frigate,
with a small detachment of lighter ships: they were all he could spare.

Of even greater concern were developments at Constantinople,
where the French Ambassador, Sebastiani, had succeeded in per-
suading the Sublime Porte to end her alliance with Britain and
threaten the Russians with closing the Bosphorus to her shipping.
Russia for her part had seized the Ionian Islands and occupied
Bucharest. Her failure at Austerlitz had made the Tsar more sensitive
to France's Mediterranean ambitions, and he also believed Britain
would attempt to annex Sicily. It was a heady and complicated mix of
relationships that required extreme subtlety and foresight to manage.
It was further stirred by an ill-timed British imposition of a total
naval blockade against northern France and the Low Countries.
Shortly afterwards Napoleon defeated the Prussians at Jena and tri-
umphantly, from Berlin, issued a decree banning all trade between
Britain and the Continent: his so-called Continental System. This
was the final attempt to strangle Britain that Collingwood had
foreseen years before.

Now, in the late autumn of 1806, Collingwood saw that he must pre-empt developments in Turkey to prevent their becoming a full ally of the French, leaving Egypt and the Middle East open to Napoleon's domination once more. So he sent as large a force as he could spare, three ships of the line under Rear-Admiral Louis, to patrol the Dardanelles and remind the Porte of Britain's naval strength (and friendship). Collingwood was concerned that the British government might not approve of his actions, and was fully prepared to be recalled or superseded. But the new First Lord, Grenville, was rather relieved than angry:

> The detaching of the squadron under Sir Thomas Louis had in a great measure anticipated the wishes of the King's government, and the promptitude and judgement with which that step had been taken could not but be highly satisfactory to His Majesty.[37]

Grenville insisted, in fact, that another two ships of the line be sent to the Dardanelles to reinforce the squadron. Against Collingwood's better judgement he ordered Sir John Duckworth to take command. Duckworth's success against the French after Trafalgar had made him a popular choice, but he did not possess the political skills required in such a sensitive situation. What was more, he was known to be indiscreet, and there was something of the Sidney Smith about him: a dash approaching recklessness. However detailed Colling-wood's orders might be (and, as usual, they were minute and very clear), he was relying on Duckworth's unproven ability to adapt to circumstances as they arose, and on close liaison with the British minister at the Porte, Charles Arbuthnot. Collingwood should have gone himself, but he did not, at least not until it was nearly too late. He remained at sea off Cadiz, having not let go an anchor in fifteen months (and proud that there was not a sick man in the ship), admitting to his father-in-law that if he ever did return home, he would be unfit for anything but the quiet society of his close family. In truth, he was in conflict with himself. Much as he dreamed of a return to his family, he was quick to resent any suggestion that he might leave his post; even more so to the idea that he was politicking. There is also a hint of paranoia:

> MY DEAR SISTER, – It is so long since I heard from you that I think you must have been deceived by the current report which I have heard was circulated with great industry in England 'that I was coming home.' I have not yet thought of such a thing, but I suppose it originated with those who wished to succeed to my command. I came here, not of my own solicitation, or to answer my own private purposes, but because I was ordered as a proper person to conduct the service, and I have such a contempt for anything like chicanery that I will certainly disappoint the authors …
> It is not that I delight in war, am ambitious of high office, or insensible to the comforts of a peaceful, quiet home, and the enjoyments of domestic life, but that I consider the war such that every man capable of serving is bound to render his best services.[38]

On New Year's Day 1807 Collingwood wrote to John Blackett hoping that he might live long 'uninvaded by the sounds of war'. He asked him to tell the girls that Bounce was very well and very fat:

> Yet he seems not to be content, and sighs so piteously these long evenings, that I am obliged to sing him to sleep, and have sent them the song.
>
>> Sigh no more, Bouncey, sigh no more,
>> Dogs were deceivers never;
>> Though ne'er you put one foot on shore,
>> True to your master ever.
>> Then sigh not so, but let us go,
>> Where dinner's daily ready,
>> Converting all the sounds of woe
>> To heigh phiddy diddy.[39]

The song reveals more than Collingwood's affection for his old companion; it is a clever parody on Balthasar's song in *Much Ado about Nothing*.[40] Whatever else Collingwood may have lost in the way of comforts at Trafalgar (and finally Sarah had sent him some knives and forks, at least), he had managed to keep his Shakespeare – and his humour. As he had done before on long Mediterranean commands, Collingwood encouraged his men to put on entertainments, to relieve the boredom both for themselves and the officers of the fleet. One such event led to an embarrassing misunderstanding involving *Ocean*'s resident drag act:

> We have an exceedingly good company of comedians, some dancers that might exhibit at an opera, and probably have done so at Sadlers Wells, and a band consisting of twelve very fine performers. Every Thursday night is a play night, and they act as well as your Newcastle company. A Moorish officer, who was sent to me by the Governor of the province of Tetuan, was carried to the play. The astonishment which this man expressed at the assembly of people, and their order, was itself a comedy.
>
> When the music began, he was enchanted; but during the acting, he was so transported with delight, that he could not keep his seat. His admiration of the 'ladies' was quite ridiculous; and he is gone to the Prince fully convinced that we carry players to sea for the entertainment of the sailors; for though he could not find the ladies after the entertainment, he is not convinced that they are not put up in some snug place till the next play night.[41]

As far as the war was concerned, Collingwood was feeling far from flippant. He saw no end to Napoleon's wickedness or ambition:

> Emperor of the French was well, Emperor 'of the West', or perhaps 'of Europe' he thinks will be better, what a wretched life must so much ambition cause him.[42]

To Lord Radstock, at the beginning of 1807, he offered this opinion:

> Wherever Buonaparte reigns, there is the domination of power,
> which is felt or dreaded by all. His rule is repugnant to the interests
> and welfare of the people; and whenever his tide of greatness be
> at the full, his ebb will be more rapid than his rise. I cannot help
> thinking that epoch is not distant. In that event, the world may hope
> for peace for a few years, until ease and wealth make them
> licentious and insolent, and then our grand-children may begin the
> battle again.[43]

With history in mind, Collingwood was convinced Napoleon would
attempt another invasion of Egypt. Therefore he prepared an
amphibious force to be ready at Malta to sail at a day's notice. But
bad news was now arriving of the fate of Duckworth's expedition
to the Dardanelles:

> The attempt at Constantinople has not succeeded at all; and yet, as
> far as depended on me, we were well prepared. Sir John Duckworth,
> you will have heard, passed the Dardanelles, and burned the ships
> which lay above them. The squadron stopped at Prince's Island;
> the winds, the currents, and every thing, being unfavourable for
> their getting up to the town. The ten days they were there were
> spent in an attempt, by negotiation, to prevent the war, and detach
> the Turks from the French.
>
> On our part it was faithful; on theirs, it was an expedient to
> gain time, until their defences were completed, and their fleet
> secured in the Bosphorus. When they had fully accomplished this,
> they dropped all further intercourse, and the squadron returned.[44]

Collingwood was privately angry with Duckworth; not for the failure
of the expedition, because Collingwood knew himself how much
such things depended on luck and fate, but for leaking his orders
beforehand so that the French, and therefore the Turks, were fore-
warned of them. He had also overstepped his orders, taking upon

himself a negotiating role when Collingwood had forbidden him
to. But Collingwood did not censure Duckworth except in a letter
to his sister, always his most favoured confidante in service matters.
In the same letter he referred to an extraordinary episode in which his
brother Wilfred had been presented with a posthumous paternity
suit. Collingwood's view was that he should not have paid a penny to
the woman:

> I believe I am not mistaken about the young woman at Deptford,
> and my brother was of the same opinion, but was under circum-
> stances which made that necessary for him to do what I do not feel
> at all necessary to continue. The woman had this child exactly nine
> months after my brother left London – so far she was in luck. But
> long before he left London he had been in a state of health that
> having children was quite [out] of [the] question and those cir-
> cumstances I found fully stated to her in letters. But he was more
> convenient to her than another and Sykes was at hand, who dealt
> out to her with a liberal hand much more than my brother could
> afford. When she pleaded the debts she had incurred I gave her
> money to clear her of the world, with which she seemed so satisfied
> that I never heard any more of her and never considered it other
> than as ending an imposition ...
>
> I could not but laugh at the idea of bringing the girl to
> Ommany's house to examine her as to her parentage, poor thing.
> There are many wiser than her who would be puzzled to know who
> their fathers were.[45]

The reference to Ommany is interesting. He was Collingwood's
prize agent and 'man of business'. The same name was chosen by
Patrick O'Brian for Jack Aubrey's agent.[46]

The Constantinople affair was not the only disaster that year.
The expedition to Egypt, which Collingwood had encouraged and
which was initially successful, became enmeshed in Egyptian politics:

'Our troops went on adventures where they certainly had no business and they suffered most severely.'[47] The Ministry of all the Talents fell, to be followed by the Portland administration, who ordered the evacuation of the expedition. Across the Atlantic, in an ominous portent of things to come, the captain of the 50-gun fourth-rate *Leopard*, seeking the recovery of deserters, attacked the American frigate *Chesapeake* off the coast of Virginia.[48] And Russia signed the Treaty of Tilsit with France which ended any hope of her remaining an ally of the British. One result was a new Northern Alliance: in the Baltic tension was raised to the point where Copenhagen was shelled by a British force aiming to prevent the Danish fleet from being handed over to the French. Only Portugal was left as an ally, and relations with her court, pressurised as it was by France, were neutral at best. But here Bonaparte was about to make his big mistake. By the end of 1807 his armies had invaded Portugal and set in train the long and bloody series of events that would culminate at Waterloo eight years later.

Amidst this explosively tense political scene, and under a climate of 'to the death' international economic warfare, the year 1807 is remembered more for the abolition, by Britain and much of the United States, of the slave trade. It is ironic that this outbreak of humanity was fostered by the revolutionary ideals of the enlightenment; in France these had led to revolution, terror, the abolition of slavery and its restitution by Bonaparte. In the more 'democratic' West, it had led to political entrenchment and the triumph of mercantile interests. In England habeas corpus had been suspended and the government spied on its own people. And yet, those same interests which sanctioned the press gang, hanging for theft and the Riot Act, had finally concluded that slavery was immoral. Even in the navy a reflection of this progressive humanity began to appear. By 1806 the Admiralty was instructing commanders not to flog 'without sufficient cause, nor ever with greater severity than the offence shall really deserve';[49] and 'starting', the practice of boatswains and their mates caning seamen arbitrarily, was also to be outlawed.[50] Collingwood, an instinctive humanitarian as much as he was a canny manager of men, had played a part in this social shift in attitudes. He had proved, and famously, that men did not need to be beaten into a state of humiliation in order to keep their ships' decks clean or fire their guns with speed and accuracy.

Collingwood's influence in the navy had increased after Trafalgar, not just because of his seniority, but also because of the sheer numbers of men who served under his ultimate command – perhaps as many as thirty thousand in his last years. His fleet, dissipated as it was with squadrons off Cadiz, at Malta, in the Adriatic and elsewhere, numbered close to eighty ships – perhaps the largest and most difficult fleet a naval commander ever had to manage.[51] Collingwood's views on discipline among both officers and men were only too well known, and if they caused resentment here and there, no one was in any doubt of the outcome if they incurred the Commander-in-Chief's displeasure.

In the late summer of 1807 Collingwood at last left the Cadiz blockade. With Viscount Castlereagh as new Minister for War and the Colonies, and his bitter rival Canning as Foreign Secretary, a more proactive Mediterranean policy began to be shaped, with the aim of taking the war to Napoleon. Collingwood was ordered to sail east via Malta, and take matters at the Sublime Porte into his own hands. His talents had been too long wasted on blockade.

By August *Ocean* was off the Dardanelles, and Collingwood had written a detailed appraisal of the situation to Lord Mulgrave, the Duke of Portland's new First Lord.[52] He had already, again on his own initiative, countermanded the Admiralty's evacuation of Egypt. The army there was now secure, and its continued presence at

Alexandria would, Collingwood believed, effectively concentrate the minds of the Turkish government. A blockade of Constantinople was pointless. The city was supplied by overland caravan, and the only effect of the blockade would be to increase hardship among the Greek islands.

Dealing with the Sublime Porte was a matter of subtlety and patience, to be combined with Collingwood's own policy of alliance through mutual self-interest. Frustrating as the protocols must have been for a man of Collingwood's directness, he was perfectly capable of adapting to the strangest ways, as he told Sarah in a letter describing his arrival:

> When we were very near, they put out the flag of truce from all quarters, and a Capagi Bashi (a sort of Lord Chamberlain of the Seraglio) came off to me with letters to the Embassador, of a pacific import: and had we only ourselves to treat for, I believe there would be few impediments; but as it is, I am not sanguine.[53] I gave him coffee, sherbet, and smoked a pipe with him. The day after, the answer was sent to them by the Dragoman. The ship that carried it anchored in the port, and the Captain was invited to dine with the Capitan Pacha, who is the Lord High Admiral. There were only five at table; the Capitan Pacha, the Pacha of the Dardanelles, my friend the Capagi Bashi, with beards down to their girdles, Captain Otway, and the Dragoman. There were neither plates nor knives and forks but each had a tortoise shell spoon. In the middle of the table was a rich embroidered cushion, on which was a large gold salver, and every dish, to the number of about forty, was brought in singly, and placed upon the salver, when the company helped themselves with their fingers, or, if it was fricasée, with their spoon. One of the dishes was a roasted lamb, stuffed with a pudding of rice: the Capitan Pacha took it by the limbs and tore it to pieces to help his guests; so that you see the art of carving has not arrived at any great perfection in Turkey ...[54]

Shortly afterwards the Russians departed, and it became clear to Collingwood that Turkish policy was now almost completely under the direction of Sebastiani, the French Ambassador. Collingwood's fear, now that the full extent of the terms of Tilsit had become apparent, was that he was being deliberately distracted in Constantinople from a joint Franco-Russian attempt on Sicily, with a French army to be embarked by Russian ships stationed at Corfu. This was a moment of extreme crisis. Collingwood was never a lover of diplomats, as he later confessed to his sister:

> God keep me from the diplomatics! In my mind there cannot be a greater error than to introduce chicane and deceptions into politics. I am persuaded from what I have seen that honesty is the best policy, and yet the great art of diplomacy is, that nothing they do should be understood.[55]

Now he took matters into his own hands, writing to the Capitan Pacha a letter of transparent directness, determined to bring matters to a head and expecting, not for the first time, to be recalled by the Admiralty as a result:

> Will the Sublime Porte accept the friendship offered by England, with a renewal of all the relations of peace and amity, the particular terms of which may be settled by the Plenipotentiaries? Or do they reject the proposal, and, influenced by malign councils, determine on a state of war?[56]

The best he could hope for was that Turkey would not interfere, and to that extent the letter succeeded. It undoubtedly won the approval of the British government, as Collingwood was flattered to find out some time later:

> I have been told by a gentleman from England[57] that Mr Canning said, 'If Mr Pitt had lived to read the letter I wrote to the Capitan Pasha ... he never would have lost sight of the person who wrote

it.' The measure was bold but it seems it was approved. He[58] was tenacious of diplomatic forms. I overthrew them to maintain the country's honour and determined in a day what he would have prosed over for a year.[59]

By October Collingwood was stationed off Syracuse doing his best, with limited intelligence and too few frigates, to determine where the Russian fleet had got to, and what French plans were maturing for an assault. He had heard that ten thousand troops were poised to embark at Leghorn. But were they destined for Africa, Gibraltar, Malta or Sicily? A squadron was preparing at Toulon, but where were they bound – were they designed to draw Collingwood's attention from the Strait of Messina?

Collingwood himself sailed to Toulon, but receiving no new intelligence from that quarter, and facing the onset of severe winter gales, retired to Syracuse to refit. Here he again received letters of supplication from Queen Maria Carolina, wanting the British to invade Calabria; from the King of Sardinia, nervous at the possibility of a French invasion, and from Ali Pacha of Joannina, ruler of part of Albania, who was nervous about the proximity of the French and Russians in the Ionian Islands. He confessed to his sister:

> I think very much of getting home if I know well how to manage it.
> I grow very weak with the continuing harassing of my mind. All
> our affairs are grey here; no bright spots in them.[60]

If Collingwood ended the year hoping he might soon be able to return to England and his family, he was very much mistaken. The year 1808 would be one of 'great and complicated objects',[61] and once again he would find himself at the centre of them.

CHAPTER TEN

Viva Collingwood

1808-1810

I am going on here wearing myself out very fast and do not care
[about] it, for really the situation of our country, and the condition
of the times, is such that people should not be coy whether they
live or not, but as they can contribute to mend them. I have at this
moment more depending than perhaps ever any person in my
situation had – an artful enemy to oppose, a sluggish country to
preserve from being his prey, and not the smallest information from
any quarter.[1]

In the first week of January 1808 Collingwood was enjoying a rare
and welcome break, ashore in Syracuse, when word came from
Palermo that the French fleet was out, having evaded the watching
frigates at Toulon. Believing their destination to be the Adriatic,

Collingwood sailed immediately to intercept them, stationing his squadron off Cape Sapienza, south of the Ionian Islands.[2] The rumours turned out to be false, so he returned to Syracuse in the hope of receiving better intelligence there from cruisers stationed at key points in the Mediterranean and Adriatic. Collingwood wrote to Sal and Mary Patience that he had been splendidly received in Syracuse, and had just had time to visit a few of its ancient wonders before the news arrived. The nobility there were uncorrupted by the vices of the court, he told them, and truly polite. He had himself been attended by a levee of priests, 'all fat, portly-looking gentlemen'.[3] He had been shown around the classical ruins and, keen geographer that he was, he took a close interest in them:

> Where the palace of Dionysius was, there are now a little mill and a pig-sty. The foundations remain of the amphitheatre, where formerly 100,000 people assembled to view the public spectacles. The cavern called Dionysius's ear is perfect and curious. Sound is so reverberated and increased from its sides, that the least whisper is made as loud as a trumpet; and a little pistol with a thimbleful of gunpowder roars like thunder. In this cavern Dionysius is said to have kept his state prisoners, and by means of a hole in the side near the top to have discovered all their secrets and plans. Within the ancient wall there are farms, and vineyards, and pastures, as in the course of time, there may be corn-fields and hop-grounds in St James's Street or the Royal Exchange.[4]

More importantly for a naval commander, Syracuse had a large land-locked harbour, which Collingwood thought the British government ought to invest in as a long-term security measure. Its peninsula, the Ortygia, was well defended against attack by sea and even offered abundant fresh spring water which gushed, and still gushes, into the Fontana Arethusa next to the harbour wall. This was where the mythical Arethusa arose, having been turned into a spring by Artemis to avoid the unwanted attentions of the river god Alpheus.[5] It was at this spring that Nelson watered his fleet before departing for Aboukir Bay in 1799.

On 7 February 1808 Collingwood finally received news of the French, and it was bad news. The Rochefort squadron under Admiral Allemand had escaped Admiral Strachan's watch while his ships were away provisioning, and were now heading for the Mediterranean. Napoleon, sensing that the moment must be seized, ordered the Toulon squadron under Admiral Ganteaume to put to sea and rendezvous with Allemand. The Emperor told his brother Joseph to prepare for an attack on Sicily across the Strait of Messina. But while the squadrons were at sea, Napoleon changed his mind. He would, instead, use Joseph's army as a feint. General Reynier was therefore ordered to seize key positions in Calabria in preparation for the assault, while the French fleet, now numbering ten sail of the line, headed instead for Corfu. This strategically important base, recently abandoned by the Russians, was vulnerable to British attack; now Ganteaume was required to reinforce and reprovision its garrison.

It was as if Collingwood was fighting grass fires, never knowing where the next one would spring up. Now the French squadrons appeared to have united, he too concentrated his resources at a rendezvous west of Sicily off Maritimo: squadrons under Admirals Purvis, Strachan (who had chased Allemand from Rochefort and lost him) and Thornbrough, and his own from Syracuse. Fifteen sail of the line, enough to defeat a French force of twenty or more. But where would they strike? Luckily the French fleet had been scattered by heavy weather. They had missed their rendezvous, and were only reunited at Corfu in the middle of March. This was the sort of eventuality that infuriated Napoleon, whose tactics required the utmost precision of movement; no naval commander had been able to persuade him of the fickleness of the sea.

Collingwood was desperate for intelligence. He had posted a 74-gun two-decker at Messina with four frigates to prevent Reynier from crossing the Strait. But should the rest of Ganteaume's fleet arrive there while Collingwood was elsewhere, they would be driven off and Sicily would be lost. It was not until 6 March that Collingwood received word of their movements, and even then the intelligence was ambiguous. The frigate *Standard* had been chased by four sail of the line at the mouth of the Adriatic. They might have been the Russian Adriatic fleet, now based at Trieste, but Collingwood was convinced they were part of Ganteaume's force. If they were, where were the other six? Hoping to draw Collingwood to the east while they made what seemed like an inevitable attempt on Messina?

Now news came of another French squadron, this time at Elba – and preparations appeared to be under way in Naples to receive a fleet – perhaps to embark part of Joseph's army. Another feint, or part of a double attack, from both east and west? Collingwood decided to reconnoitre Naples for himself. There was no French fleet there but there was news, or rather rumour, that Ganteaume's entire force was now gathered at Taranto[6] near the mouth of the Adriatic and was poised to fall on Sicily.

This was the best news Collingwood could have had. If he found the enemy fleet at Taranto, he could bring them to battle, either there, or having forced them into the Adriatic. There would be no escape. Now he issued his battle orders – no song and dance, no charismatic Nelson touch, just a tactical memorandum which, typically in great detail, told his captains how he expected a battle to be fought and won. It was a further evolution of the tactics which the navy's leading officers had been developing over the last fifteen years: an attack in two columns designed to break the enemy's line into three, cut off the van, and bring on a mêlée. The only major variation was that Collingwood, in the light of Trafalgar, wanted the columns to attack at a less perpendicular angle to the enemy line, to avoid the long exposure to raking fire endured by both *Victory* and *Royal Sovereign* in October 1805.[7]

Collingwood, feeling increasingly old and worn out, was suddenly revived by the prospect of beating the French one more time and ending their naval threat in the Mediterranean for good:

> Constant application has made me very weak, and the illness which always attacks my bowels has reduced my strength very much. My situation will not admit of sickness, and if I could but get hold of the Frenchmen once more, I would then come home.[8]

This was not the first time Collingwood had complained of his bowels. They had been a source of pain and discomfort to him periodically over the years. He was becoming frail with lack of exercise, cooped up in his cabin for twenty or so hours every day – often he only came on deck for an hour or so at twilight. Nevertheless, his spirits were roused by the thought of battle. He wrote to Sarah:

> You know, when I am earnest on any subject, how truly I devote myself to it; and the first object of my life, and what my heart is most bent on (I hope you will excuse me) is the glory of my country. To stand a barrier between the ambition of France and the independence of England, is the first wish of my life; and in my death, I would rather that my body, if it were possible, should be added to the rampart, than trailed in useless pomp through an idle throng.[9]

Sarah seemed to have resigned herself to having no husband. She was spending much of her time arranging the comforts of her new house at Chirton, and enjoying society. Sarah's uncles, the Blacketts, were even corresponding on the matter. Lady C. and the girls were at Brighton that summer, dancing very publicly at the Prince of Wales' fancy balls: hardly the thing when her husband was laying down his life for their country. Collingwood was himself beginning to be concerned at what he heard. Sarah and her father were both spending far too much money, and conspicuously so.

Napoleon's plan, and Collingwood's defence against it, had been conceived with deadly intent. It was the sea and the elements, which Collingwood knew so much more intimately than his opponent, which decided that the execution of these objects would end in a comedy of fates. And not for the first time, just as one phase of the war came to a natural conclusion, so another sprang to life.

Even as the English fleet arrived at the mouth of the Adriatic, news came that the Spanish squadron at Cartagena was out, destined for Majorca. Suspicious that they might make for Naples and revive the invasion plan from the west, Collingwood detached a small group of ships to reinforce those already at Palermo, and sent his precious frigates out to find the French among the Ionian Islands, or at Corfu itself. They returned with the devastating news that the French were nowhere to be found. They had been and gone. Ganteaume, horrified at the prospect of Collingwood catching him in a *cul de sac*, had rapidly landed his cargoes at Corfu and sailed for France, even at the risk of incurring the Emperor's wrath. The two fleets must have passed within fifty or so miles; but neither was aware of the other. Collingwood admitted himself 'mortified'.[10] But he had achieved his objective, and with Sicily once again safe for the time being, the fleet sailed to the Balearics to find the Spanish fleet secure, but unready for sea, at Mahon. The French were nowhere to be seen – they had returned to Toulon. It was the last time they would come to sea in force. Even with luck against him Collingwood, by anticipating every possible eventuality, had again thwarted Napoleon's Mediterranean plans.

Once more off the west of Sicily, Collingwood wrote to Rear-Admiral Purvis of his frustrations. All his frigates bar one had been dispersed in pursuit of the French, and now he was, as it were, cut off from all knowledge of the outside world. Or almost all. Rumours had reached him of great events in Spain and once again, as so often before in the wars against France, as one fire was extinguished, another burst into flames.

The 'Spanish ulcer', as it became known, was entirely of Napoleon's own making. He had been pressurising Portugal to suspend her friendship with Britain since before Trafalgar. Relations had been tense, but British ships were still being allowed into the Tagus at Lisbon. However, in October 1807 Napoleon dispatched General Junot with thirty thousand men across the Pyrenees with orders to advance on Lisbon. Spain acquiesced in the passage of French troops: she (and specifically the so-called Prince of Peace, Manuel de Godoy – lover of the Queen, and reviled traitor) had agreed in secret to support the invasion, and to partition Portugal between herself and France. Napoleon had already been interfering with Spanish politics, and succeeded in destabilising the ruling Bourbon monarchy. Charles IV had been prevailed upon to abdicate in favour of his son Ferdinand. Now Napoleon invited them to Bayonne, forced them both to abdicate, and took them prisoner. He recalled his brother Joseph from Naples and placed him on the throne of Spain.

On 2 May 1808, the *Dos de Mayo* of Goya's famous painting, Madrid rose against the French. The first rising was put down with great savagery, but there was another, and soon many Spanish cities were in a state of insurrection. In Portugal the British ambassador had persuaded the royal family to embark themselves and their treasury and sail with their navy to Brazil under the protection of none other than Sir Sidney Smith. Having escorted his charges to safety, Smith returned to the Tagus to find a Russian squadron there, and blockaded them.

The British government first got wind of the *Dos de Mayo* uprising on 4 June.[11] A month later Lieutenant-General Sir Arthur Wellesley, fresh from the bombardment of Copenhagen in which he had shown something of his future promise, was sent from England to Portugal at the head of an expeditionary force comprising nine thousand men. The government realised that in the Iberian peninsula they might at last gain a foothold on the Continent, and they responded with speed. They were lucky. In Collingwood they had a Commander-in-Chief who could and did anticipate their moves; and long before Wellesley's arrival north of Lisbon in August, Collingwood had taken it upon himself to do whatever he could to support the uprising. His means were considerable. But even more valuable was his personal stature in a country which had not forgotten his behaviour after Trafalgar.

Collingwood was cruising off Toulon when, on 1 June, he heard of the *Dos de Mayo*. He left Admiral Thornbrough to watch the French fleet and headed directly for Cadiz, where he arrived eleven days later. The Spanish quickly accepted his squadron's entry to the harbour, and then summoned the six French ships which lay there to surrender. When they refused, the Spanish batteries opened up on them:

> After two days firing, in which they do not seem to have done much harm, the French made a truce and proposed that they should be allowed to leave the port, and the English to engage not to follow them for four days. The Spaniard sent me this proposal, to which I replied the French were amusing him to gain time ...[12]

The French fleet duly surrendered. Collingwood now offered the Spanish whatever assistance they required, though he soon found the organisation behind the uprising to be almost non-existent. Their ideas of armed resistance were laughable in his eyes, though he thoroughly admired the patriotic spirit and bravery of the populace. Led largely by the priesthood, and with hatred of the French and disgust at the ruling juntas fuelling them in almost equal measure, they were to evolve over the next five years the hit-and-run tactics which won them the name *Guerrilleros*.

One of the first practical measures Collingwood took was to offer the garrison at Cadiz all the gunpowder he could spare from his fleet:

> The gunpowder which was first furnished by the English fleet was immediately fired away by the Spaniards in honour of a local saint whose festival they were then celebrating; and when they requested a further supply, Lord Collingwood informed them that he could spare no more, unless they would promise to reserve it for sinners, and not saints.[13]

Collingwood's view of the ultimate prospects for the uprising was pessimistic – he saw nothing in the country to remind him of the determined and efficient rebels at Bunker's Hill. Spain, though, was in a state of exuberance:

> They say that Buonaparte has hitherto had only armies to contend with, but that now he has a nation where every man is a soldier. I sincerely hope it may give a turn to our affairs, and an example to other nations which have been oppressed, how, by a vigorous effort, they may recover their independence.[14]

Collingwood did not have time to set foot in Cadiz until August, at the height of Spanish successes against the French. The result was that forty thousand Spaniards turned out to cheer him through the streets, as he told little Sal (now not so little: she was sixteen).[15] There were everywhere cries of 'Viva Collingwood', and when he attended the opera, he received a fifteen-minute standing ovation.[16] Typically, he played down this Nelsonian reception – public praise always embarrassed him. In his letter to Sal he also had news of Bounce, who he admitted was growing very old. He regretted he had never had his dog's 'picture taken': 'he had the good fortune to escape that', declining to go ashore with his master. Collingwood himself was now weak and nearly blind. His daughters, he said, would have to look after him when he came home.

By now General Wellesley was advancing towards Junot's army as it marched on Lisbon. The British were outnumbered, but Wellesley had already honed his legendary positional sense during his Indian campaigns and his troops were well-drilled, like their naval counterparts. The two armies met at the village of Vimeiro, thirty miles north of Lisbon, and Junot was decisively defeated. Absurdly, Wellesley's superiors agreed to a truce at Cintra which allowed the French army to embark and sail for France so they could fight another day. It caused a huge scandal in England. Collingwood was appalled: what was the point in beating an enemy merely to allow him to go home and regroup?

Wellesley returned to England in disgust. He was replaced by another talented young general, Sir John Moore, who had as many as thirty thousand men at his disposal. After a successful cavalry action at Sahagun he was confronted by Marshal Soult at the head of a large army of French reinforcements which Napoleon was pouring into the country, and cornered. The resultant disastrous retreat to Corunna was followed by the forerunner of the Dunkirk evacuation of 130 years later – again with the navy as the army's saviour. Moore was fatally injured there in January 1809. It looked as if this might be the end of the British Army's expedition to the Peninsula, but Wellesley, pulling all the political strings he could lay his hands on, persuaded the government to allow him to return to Portugal in the spring with a new army. This time he would stay.

Collingwood spent the summer dealing with the junta of Cadiz, and with the political and military repercussions of the uprising.

He tried to arrange a supply of horses for the Cadiz militia with the Emperor of Morocco. He dispatched cruisers to harry French privateers along the Spanish coast (one of these, *Impérieuse*, was commanded by Lord Cochrane, whom Collingwood warmly commended for his initiative) and support rebels where they could. In particular he sought supplies of guns and ammunition, begging two thousand muskets from his friend Ball at Malta. He also ensured the protection and resupply of the army in Portugal; and, as ever, he saw that the French fleet at Toulon were watched day and night.

All these operations had to be carried out with great delicacy. On the matter of the horses, his initial approach was turned down by the Emperor on religious grounds. But Collingwood was far too well informed to be intimidated by such a response. He wrote, with a tremendous moral force only too well-known to those who served with him:

> I regret that granting to your neighbour this great good should be considered as in any degree militating against the tenets of your holy religion. I respect all those who are true to their faith. Mahomet was a wise and great law-giver; – he knew how fallible and weak mankind were; – he knew how much they required the assistance of each other: and one of his commands to his people was, (and it is a sacred tenet in all religions,) 'To do good to all'. What greater good can His Imperial Majesty do, than assist a loyal people in repelling an enemy, who regards not the laws of God, and maintaining their existence as a nation.[17]

Understandably, the Spanish on their part wanted to feel it was their armies and their sense of independence which were so disrupting the French occupation of their country – as indeed it largely was. It was crucial to tread carefully, and proposals to land a British force at Cadiz to garrison the forts in the port, which had been handled poorly by diplomats, required Collingwood's light touch, and his reputation with the Spanish, to carry them through. The trust in which Collingwood was held by the Spanish was of additional benefit to the British government. It meant that he became the most useful source of political intelligence on the Peninsula. His performance met with the approval of the First Lord, Lord Mulgrave, who wrote admiringly to him in July, albeit with a prolixity and awkwardness which contrast with the economy and elegance of Collingwood's own phrases:

> No object can be of equal importance to this Country with the vigorous and preserving exertions of Spain, and that entire confidence in the zealous and disinterested aid of Great Britain, without which it is hardly to be hoped that the Spaniards will make such efforts as will be indispensably necessary to the successful conclusion of the great and interesting struggle in which that nation is engaged. I feel most highly gratified in considering that the establishment of that confidence, and the encouragement in their efforts, will depend so much upon the exertion of your Lordship's talents and zeal, and shall be happy to hear that your health has not suffered from the anxious vigilance which you have had to exercise for so many months.[18]

For elegance and warmth the First Lord of the Admiralty was effortlessly out-done by the Supreme Council of Seville, who sensibly admired:

> the talents and penetration of the English Admiral, which they have seen displayed in the capacity with which he comprehends all our interests, and the foresight by which he would avert every danger. No Spaniard could have pleaded the interests of Spain with a warmer zeal than Lord Collingwood has done. Our gratitude to him will be eternal.[19]

There was a much less approving letter from Sarah, to whom Cuthbert had sent a portrait of himself, painted at Syracuse by

Giuseppe Sorcevani. Collingwood reckoned it a good likeness; but then, he had not seen his wife for more than five years, and he had aged at least ten in that time. It is, to be sure, an unprepossessing likeness, and she was shocked. He replied, with more than a hint of pique:

> I am sorry to find my picture was not an agreeable surprise ... you expected to find me a smooth-skinned, clear-complexioned gentleman, such as I was when I left home, dressed in the newest taste, and like the fine people who live gay lives ashore. Alas! it is far otherwise with me ... The painter represented me as I am, not as I once was. It is time and toil that have worked the change, and not his want of skill.[20]

Collingwood tried to raise Sarah's and his own spirits by changing the subject to his musings on Mrs Currell's son Tom.[21] This was the young man, a midshipman, who was so hopeless and lethargic that Collingwood thought he ought to be apprenticed to an apothecary, where his grave manner might suit. Now he wrote of the boy that 'he is of no more use here as an officer than Bounce, and not near so entertaining.'[22] Lady Collingwood's acquaintance with the Currells brought her into contact with the unfortunate son some years later, and it seems the whole family came to share Collingwood's opinion of him. Sal wrote to a friend:

> Mrs Currell dined with us on Tuesday; but not her son. She says he has got boils on his neck, which prevents his calling. My mother saw him when she called, and she thinks nothing can be worse than he is. We have not had the pleasure of seeing him yet.[23]

By the early autumn of 1808 Collingwood was back on the Toulon blockade. At Cadiz he was too readily available as a sort of universal saviour; attempts had been made to manipulate him politically, and although he saw through them all (he had, after all, been acquainted with midshipmen in the Royal Navy for forty years: he knew trickery when he saw it), he longed to escape the machinations of the juntas. Besides, both for the safety of Sicily and for the support of the Spanish insurrection in Catalonia, it was once again critical that the French fleet be bottled up. And as ever, Collingwood trusted no one more than himself. But despite his support, affairs in Spain continued to promise more than they delivered. At Rosas, just south of the French border, a garrison had held out for several months, supported by the indefatigable efforts of, among others, Lord Cochrane. But in December the town fell for want of good leadership, and soon Catalonia was overrun:

> In my prospect of Spanish affairs, from the beginning, I have not been mistaken. Their country is without Government, their armies without Generals; the only classes who are and have been true to the cause, which all talked of, were the priests and the people – they are brave, love their country, and detest the French.[24]

Once more the internal affairs of the Sicilian court had surfaced too. Queen Maria Carolina and King Ferdinand had sent Collingwood their son, Prince Leopold, with a view to planting him as a Bourbon regent on the Spanish throne – a plot so stupid that Collingwood dismissed it out of hand. Collingwood's sister wrote to him asking if he had not been a little high-handed with the King of Sicily:

> There is no fear of the King of Sicily being offended with me – nothing can be greater friends than we are. I had one of the kindest letters possible from him a week since, but very desirous that I come to Palermo, and I will go there whenever I can. All the people of Palermo are impatient to see me.[25]

No doubt they were: Collingwood had managed to avoid attending the court at Palermo for two years. He had no intention of going there now, for he had written to the Admiralty saying that he was too ill to continue as Commander-in-Chief, and must come home. Mulgrave, the First Lord, deployed a mixture of flattery and blackmail in response:

> I lament to learn that your health and strength have [been] impaired from the long and interrupted exertions by which you have so ably conducted the delicate, difficult, and important duties of your command; upon a former intimation of the injury which your health had received I took the liberty to press strongly upon your Lordship's consideration the importance which I attach to your continuance in a situation in which through a variety of great and complicated objects, of difficult and delicate arrangements of political as well as professional considerations, your Lordship had in no instance failed to adopt the most judicious and the best concerted measures. Impressed as I was and am, with the difficulty of supplying your place, I cannot forbear (which I hope you will excuse) suspending the recall which you have required, till I hear again from you.[26]

Collingwood cannot have been much surprised by this response; he may even have been relieved, because at least part of him wanted to stay until he had had one last go at the French. Even so, he must have bitterly regretted that after his extraordinary record of service, it had not so far proved possible to change the terms of his peerage to ensure the girls their inheritance, and the continuity of his title. And to Sarah he wrote of the dilemmas faced by a man of his complex emotions, when charged with great responsibility:

> Perhaps you may think I am grown very conceited in my old age, and fancy myself a mighty politician; but indeed it is not so. However lofty a tone the subject may require and my language assume, I assure you it is in great humility of heart that I utter it, and often in fear and trembling, lest I should exceed my bounds … I do everything for myself, and never distract my mind with other

people's opinions. To the credit of any good which happens I may lay claim, and I will never shift upon another the discredit, when the result is bad ... that the public service might not suffer from my holding a station, and performing its duties feebly, I applied for leave to return to you, to be cherished and restored ...[27]

With so many worries both at home and at sea, it is unsurprising that he now opened his heart to his oldest friend, Mary Moutray, in the most intimate terms:

MY DEAR FRIEND, – I wish you had one of those fairy telescopes that can look into the hearts and souls of people a thousand leagues off, then you might see how much you possess my mind and how sincere an interest I take in whatever relates to your happiness and that of your dear Kate ... it is evident that I shall not get home very soon and my heart was bent on it. My girls are young women; my wife an old one, and I have hardly seen them I may say for sixteen years. If this is not giving up comforts for my duty tell me what is.[28]

If Collingwood was wearing out fast, he had at least lasted longer than his flag ship. *Ocean* was only three years old but already falling apart at the seams, unable to cope with an unusually stormy autumn off Toulon. Collingwood put this down to 'the new whimsies and absurd inventions of those who, having little science, would be thought to have it because they have an office from which science should proceed.'[29] In particular he disdained the new fashion for 'wall-sided' ships, preferring the old-fashioned tumblehome where the ships' sides curved inwards. It was a design developed over centuries which had arrived at a state of near perfection, and that body of knowledge was being tampered with in favour of 'philosophic plans'. *Ocean* would not survive the winter on blockade duty, so Collingwood sailed to Malta, where the ship was 'new-bolted' with iron. This at least gave him the chance to meet his very old friend Alexander Ball, whose governorship of Malta had proved a political and economic revelation. In the few years since the island's recapture, it had become the hub of Mediterranean trade, thriving under a man whose honesty and decency won him wide regard.

While he was at Malta, in January 1809, Collingwood received news that he had been appointed Major-General of Marines. This was a sinecure, until recently held by the late Admiral Gardner. It involved no specific duties, and paid a reasonably handsome stipend of £1,200–1,400 a year – though as Collingwood pointed out to his sister, it would be offset against his half-pay if and when he retired. As usual, he was quick to recognise a bribe when he saw it, and to take it as an insult to his pride: 'I am jealous of their supposing such an excitement necessary to retain me.'[30] Nevertheless, the money would prove useful in defraying the increasing debt being generated at Chirton. It was around this time that Collingwood found out that Sarah's father, in attempting to pay off the debts of a collateral member of the family, had borrowed £2,200 off Collingwood, and repaid it with shares in a fire insurance company.[31] To be associated with such low commerce must have reminded him very painfully of his own upbringing, and he was furious. How could the King possibly respect a gentleman who dealt in insurance?

The high society life of Valetta was no more to Collingwood's taste than that of Gibraltar or Cadiz, so he was not unhappy to leave. But he could no longer put off a visit to Palermo and sailed there in February, ostensibly to confer with the commanding officer of British forces there, Sir John Stuart. Collingwood wanted to detach part of his force to Spain, where he thought an efficient, well-led British unit might shore up Spanish military morale. Once again showing acute foresight, Collingwood emphasised that in order to defend Sicily (and the same went for Corfu, Malta, Algiers, Morocco, Egypt and the Ottoman Empire) France had to be strangled, or at least tied up. He had been almost the first to realise that exploiting the *Dos de Mayo* was critical: 'The fate of Europe depends on Spain, and lesser interests should be subservient to our efforts there,' he had written.[32] But Stuart, probably influenced by the Queen's obsession with recovering her lost kingdom, would have none of it, insisting that the threat from Naples was too great. Sending British troops to Catalonia would be throwing bad money after good. In the meantime, Collingwood wrote to his sister:

> I took the opportunity to pay my respects to the King and Queen. I arrived on Tuesday before Ash Wednesday, when by closing the jollities of the carnival the Queen gave a ball to the nobility. I rec'd an invitation the moment we anchored. We went and were most graciously received. The King is a good humoured man, free and affable in his manners, and had he not unhappily been born to be a king would have been a respectable country gentleman. Matters of state weary him, and I understand he does not attend much to them. His country amusements of hunting and shooting occupy him. On the other hand, the Queen is the great politician and is continually engaged in intrigues for the recovery of their lost [kingdom] of Naples ...[33]

Abraham Crawford, visiting Palermo around the same time, called it 'gay, idle and rich ... having ... the air of a metropolis, but with that mixture of squalor and splendour, meanness and magnificence, which characterize all great towns – those of the south of Europe, perhaps, more than others.'[34] Crawford was a lieutenant under Admiral Duckworth in the *Royal George*. He met Collingwood several times, greatly admired him, and wrote the most penetrating existing portrait of the Admiral in his last years. The King of Sicily, meanwhile, recognising in Collingwood a keen fellow gardener, took him to dine at his country lodge just outside Palermo: *La Palazzina Cinese*. It was an extravagant caprice in the Chinese style, with beautiful formal gardens, and hunting grounds close by in the hills: 'the prettiest thing you can conceive' according to Collingwood.[35] He must have been delighted and appalled in equal measure by the dining arrangements. There was a round table with a central section, supported on some mechanical device which allowed it to be lowered to the kitchen, where it would be cleared and replenished and then raised up again.

Nevertheless, Collingwood was not fooled by the royal attention paid to him. The Queen was still seething over the snub Collingwood had delivered to Prince Leopold, and such was her pathological addiction to intrigue that she was sure he was plotting to rid the court of all her French advisors. Nothing could have been further from Collingwood's mind, and he was as glad to see the back of Palermo as the Queen was to see him go. As he wrote in semi-disbelief to Admiral Purvis:

> God protect them: I wish you had seen that court. I consider it as a sort of curiosity, and how such a one can exist in civilised Europe is a matter of great astonishment.[36]

In March, it became obvious that *Ocean* was simply not up to the rigours of Mediterranean service. She would have to return to England for a complete overhaul. A replacement was sent out to Collingwood, and she arrived when he was taking shelter in the lee of Menorca. So for the first time since 1799 Collingwood returned to Port Mahon, whose harbour he had surveyed as a midshipman in his late teens aboard *Liverpool*, and there he transferred to his last flag ship, *Ville de Paris*. She was a huge 110-gun three-decker, built in 1795 and named after the French flag ship captured by Rodney at the battle of the Saintes in 1782.

Access to Mahon's magnificent deep-water harbour was the navy's reward for its support of the Spanish uprising. Returned to

Spanish control under the terms of the Peace of Amiens, Menorca's governors and people found they enjoyed French influence even less than the previous century of British possession. It had taken a few months of delicate negotiation to ensure a welcome for British warships there, but for both parties it was a matter of necessity. The Spanish garrison had been reduced to less than a hundred men[37] and, as ever, the island was vulnerable to attack because of its rocky coastline and numerous coves and inlets. Not only did Mahon provide shelter for the storm-battered ships of the British fleet, but it was close enough to the coast of Catalonia, and to Toulon, to keep an eye on the French fleet without maintaining the constant rigours of a full blockade. Collingwood needed all the advantages he could get, as he wrote to Sarah:

> The Admiralty have been exceedingly kind and attentive to me; they have sent me the best ship in the navy, and have reinforced my squadron; but what I most want is a new pair of legs, and a new pair of eyes. My eyes are very feeble; my legs and feet swell so much every day, that it is pretty clear they will not last long.[38]

Collingwood might surely have stayed in Menorca now. It was a place he liked, he was welcome there, and it was a sound base from which to order operations. He chose, instead, to rejoin the Toulon blockade, where he stayed for the whole summer. Not that he was idle. His political and strategic brain was as active as ever, and there exist hundreds of letters and dispatches, mostly in his own hand still, which testify to the scope of his responsibilities and the attention he paid to every one of them.

One preoccupation was what he saw as ineffective leadership in the army. Of one general, a relative of his sister-in-law, he wrote:

> What do you think of your cousin Gen. Clavering? What a delightful head that man must have for the front rank of an army! It needs

no helmet, they might hack their swords to saws without harm to it. I always thought Sir Thomas had the most distinguished head in that family, but I have been mistaken.[39]

Collingwood was becoming increasingly frustrated with another army officer, Sir John Stuart, the general in charge of the British force in Sicily. Stuart, under the influence of the court at Palermo, undertook to capture the two little islands of Ischia and Procida that lay in the Bay of Naples. It made him popular with the court, but as Collingwood pointed out to him in a polite but brutally honest letter, their possession was of no use to anyone who did not possess Naples, and they required garrisons who would have been better employed in Sicily or elsewhere. Much more valuable was Collingwood's idea of using marines to make lightning amphibious assaults all along the Italian coast, to disrupt French forces and divert them from engaging the Austrian army. The Austrians, encouraged as all Europe was by events in Spain, were beginning once more to undertake offensive operations on the Italian peninsula, and Collingwood had been in communication with them to offer just such support. It was from this time that the Royal Marines began to establish their reputation for small, secretive and highly effective coastal operations. As it happened, Austria's campaign against Napoleon, which had started with promise in Bavaria in the spring, had gone disastrously wrong, ending with defeat at Wagram in July, one of the bloodiest encounters in the entire war.

As for General Stuart's land forces, Collingwood thought they would be far better deployed in an attack on the Ionian Islands, specifically Xante and Cephalonia, where intelligence suggested the people would happily combine with them to turn the French out. Possession of the islands, especially Corfu, by Britain, would be of inestimable benefit in supporting operations in the Adriatic, and in discouraging Napoleon from any ideas of invading the Greek mainland. More discreetly, Collingwood had prepared secret orders for the Pope to be evacuated from Rome, and Archduke John to be rescued from Trieste. Above all, he was exercising what he called 'the patient courage which waits for the opportunity which it cannot create', trying to maintain a presence in all places and at all times, ready to pounce when the time was right. It had served him well in his relations with Spain, and it would serve him well twice more – though it would never have done for Nelson.

However obsessed Collingwood was with the destruction of his arch-foe, he managed never to lose sight of the objects for which war was fought, namely to obtain an honourable peace for the benefit of all mankind. This was the diplomatic moral force which he applied in his dealings with all foreign powers, and the deys, beys, pashas and emperors with whom he dealt instinctively recognised the fundamental honesty of his position. But whether the objects in his view were large or small, simple or complex, he never forgot what war meant for ordinary people, as he confided to his sister-in-law in April 1809:

> When I look abroad, the prospect is bad: when I look to home, it is worse. And unless mankind can be made honest and to act from public spirit, uncontaminated by their individual interest, and reconcile themselves to justice though to their own disadvantage, the longer we live the worse we shall see it. I am thankful my head is grey. The people in England know nothing of war but the taxes, and what they read in a newspaper of the destruction of twenty-eight or thirty thousand men, the impression is slightly felt at Charing Cross. But were we to witness the inhabitants flying from their town in flames, and before they gain the next discover it in the same state, women and children running from death and when they come to the Po or the Pavia find the bridges broken down, it

was scenes like these, to which human creatures are now daily
exposed, that made me so desirous my girls should learn to swim,
then they might have set such chance and circumstance at defiance,
and a river or two would have been no bar to their safety.[40]

Collingwood amplified this theme in another letter to his sister-in-law
later that year. It not only shows that his sense of humour was intact,
and as dry as ever, but it encapsulates what, for an eighteenth-century
gentleman, was a surprisingly modern attitude towards women in
general, and daughters in particular. It makes the irony of their dis-
inheritance all the more poignant:

> The women [under siege at Gerona] are dressed in the habits of
> men, are armed with muskets and behave with the greatest
> gallantry. The soul of a woman is the excellence of creation, but
> how they would spoil it by foolish fashion, affecting a timidity which
> they do not feel. I wish my girls were taught their exercise and to
> be good shots. I think it will be useful to them before long. I am
> sure Sarah would be a sharp shooter, a credit to any Light Corps.[41]

While Stuart invented more excuses for deferring an expedition to
the Ionian Islands, Collingwood sensed another opportunity for disrupting French schemes. This time it was in his own hands, and
although he wrote to the Admiralty informing them of his plans,
he did not wait for approval when the time came to strike. It was a
masterly *coup de main* in which Collingwood used his knowledge of
the French intelligence network to his own advantage. He had
known for some time that the French were to attempt to resupply
their garrison at Barcelona with a convoy from Toulon. It was
perfectly clear this convoy would not sail with the blockading
squadron stationed off Toulon. If the British were driven off the
station by autumn gales, the convoy would very likely get through.
So it was of the first importance that Collingwood determined the

timing of the convoy's departure: it must sail when he wanted it to.

In October he sailed from Toulon for Menorca to water and provision his ships. It was an obvious ruse to tempt the French out, and on its own would not have worked. But Collingwood anticipated French reaction. At Mahon, a few days after the fleet's arrival, he received a French spy who had fed him reliable information on a number of occasions in the past. The spy told him that a convoy would sail from Toulon to relieve Barcelona in two or three weeks. Collingwood perfectly distrusted this man who, he was sure, had come to Mahon to determine the state of the British fleet. Now Collingwood executed the first part of his 'sting', as Abraham Crawford recalled:

> [The fleet's] condition, however, when he arrived at Mahon, was well calculated to deceive a better judge than the Frenchman as to the probable time of its being ready for sea. Some of the ships, with sails unbent, were blacking yards and rigging; some with scaffolding over the sides, were caulking; some painting; while a few, with yards and topmasts struck, seemed almost dismantled. In fact, it looked as if the fleet had gone into harbour for the purpose of re-fitting, and that the time of its again sailing was quite indefinite.
>
> In an hour or so after his arrival, the Frenchman was dismissed, and the frigate which brought him again made sail for Toulon. Scarcely, however, had she left Cape Mola a league astern, when the signal was flying on board *Ville de Paris* for all Captains, and immediately after for the fleet to prepare for sea.[42]

The result of Collingwood's rather brilliant deception was that the British fleet came up with the convoy, escorted by three sail of the line and two frigates, on 23 October 1809, two days after the anniversary of Trafalgar. The convoy made off, and during an unpleasantly long night Collingwood thought he had lost them. But Admiral Martin's detachment found them the following day, and gave chase.

A French 80-gun ship and a 74 ran ashore and were destroyed by the French admiral. Another 74 ran ashore at Cette and five of the convoy ships were burnt. In the event the second 74 got away, but the final tally of the action was the destruction of two line ships and thirteen of the convoy (including a powder ship that blew up), while four other convoy ships were captured.[43]

Collingwood may have hoped for something a little more spectacular, and it is true that this episode has never excited historians to hyperbole. Nevertheless, it was a highly effective action, and showed once again that Collingwood at sea was a match for any French plans in the Mediterranean. The Duke of Northumberland, on hearing of this success, wrote to him to say:

> I never can forget the accuracy with which you viewed the whole of this Spanish Business from the very first, and I only lament the Ministers shou'd give their confidence to those who, from their former situations, are not able to give them such good Information, as others, on whose Judgement they might more safely depend.[44]

That was not all. Finally, Collingwood had prevailed on the reluctant Stuart to embark on offensive operations in the Ionian Islands, with the result that four of them had been wrested from the French. It was another triumph for a naval commander who had truly become, as the political diarist Thomas Creevey said ...

> the prime and sole minister of England, acting upon the seas, corresponding himself with all surrounding States, and ordering and executing everything upon his own responsibility.[45]

The cost to his own health and happiness had been terrible, but Collingwood accepted that as part of the duty of service he owed his country. But as if to twist the knife, the fates now contrived to deprive him of his most cherished companion, as he told his sister:

> You will be sorry to hear my poor dog Bounce is dead. I am afraid he

fell overboard in the night. He is a great loss to me. I have few comforts, but he was one, for he loved me. Everybody sorrows for him. He was wiser than [many] who hold their heads higher and was grateful [to those] who were kind to him.[46]

Bounce was, of course, irreplaceable. After an animal of such shining parts, Collingwood 'could not bear a common creature'.[47] He was to lose other friends as well. Alexander Ball had died at Malta, much lamented not just by Collingwood, but by the Maltese themselves. And he had finally determined to sell his beloved house on Oldgate, in Morpeth – partly because Sarah, now installed at Chirton, was spending so much money. And if she was not, then her father had become very free with it. But Collingwood assured his sister (evidently concerned at the apparent dissoluteness prevailing at Chirton) in a long and very detailed letter, that his daughters' futures were secure, the title apart, and that he had taken steps to regain control over his finances from his wife's family. He found the whole domestic situation depressing; it made him feel impotent and even more dislocated from the world than he was already. He had been at sea, almost unbroken, for nearly seven years, without having seen England or his family once. He had survived the battle of Trafalgar and two smaller fleet actions. He had kept the French fleet bottled up in Toulon, apart from two failed excursions, for four years. He had conducted a diplomatic and political plate-spinning exercise that is breathtaking in its scope and achievement. As the most eminent historian of the Mediterranean theatre, Piers Mackesy, wrote: 'The scale was heroic; and over the vast canvas towers the figure of Collingwood.'[48]

By the middle of November Collingwood had returned to Port Mahon. He was now very ill, weak and unsteady in his limbs, and suffering almost continually from his painful bowels. It was probably now that he rented the house at El Fonduco, though how much time he spent ashore is impossible to know. His doctors recommended that he try riding a horse, but it was too painful for him. He could barely eat, as the tumour in his stomach took hold and strangled his digestive system. At least from the house he could see *Ville de Paris*, moored in the deep clear waters of the harbour.

Menorca can be a surprisingly grim place in winter. At this time Mahon was 'a respectable little city, clean with no appearance of poverty or meanness about it'[49] and a population of nearly sixteen thousand. But from October to April it is blasted by the tramontana and the mistral, and during the stormy season of 1809–10, with the Commander-in-Chief in failing health and with little sign of progress in the war (despite Wellesley's victory at Talavera in July; now he had fallen back on Torres Vedras), good cheer must have been in short supply. British officers, who in summer and at carnival time would congregate at the Posada Alexandra in Mahon, to be taught their first, faltering steps in the *contradansa Espanola*,[50] now kept to their ships and eked out their precious luxuries with little hope of being resupplied until spring.

At the end of February 1810, now almost unable to walk, and forced to dictate letters for the first time in his life, Collingwood wrote to Lord Mulgrave resigning his commission as Commander-in-Chief. The game was up. The British government and the Admiralty had squeezed all the blood that could be squeezed from that stone.

On 3 March Collingwood wrote a last letter to his brother:

MY DEAR BROTHER, – My health has become so bad, and I am so weak that application to business is impossible. I have therefore informed the Admiralty that I shall leave this port tomorrow for Spithead, as the medical gentlemen here inform me my return home is the only means I have for a prospect of recovery.

I should be glad to have Lady Collingwood and my daughters, or some of my family, in London, ready to join me at the port I arrive at, from whence I shall write to them (addressed at Ommaney's) to tell them whither I intend to go for advice, and as soon as they arrive in London, I beg them to write a letter addressed to me at the Port Admiral's at Portsmouth and one for Plymouth, so that I may know when I arrive whether they are in Town or not. Ever, my dear brother, Your affectionate, COLLINGWOOD.[51]

Enclosed with this letter was one from Collingwood's secretary, William Cosway, which needs no comment:

SIR, – Your brother, Lord Collingwood, is extremely ill, and very much reduced. I believe it is supposed that Bath would be the best place for him to go, and if that should be decided on, we shall put into Plymouth. I shall in such case go with him to Bath and write to Ommaney the moment we get to port, or before if we meet any thing going home to inform you how it is.

I think, Sir, you will judge it right to prepare Lady Collingwood and the Admiral's daughters and family, for any event. His complaint is of that nature that it is impossible to foresee the result, and the Admiral aware of it, has arranged his affairs, which I am in possession of. His mind is as calm and serene as possible ...[52]

On the same day, 3 March 1810, Collingwood surrendered his command of the Mediterranean to Rear-Admiral Martin:

The two following days were spent in unsuccessful attempts to warp the Ville de Paris out of Port Mahon; but on the 6th the wind came round to the westward, and at sunset the ship succeeded in clearing the harbour, and made sail for England. When Lord Collingwood was informed that he was again at sea, he rallied for a time his exhausted strength, and said to those around him, 'Then I may yet live to meet the French once more.' On the morning of the 7th there was a considerable swell, and his friend Captain Thomas, on entering his cabin, observed that he feared the motion of the vessel disturbed him. 'No, Thomas,' he replied, 'I am now in a state in which nothing in this world can disturb me more. I am dying; and I am sure it must be consolatory to you, and all who love me, to see how comfortably I am coming to my end.'[53]

Collingwood died at eight in the evening, on 7 March. On 21 April the *Newcastle Courant* reported:

A mail from Malta and Gibraltar arrived on Tuesday; it has brought intelligence which will be received with the deepest concern, viz. the death of our highly distinguished and gallant townsman, Admiral Lord Collingwood. His health had long been in a declining state, but he persisted in keeping the sea, being anxious to bring the Toulon fleet to action, and by the defeat of the last naval force of the enemy, to complete the destruction of the French navy. He had not above once set his foot on shore since the great battle of Trafalgar. At length his health declined so much that he was under the necessity of determining to return to England. It pleased Heaven, however, that he should see his native land no more. On the 6th ult. He left Menorca, on board the *Ville de Paris*, and on the 7th he breathed his last. The *Ville de Paris* brought his honoured remains to Gibraltar; and on Monday they arived at Portsmouth on board the *Nereus* frigate ... For some time before his death he was incapable of taking any sustenance whatever. Leaving only two daughters, the title dies with his Lordship; but his services will forever live in the memory of a grateful country.

From Portsmouth *Nereus* carried the Admiral's body to the Great Nore, where it was transferred into a barge and taken up the Thames to Greenwich. There it lay in state from 26 April to 11 May when the coffin was borne to St Paul's cathedral by carriage, and buried next to that of Nelson in a plain and simple tomb, the coffin itself bizarrely enclosed in Cardinal Wolsey's sarcophagus, donated by the

Duke of Clarence. Mourners at the funeral included Lord Eldon, on whose arm a common seaman wept through the entire ceremony; Lord Cochrane, and Earl St Vincent: Old Jarvie – still alive and tough as old boots. Thirty admirals and captains of the fleet were also in attendance, along with scores of seamen of all ranks. Many he had served with, and many more may simply have turned up to see 'Old Cuddy' off in style. Even if they had never served under him, his reputation for humanity and fairness, for severe discipline tempered by humour and kindness, honed in more than forty years at sea, must have been known to all of them. It was a grand state occasion, even if it did not quite have the pathos or bathos of Nelson's funeral. But by naval custom Collingwood's servant Smith, who had been so astonished by the Admiral's calmness before battle, was given the privilege of placing his baron's coronet on the coffin.

Sarah, Lady Collingwood, who on hearing of her husband's death was so distraught that she had to be put to bed immediately and 'given a great deal of laudanum',[54] survived her husband by nine years, surrounded by her family and bolstered by the nation's gratitude for her sacrifice. Her husband, whose admiral's pay had been £1,000 per annum, managed to leave her £163,743 in his will, with £40,000 to each of his daughters – almost all of it accumulated after Trafalgar.

CHAPTER ELEVEN

Fame's trumpet

'Fames' trumpet makes a great noise, but the notes do not dwell long on the ear.'[1] Collingwood was replying to Mary Moutray in a letter written in the spring of 1807. Mary had asked her old friend for a piece of wood from *Royal Sovereign*, as a souvenir of Trafalgar. Collingwood was surprised – he thought people had already forgotten the Action (as he called it), and wondered that Mary should want to be reminded of a battle whose memory, for both of them, was at least as painful as it was pleasurable. They had, after all, both lost a dear friend – 'a hero whose name will be immortal'.[2]

Two hundred years of hindsight confirms that Collingwood was wrong about Trafalgar, but right when he spoke of his friend Nelson's immortality. Nelson is *the* English secular hero, comparable to

George Washington, Jeanne d'Arc, Garibaldi – and perhaps all those figures rolled into one semi-mythical creation. The lasting notes of Nelson's fame would please Collingwood, if only on his friend's behalf; he himself played a part in the creation of that myth. But he could only be astonished at the thought that his own Trafalgar dispatch would be celebrated two hundred years on, in a reconstruction of Lieutenant Lapenotiere's journey in the schooner *Pickle* from Trafalgar to Falmouth, and then by coach from Falmouth to the Admiralty in London.

Collingwood is not a national hero. His memorials are a naval school of gunnery, one or two monuments, and twenty-seven streets, schools and public houses named after him in Newcastle. Even here, though, Nelson beats him with twenty-eight. Collingwood, like Nelson, died at sea. But he did not die gloriously in battle and his achievements as Commander-in-Chief of the Mediterranean fleet, though crucial to the progress of the war, did not set trumpets blaring on the Strand, nor yet at Charing Cross. If his life was heroic (and it is an over-used term) it was not popularly so.

A small group of people knew very well what Collingwood had achieved. The government may have taken his services for granted, denied his officers any number of promotions and disinherited his daughters, but they at least knew they could not have conducted the Mediterranean theatre without him. They were told so by men who knew what they were talking about: St Vincent for one; the Duke of Northumberland, the Spanish juntas, and successive First Lords of the Admiralty. Wellington, as Arthur Wellesley became shortly before Collingwood's death, appreciated his role in the first years of the Peninsular War, knowing only too well how important the navy's support was to land operations.

For a wider group of politically aware men and women the full breadth of Collingwood's astonishing record and abilities became much more apparent in 1827 with the publication of G. L. Newn-ham-Collingwood's memoir. Collingwood had been asked to provide information for a memoir after Trafalgar, but couldn't think of very much to say about himself, never having been in the public eye before. His son-in-law, who married Sal in 1816 and added her name to his, produced a 'life and letters' biography that ran to nearly six hundred pages and five editions – the last of these in 1837 including many additional letters.

The work was an instant success, for it opened the world's eyes to a man whose character was only thinly sketched in the nation's imagination. Of Trafalgar they knew much; of his other actions less than they thought. Of his humanity there were anecdotes, and some had heard of a grave humour. But the depth of his knowledge, of his skill in managing men, and his delightful wit, came as a surprise to many. One of these was Thomas Creevey, a Whig politician who had played a small part in the 'Ministry of all the Talents', was politically well-connected without ever himself wielding power, and who knew everyone. His diary entry for 11 August 1827 is worth quoting in full:

Dolphin Inn, Chichester: to Miss Ord[3]
You may judge of our weather at Stoke when I tell you that, with all their courage and contempt of rain, we were on horseback only once, and for less than one hour, and then were wet thro'. But if the body was not regaled, the mind was – at least by me – for I pitched my tent daily in the greenhouse, read Lord Collingwood and his life and letters right thro', and was delighted with him. You must excuse me if I am rather pompous and boring upon this subject. You see, my dear, that altho' the poor man was the bravest and best and most amiable of men, this personal character of his is nothing compared with the part he acts in history for the four or five years intervening between Nelson's death and his. At that time

the army was nothing compared with what it later became immediately after and Collingwood *alone* by his sagacity and decision –
his prudence and moderation – sustained the interests of England
and eternally defeated the projects of France. He was, in truth, the
prime and sole minister of England, acting upon the seas, corresponding himself with all surrounding States, and ordering and
executing everything on his own responsibility ...

One has scarcely patience to think that, whilst our Government
had the sense to see, and to tell him again and again, that his value
to them and the country was such as never could be replaced, and to
implore him actually to continue his services at the known and
certain sacrifice of his life, still the villains were base enough to
refuse every recommendation of his in favor [sic] of meritorious
officers, as he justly observes, when *parliamentary* pretensions were
to be put in competition.

The agreeableness of the work is greatly added to by the
constant proof it affords of the early, long and intimate union
between Nelson and Collingwood. Even in the novel line, I have
found nothing so calculated to *lumpify* one's throat as when one of
those great men of war, poor Nelson, in his dying moments desires
his captain to give his *love* to Collingwood.[4]

Newnham-Collingwood's memoir was compiled using more than
four hundred letters, both to and from the Admiral. These are interspersed with anecdotes, many of them from Sal herself, naturally.
Other stories came from correspondents who knew the Admiral:
from his secretary William Cosway, from Lieutenant Clavell and
from Smith, his servant. None of these can be taken entirely at face
value. For one thing, we know Newnham-Collingwood edited and
'improved' some of the letters. Where they are to be compared with
the later collection of letters edited by Edward Hughes in 1957, it is
obvious that the son-in-law thought their style needed lightening.
His selection of material is clearly intended to portray his father-in-

law as a very serious naval commander with a very human side to his nature. It is an indulgent portrait, heavily informed by family tales of kindness and moral rectitude. But it is not a hagiography, and the Collingwood it produces is three-dimensional, fallible, and human.

As Collingwood's junior officers matured and retired, a number of affectionate accounts of their days with him emerged in the middle of the nineteenth century. Jeffrey Raigersfeld, Hercules Robinson, Abraham Crawford and Robert Hay had all become as close to him as irreverent young men can, and all four paint a very similar picture of a man whose stern reserve strangled his relations with captains and most lieutenants, but whose indulgence to midshipmen, and to ordinary sailors, was undiminished until his death. They are immensely valuable accounts, to be set against the much less enthusiastic portrayals of some of his contemporaries. Men like Codrington, Elliot and Hoste, who thought him provincial and meddling and, evidently knowing something of his background, did not believe him to be a true gentleman, whatever his accomplishments. That these views are prejudicial is unsurprising. The navy was a competitive, gossiping, rank-driven and highly self-conscious profession. Not only did Collingwood attain huge, almost untouchable power at sea, he also possessed what thousands of men desired: the friendship of Nelson.

Men who had not suffered Collingwood's micro-management at sea could sit comfortably back in their armchairs and place him among other great figures on a mantelpiece of virtue. Thackeray, who celebrated British life of that period in history as well as fiction, gave him a very prominent place indeed:

> I think, since heaven made gentlemen, there is no record of a better one than that. Of brighter deeds, I grant you, we may read performed by others; but where of a nobler, kinder, more beautiful

life of duty, of a gentler, truer heart? Beyond dazzle of success and blaze of genius, I fancy shining a hundred and a hundred times higher, the sublime purity of Collingwood's gentle glory.[5]

Thackeray, writing at a time when the sort of selfless duty that Collingwood displayed was more valued than in his own lifetime, may be forgiven for such misty hyperbole. So can William Clark Russell, who wrote the first pure biography of Collingwood in 1891. It draws very heavily on Newnham-Collingwood, quite naturally, and it is firmly within the Victorian tradition of solemnity and imperial dignity.

Collingwood remains his own most credible witness. We have six hundred or so of his letters, along with his journals, official dispatches and logs from many of the ships in which he served.[6] As a record of his life these sources are rich beyond the dreams of many biographers. Their contents are frequently corroborated by the vast quantity of official papers which exist for the period, the more so because of the navy's obsession with recording the business of its ships in what, to their commanders, was excruciating detail. Collingwood was himself a pioneer in this respect: one of the very first commanders to keep a record of the punishments which he ordered.

The spread of this material is uneven in the extreme. Famous people are rarely born to that station. Collingwood's family was one of thousands whose sons went to sea at an early age and whose correspondence, if it was at all regular, did not immediately demand to be saved for posterity. The first of Collingwood's letters that survives dates from 1776 when he was already twenty-eight years old, and that is no coincidence. It was the year after his involvement in the American War of Independence which led to his promotion on the day the battle was fought at Bunker's Hill. No letters written to either his mother or father survive. It seems likely that such an assiduous letter-writer did write to his parents; it is equally easy to imagine that on their deaths (his father in 1775; his mother by 1790) boxes full of old correspondence were discarded – their son was not yet famous. A number of his letters to Sarah survive, but none of hers to him. Surely he must have kept them. But did he destroy them when he knew he was dying, or were they destroyed by Sarah herself after his death? Or by his daughters much later? We do not know.

From 1776 until 1785, when Collingwood was stationed in the West Indies, we have just seven letters, and these are addressed either to his brother John or his sister Betsy. 1785 is the year of the first letter between Nelson and Collingwood, when the latter was in his late thirties. Such is the concentration of surviving correspondence from his later years, that half of all the letters edited and printed by Newnham-Collingwood date from the period between January 1807 and the Admiral's death in March 1810.

Collingwood's private letters to his closest confidants appear on the surface to be randomly chatty, containing all sorts of items of news, personal and professional, together with reactions to letters which he had received and his desires for his daughters' upbringing. There is a wealth of family gossip, and whichever correspondent the letter was addressed to, it was assumed by both the sender and the recipient that it would be circulated to Cuthbert's brother, his sisters, his wife and sister-in-law; and probably his uncles and father-in-law too. Closer analysis reveals not only that Collingwood wrote in subtly different ways to each of them, but also that his letters were structured in a consciously rhetorical way. These traits are evidence of complex undercurrents in his emotional and intellectual life.

One of the most pronounced features of the letters is that Collingwood's most intimate confidants were women: his wife, his sisters and his sister-in-law Mrs Stead. He by no means restricted himself to domestic and personal matters with them. A letter written to one of his sisters (either Bess or Mary) from *Excellent*, off Toulon, in 1796, has a typical structure.[7] It begins with an apology: he has not written to her for a while, but assumes she has kept up with his news by reading his letters to Sarah. Then comes a statement of his health which also summarises his views of the station:

> I have good health, indeed a sort of constitution that all countries agree with. For the rest, it is but a languid sort of life, always at sea and little to do, but as this will only be while the French are not in condition to come out with their fleet, the state of affairs may soon take a change as they are daily getting forward in their preparation ...

Collingwood goes on to describe how the ships lay at the entrance to Toulon harbour, and how one of the French frigates has been taken in a cutting-out expedition. Then a line or two on Nelson (not yet, at this time, England's Saviour), who has been harrying French trade along the coast with a small squadron. This is the sort of news which will have found its way into the coffee houses of Newcastle: one imagines ... 'Miss Collingwood tells me her brother and Nelson are harrying the French off Toulon ...', and so on.

Next comes family gossip. Edward Collingwood (the cousin who left the Admiral the house and coal mine) has been building a house at Dissington, but Cuthbert thinks he will always keep Chirton for his main residence. He hears that Admiral Roddam is not in good health, but hopes that his new wife will make his last days comfortable, and 'spare him many a long journey in pursuit of pleasures'. It is one of Collingwood's gentler barbs.

Then there is news of an old acquaintance, Signor Spannochi, who was a midshipman with Collingwood in *Liverpool*, many years before. They have met for the first time in years. Spannochi has news of the progress of the war at the court of Naples (with which both Collingwood and Nelson will become only too familiar in later years), and this leads Collingwood on to a consideration of the general state of political affairs in Europe. Here he employs a rhetorical technique very familiar from other letters. In a recent letter Spannochi was:

> lamenting the probable fate of Italy, to be ransack'd by a set of plunderers who carry desolation and misery wherever they come. Nothing can save those states but a great turn of fortune ...

Having relieved himself of his opinions on the war, Collingwood passed on to rumours of a general promotion in the navy, and brought the subject back to himself:

> I cannot say I feel much interested about [it], for though I should be very glad to be an Adml, I shou'd leave this service we are engaged in with regret and the more from the difficulty I shall have in getting employment amongst so many flag officers.

The tone has turned from rhetoric to lugubriousness; it descends to self-pity:

> I shou'd return with more pleasure was the war quite at an end and peace established for the rest of our days: but we must take events as they come and make the best of them.

Aware of his own negativity, Collingwood ends the letter with an upbeat list of family and friends to whom he begs his sister will remember him, and a joke about his rather too choosy unmarried cousins. While the weight of his letters was adapted to each reader, and the content changed according to the state of the war, and how busy he was, the structures are remarkably consistent. They expose a man conscious of the weight of the world's problems on his shoulders, deeply concerned with the fate of the world, and able to switch attention instantly from global events to the most trivial matters of family gossip. He was perfectly aware of the irony, and relished it. It appealed to his sense of the ridiculous, his playful and sometimes bitter humour, and his belief that a life of war was ultimately a ludicrous but essential search for peace and the happiness of mankind. He portrayed himself variously as stoical, inadequate, self-pitying, obsessive, but caring and determined, and possessing huge relish for a fair fight.

Such traits might perhaps explain why he and Nelson, ostensibly such different characters, were so close. Nelson too possessed many of these traits. Was it that Collingwood shared many of Nelson's passions, but that he had trained himself to control them, so much so that to all external appearance he had no passion at all? Certainly, when he was an admiral several of his captains found him humourless, dull and unforgiving, while his moral lectures were quite awful. But the evidence of his junior officers shows quite another side of him, as of course his letters do. Perhaps fundamentally what separated Collingwood and Nelson was their self-control – which Nelson longed for, and which Collingwood resented in himself for the shackles it bound him with. Nelson, of course, was fragile in the extreme, both physically (he was known to start at the fall of a rope's end; his illnesses and depressions were frequent) and emotionally. He veered from crippling self-doubt to an unshakeable belief in his abilities and his destiny. Collingwood intellectualised, recognising these extremes in himself and, to a large extent, smoothing them out – at least as far as his external world was concerned. His letters allowed him to play out these contradictions so that, in his public persona as a naval officer, he might appear to be always one and the same.

Given his devotion to active service, and his reluctance to give it up even in the most extreme circumstances, it is tempting to speculate on what Collingwood's future might have held had he survived and kept his health. He had been offered a shore post at Plymouth, but it would scarcely have interested a man who had discovered a taste for high diplomacy. Surely, after a spell of recuperation at Chirton, he would have taken his seat in the House of Lords. It was a turbulent time for British politics. The Peninsular War had not, by a long shot, reached the heroic momentum of 1812. From 1811 the King's illness and increasing senility meant that the entirely unsuitable 'Prinny' became Regent. A year later the prime minister, Spencer Perceval, was assassinated by a bankrupt Liverpool broker. Confusion reigned. Collingwood, whose party was avowedly neither Whig nor Tory but 'Old England', would have made an obvious choice as a non-partisan First Lord. He would have instituted reforms in ship construction and in seamen's conditions; above all he would have made an astute naval strategist, with a breadth of experience that only St Vincent, if anyone, could have matched. One can only speculate what influence he might have had on the outbreak – and outcome – of the disastrous war of 1812–14 with the United States of America; it was a war he had himself predicted[8] and which, having been so intimately involved with the American struggle for independence, he deplored.

The family, surely, would have moved from Chirton down to London (after Collingwood's death the estate reverted to John, and Sarah and the girls moved to Tynemouth): both Sarah and her girls loved the social round that Collingwood's fame and relative wealth had introduced them to. As it was, they became acquainted with many influential and socially active people. Among them were the Nelsons:

> Portman Square, London: Letter to Miss Mary Woodman
> 10th May 1812
> Yesterday we dined at Crespigny's and met Lord and Lady Nelson …
> Lord Nelson is a most vulgar disagreeable man. The widow Viscountess Nelson has been in town, and we saw a great deal of her.
> She is a most agreeable woman.[9]

Had Collingwood lived, like 'Old Jarvie' (Sir John Jervis, Earl St Vincent), into his eighties, he would have found himself a favourite at court. William, Duke of Clarence, had served with Nelson in the West Indies, and at one time hoped (to the ministry's horror) to succeed Collingwood as Commander-in-Chief of the Mediterranean. He had written many admiring letters to him over the years. After the death of his brother George IV he became King William IV, the Sailor King, in 1830. Nelson's closest friend, and the 'other' hero of Trafalgar, would have been displayed at Windsor to great advantage. Two years after William's accession, it was Collingwood's fellow Northumbrian, Earl Grey (First Lord of the Admiralty in 1806), who forced through the Reform Bill of which Collingwood, despite his traditional Tory values, might well have approved, even if his old friend Eldon opposed it.

Collingwood's death at sea, after an absence of seven years from England, may have played a part in his subsequent treatment by historians. In James' *Naval History* he was censured for not anchoring the prizes after Trafalgar, though there is the ample testimony of his own account to show why that was not possible or desirable. No doubt the loss of prize money had some effect on the accounts of those captains, some of them already prejudiced against Collingwood, whom James consulted. James' history was published a year before Newnham-Collingwood's memoir, in which those arguments were vehemently countered.[10]

Considerably more damage was done to Collingwood's reputation by an entry in the *Dictionary of National Biography*, in which he was described as:

> an admirable second in command, but without the fuller genius fitting him to rise to the first rank as commander-in-chief.[11]

Such an opinion might be dismissed if it had not proved so

influential in the creation of the Holmes-Watson myth of the relationship between Nelson and Collingwood, which is unsustainable. Just as Watson is a convenient sidekick, providing an absorbent narrative foil for the genius of his master, so Collingwood fits rather well as Nelson's dependable but essentially dull second. In taking over command of the fleet just before Trafalgar, Nelson held centre stage in a gesture (wholly self-conscious) designed to admit of no doubt who the main character was. Collingwood, if he resented such treatment, as he might have done before, at the battle of Cape St Vincent, and in the West Indies, gave no hint of it to Nelson, or to his family intimates.

Nelsonian narratives have two features in common. Firstly, they tend (with notable exceptions) to exclude events in which Nelson himself did not play a part. Collingwood's brilliant though defensive action in August 1805 is rarely aired, even though at the time the Naval Chronicle regarded it as 'an instance of genius and address that is scarcely to be paralleled in the pages of our naval history'.[12] In itself it makes a very good story, but it is easy to see how it confuses the Nelson story, a story which relies heavily on there being only one hero. A second, inevitable feature of Nelsonian history is that it tends to end with his glorious death at Trafalgar and his subsequent state funeral at St Paul's cathedral. Thus, one of Nelson's biographers, in following some of the main characters in his story, described Collingwood as having, after Trafalgar, spent 'four uneventful years in the Mediterranean'.[13] This view of the naval war as effectively ending with Trafalgar is as common and facile as it is mistaken. The naval war continued after Collingwood's death, even though there were no great fleet actions, and public minds were focused squarely on the land war in the Iberian peninsula. It continued too outside the Mediterranean, especially in the Baltic where Sir James Saumarez played every bit as crucial a role as Collingwood, if on a smaller scale.

It is true that the Mediterranean theatre of those last four years was an exceedingly complicated one. Great credit for unravelling its knots must go the historian Piers Mackesy, who not only understood its multiplicities, but as a result became something of a champion of Collingwood's role there. It was, oddly, in the same year as the publication of his *War in the Mediterranean* that Edward Hughes published a collection of Collingwood's correspondence, which both complemented and enhanced the original memoir of 1828, and with much less interference.

Just two biographies of Collingwood were written in the twentieth century. Geoffrey Murray's 1936 *Life* was a popular account of a man whose story by then had largely been swallowed by the Nelson myth. In 1968 Oliver Warner, the distinguished naval historian, published a biography which allowed the work of both Hughes and Mackesy to be integrated into the most authoritative account of the admiral's life that has so far been written. Given its scope, it is unimprovable. And yet, as the two-hundredth anniversary of the Action approaches, it is still seen as legitimate to portray that battle, and indeed almost the whole of the naval wars against France, as the personal Triumph of Nelson.

That Collingwood played an important role in the events that led to Trafalgar, in the battle itself, its aftermath and the consolidation of British naval supremacy in the years afterwards, cannot seriously be in doubt. But it is still routinely asserted that Nelson 'won' the battle of Trafalgar. There were something in the region of twenty thousand men fighting on the British side, of course. Nelson, as commander, devised the strategy with which the British fleet went into battle. It has been shown that this tactic, cutting the line with two perpendicular columns, was an evolution of much that had gone before, particularly Duncan's brilliant defeat of the Dutch at Camperdown.

It was pointed out at the time that once that strategy had been determined, no act or signal on the part of the Commander-in-Chief would make much difference to the progress of the battle. Few signals were made; fewer were seen. It is unnecessary to comment on the individual bravery and skill of the naval officers and men on both sides, except in one crucial respect. What actually determined the outcome of the battle, in truth a devastating and overwhelming victory regardless of its long-term effects, was gunnery. This may be demonstrated by the relative rates of gunfire on both sides, and the casualty figures. Rates of fire are less easy to establish; much of the evidence for them is anecdotal. But it can be said that a rate of three broadsides in five minutes was considered good practice, and it can also be said that some commanders, of whom Collingwood was the outstanding exponent, achieved higher rates than this: perhaps as many as three in three and a half minutes. With their lack of battle experience and live-firing exercises, the Combined Fleet could not manage anything like these rates. One broadside in five minutes might be nearer the mark. Gunnery tactics were also different. English guns aimed at the ships' sides, a direct attempt to destroy the enemy's ships, disable their guns, and kill their gunners. French tactics, in particular, were designed to damage masts, spars and rigging by aiming high, particularly using grape and canister shot. After disabling a ship, they expected to board and carry her without having destroyed her in the process.

At Trafalgar these tactics were successful to the extent that many of the British fleet were dismasted and lost all steerage way. But not a single British ship struck her colours. That had more to do with skill and seamanship in the face of the terrible gale that followed, than it did to luck. Nevertheless, the relative casualty figures shown below paint a much truer picture of the battle's outcome.[14] The British fleet's order is that of attack, following Collingwood's own list (Appendix 1).

British fleet

VAN

Victory (100)	Nelson; Hardy	57 killed	102 wounded
Téméraire (98)	Harvey	47	76
Neptune (98)	Fremantle	10	34
Conqueror (74)	Pellew	3	9
Leviathan (74)	Bayntun	4	22
Ajax (74)	Pilfold	2	2
Orion (74)	Codrington	1	21
Agamemnon (64)	Berry	2	7
Minotaur (74)	Mansfield	3	20
Spartiate (74)	Laforey	3	17
Britannia (100)	Northesk; Bullen	10	40
Africa (64)	Digby	18	37
Division totals		**160**	**387**

REAR

Royal Sovereign (100)	Coll.; Rotheram	47	94
Mars (74)	Duff	29	69
Belleisle (74)	Hargood	33	93
Tonnant (80)	Tyler	26	50
Bellerophon (74)	Cooke	27	123
Colossus (74)	Morris	40	160
Achille (74)	King	13	59
Polyphemus (64)	Redmill	2	4
Revenge (74)	Moorsom	28	51
Swiftsure (74)	Rutherford	9	8
Defence (74)	Hope	7	29
Thunderer (98)	Stockham	4	12
Defiance (74)	Durham	17	53
Prince (98)	Grindall	–	–
Dreadnought (98)	Conn	7	26
Division totals		**289**	**831**
Fleet totals		**449**	**1218**

Combined fleet

FRENCH SHIPS

Bucentaure (80)	Wrecked	197 killed	85 wounded
Redoubtable (74)	Captured and sunk	490	81
Intrépide (74)	Captured and burned	242	?
Indomptable (84)	Ran aground	500?	?
Fougeux (74)	Captured, wrecked	546 killed and wounded	
Aigle (74)	Captured, wrecked	500? killed and wounded	
Achille (74)	Blew up	480 killed and wounded	
Berwick (74)	Captured, wrecked	700?	—
Swiftsure (74)	Captured	68	123
Formidable (80)	Escaped, recaptured	22	45
Scipion (74)	Escaped, recaptured	17	22
Duguay-Trouin (74)	Escaped, recaptured	12	24
Mont Blanc (74)	Escaped, recaptured	20	20
Pluton (74)	Sank	60	132
Héros (74)	Escaped	12	24
Neptune (84)	Escaped	15	39
Algésiras (74)	Escaped	77	142
Argonaute (80)	Escaped	55	132
French fleet totals		**4013?**	**869?**

SPANISH SHIPS

Santissima Trinidad (130)	Captured and sunk	216	116
Monarca (74)	Captured, wrecked	101	154
Argonauta (80)	Captured and sunk	100	203
Neptuno (84)	Captured, wrecked	38	35
Rayo (100)	Wrecked, burnt	4	14
San Fransisco de Asis (74)	Wrecked	5	12
San Augustin (74)	Captured and burnt	184	201
Bahama (74)	Captured	75	66
San Ildefonso (74)	Captured	36	129
San Juan Nepomuceno (74)	Captured	103	151

Santa Anna (112)	Captured, escaped	104	137
Principe d'Asturias (112)	Escaped	54	109
San Leandro (64)	Escaped	8	22
San Justo 74)	Escaped	7	
Montanes (74)	Escaped	20	29
Spanish fleet totals		**1048**	**1385**
Combined fleet totals		**5061**	**2254**

These figures do not shock any less for rereading them. A great deal can be read into them, possibly too much. As Collingwood pointed out at the time, and from his own bitter experience after the Glorious First of June, the skill and bravery of a ship's officers and men were not necessarily reflected in the casualties they suffered. But the bald facts are clear. The Combined Fleet (which had six more ships than the British) suffered something like six times the overall casualties of the British fleet. Even allowing for the very large numbers of French sailors who drowned or were blown up, the actual battle casualty rates must have been something like three or four to one. It might be too simple to equate this rate with the relative rates of gunfire, also between three and four to one. But essentially, it was superior gunnery that won the battle, as the devisers of the mêlée tactic knew it would. It was not a tactic designed to test the strength and skills of two equal opponents. It was designed to annihilate the enemy. This one action saw more casualties than all the other naval engagements of the Napoleonic Wars put together – but then, not nearly so many as were lost to disease in that period, a much more shocking figure.

Looking down those terrible lists of lives lost, and the fates of the ships, it becomes even more evident just how miraculous it was that not a single British ship was lost. That is a direct reflection of

the fact that the captains of the British ships, and of course Collingwood in particular, had been so hardened to a life of blockade, that
their consummate skill was equal to a series of gales that were the
severest many of them had ever seen. In this context, censuring
Collingwood for the loss of the prizes rather misses the point.

The navy's Mediterranean (and for that matter Baltic and
Atlantic) exploits after Trafalgar must give the lie to the often-
repeated idea that Trafalgar put an end to French naval ambition. It
was the last great naval engagement involving wooden-hulled ships.
But between 1805 and the end of the war ten years later, the essence
of the conflict at sea changed in response to Napoleon's altered
ambitions. Blockade and intelligence-gathering, coastal operations
and small frigate actions became the order of the day. The fleet was
always there to back them up, and to intimidate any enemy squadron
that might show its face. Trafalgar had achieved a major blow.
Perhaps the subtleties and complexities of the naval war in the
following years makes the navy's achievement harder to appreciate,
if not less impressive.

By the time of Collingwood's death his role as Commander-in-
Chief of the Mediterranean was, to the ministry's relief, losing its
crucial importance. The land wars were beginning in earnest. Within
a year Napoleon would be so completely absorbed by his rash com-
mitments in Spain and Russia that invasion plans for Sicily, Menorca,
Egypt and Turkey were effectively abandoned. Collingwood's role in
bringing about that scenario should not be forgotten.

Source notes

INTRODUCTION

The Collingwood touch

1 William Henry Smyth's map of 1813: Museum of Military History, Es Castell, Menorca

2 Obituary: Naval Chronicle xxiii: 350ff

3 Biographical sketch: Naval Chronicle xxiii: 380

4 'Sam', Trafalgar: the view from the lower deck, quoted by Lewis 2001: 171

5 Collingwood first mentions a dog in 1790. The distinguished naval biographer Oliver Warner was of the opinion that this dog, and Bounce, who died in 1809, could not be the same; there is no conclusive evidence either way

6 Newnham-Collingwood 1828: 429

7 Collingwood unselfishly promoted Clavell to a command in March 1806, so losing his most valuable lieutenant

8 Hope-Dodds and Hall 1954: note

9 Collingwood to Rear-Admiral Purvis (February 1809) Hughes 170, Ocean, Malta

10 Newnham-Collingwood 1828: 412

11 Newnham-Collingwood 1828: 567

12 Gregory 1990: 158

13 Collingwood to his sister (Jan 1806) Hughes 98

14 Newnham-Collingwood 1828: 570

15 George Price, The Youth's Instructor, quoted by Warner 1968: 249

16 Collingwood to Mrs Stead (April 1809) Hughes 174, Ville de Paris

17 Collingwood to John Davidson (June 1807) Hughes 129, Ocean

18 Newnham-Collingwood : i, 53. This edition, the fifth, was published in two volumes, and contains a number of additional letters not found in earlier editions

19 Lincoln and McEwen 1960: anecdote 13

20 Newnham-Collingwood 1837: ii, 434

21 Sir William Hoste, quoted by Warner 1968: xviii

22 Blackwood, quoted by Nicholas vii 26

23 Thomas Creevey, quoted by Maxwell (Ed) 1903: ii, 161. See also Chapters Ten and Eleven

24 Jane Austen: Persuasion Volume 1 Chapter iii

25 Collingwood to his sister (August 1809) Hughes 184, Ville de Paris, off Toulon

CHAPTER ONE

A large piece of plum cake 1748–1771

1 Mackesy 1957: preface, x; 395

2 Tough 1987: 174

3 Clark Russell 1891: 4

4 Warner 1968: 3

5 Hope-Dodds and Hall 1954: 30ff

6 Raigersfeld 1830: 35. Raigersfeld was a midshipman who served with the two brothers on the Leeward Islands station. See Chapter Three

7 Middlebrook 1950: 117

8 ibid

9 ibid, quoting Bourne 1736: The History of Newcastle upon Tyne, or the Ancient and present state of that town

10 Middlebrook 1950: 124

11 Newcastle Courant 24 September to 1 October 1748. Newcastle City Library

12 Fraser and Emsley 1973: 68

13 Ireland 2000: 18

14 B. Mains, personal communication

15 Mains and Tuck 1986: 59

16 Rodger 1986: 29ff

17 Under the 'Convoys and Cruizers Act' 1708 the

Crown gave up its right to captured enemy ships 'for the better and more effectual encouragement of the Sea Service'. Padfield 2003: 69

18 Warner 1968: 247

19 Hay 1953: 71

20 Newnham-Collingwood 1828: 6

21 Rodger 1986: 268

22 Collingwood to Sir Edward Blackett (August 1795) Hughes 35, *Excellent*

CHAPTER TWO

Out of all patience 1772–1777

1 Collingwood's log, *Portland*, 30 March 1773

2 Collingwood's log, *Princess Amelia*, 6 June 1773

3 According to Collingwood himself. Warner 1968: 12

4 *Boston and Country Gazette*: Monday 17 January 1774. Boston City Library

5 *Boston and Country Gazette*: Monday 10 January 1774

6 *Boston and Country Gazette*: 16 May 1774

7 *Massachusetts and Boston Weekly Gazette*: the Newsletter: 13 January 1774. Boston City Library

8 Ketchum 1962: 16

9 Ketchum 1962: 18

10 ibid

11 Morrissey 1993: 47

12 Ketchum 1962: 23

13 Collingwood to his sister (March 1776) Hughes 1, London, Castle Street. Mount Pisga is a hill which overlooks Cambridge and the Charlestown peninsula

14 According to Clark Russell (1891: 11) many veterans considered that day to have been the hottest action they ever saw

15 Vice-Admiral Graves to Captain le Clas (10 December 1775) *Preston*. Naval Documents of the American Revolutionary War, Volume 3 1968: 37

16 Naval Documents of the American Revolutionary War, Volume 3 1968: 924. 2–20 February 1776

17 Naval Documents of the American Revolutionary War, Volume 4 1969: 1008–1010

18 Newnham-Collingwood 1828: 96

19 Rodger 1986: 357

20 Collingwood to his brother John (1777) Hughes 2, *Hornet*, West Indies

21 ibid

22 Rodger 1986: 135

23 Collingwood to his brother John (1777) Hughes 2, *Hornet*, West Indies

24 Warner 1968: 12

CHAPTER THREE

The bonds of our amity 1777–1786

1 Nelson's first commission; he had passed his examination at the Admiralty the previous day

2 Syrett 1988: 185

3 Baugh 1988: 150

4 Coleman 2001: 24

5 Nicolas i, 8

6 Nicolas i, 57–8, quoted by Coleman 2001

7 Newnham-Collingwood 1828: 8 Taken from Collingwood's autobiographical memoir, printed in the Naval Chronicle

8 According to Clark Russell (1891:14) Collingwood captured a French brig of 16 guns, *Le Cerf*, and recaptured a British merchantman, while in command of *Pelican*. If so, these may have been his first naval 'actions'

9 Breen 1988: 196

10 Newnham-Collingwood 1828: 8 Collingwood later briefly hoisted his admiral's flag in *Diamond*, in 1803

11 Warner 1968: 15

12 Collingwood to his brother John (June 1782) Hughes 3, London

13 Collingwood to his sister (August 1783) Hughes 5, *Mediator*, Portsmouth

14 ibid

15 There is no record of a voyage in *Sampson*; Collingwood may have been in charge of fitting her out while waiting for *Mediator*

16 Raigersfeld 1830: 12

17 Reprinted by Cassells in 1929 from the only known, privately printed copy in the Admiralty Library, now the Caird Library at the National Maritime Museum

18 Raigersfeld 1830: 33

19 ibid: 12

20 ibid: 15

21 Pocock 1983: 778

22 ibid

23 Raigersfeld 1830: 15; Johnny Newcome was a generic name for inexperienced seamen

24 ibid: 29

25 ibid: 15

26 Robert Fulton, inventor of the submarine and the torpedo, named his underwater bomb after the eel of that name

27 ibid: 32

28 Aspinall 1912: 182, quoted by Nicholson 2002

29 Nicolas i, 110

30 Nicolas i: 112

31 Nicholson 2002: 21

32 Warner 1968: 19

33 Warner 1968: 20 (PRO/C.O/ 152/64)

34 Collingwood to his sister (January 1785) Hughes 7, *Mediator*, Antigua

35 Nicolas i: 179 June 1786

36 Warner 1968: 162

37 Collingwood to his sister (January 1785) Hughes 7, *Mediator*, Antigua

38 Pocock 1983: 780

39 Collingwood to his sister (January 1785) Hughes 7, *Mediator*, Antigua

40 Raigersfeld 1830: 36

41 ibid: 14

42 ibid: 20

43 ibid: 24

44 ibid: 27

45 Raigersfeld 1830: introduction

CHAPTER FOUR

A comfortable fire and friends 1787–1792

1 Coleman (2001) quotes the 1790 navy list, when there were 55 post ships and 427 post-captains, 172 of them senior to Nelson and even more senior to Collingwood

3 Middlebrook 1950: 146

4 Oliver1831: 176

5 *Newcastle Courant* 9 December 1786

6 Collingwood to Rear-Admiral Purvis (December 1807) Hughes 145, *Ocean* off Mauritimo

7 Newnham-Collingwood 1828: 12–13

8 Warner 1968: 23

9 Ireland 2000: 122

10 Padfield 2003: 10; 35ff

11 Collingwood to the Secretary of the Admiralty (May 1790) Hughes 7 supplementary, London

12 Plums. In naval parlance the equivalent of cherry-picking. The expression derived from a naval culinary treat, plum duff, which often had so few plums (in reality currants) among the suet, that they were prized by those fortunate enough to get one

13 Collingwood to his sister Mary (May 1790) Hughes 8, London

14 Collingwood to his sister Mary (May 1790) Hughes 9, London

15 Collingwood to his sister Mary (May 1790) Hughes 10, London

16 ibid

17 Collingwood to his sister Mary (July 1790) Hughes 11, Sheerness

18 Collingwood to his sister Mary (October 1790) Hughes 12, Portsmouth

19 Collingwood to his sister Mary (April 1791) Hughes 13, Portsmouth

20 Collingwood to his sister Mary (February 1792) Hughes 14, Musselburgh

21 Collingwood to Dr Alexander Carlyle (September 1792) Hughes 15, Morpeth

22 Padfield 2003: introduction

23 ibid: 52

24 Newnham-Collingwood 1828: 17–18

25 Padfield 2003: 57

CHAPTER FIVE

The sharp point of misfortune 1793–1795

1 A first-rate was a ship of 100 guns and more. A second-rate carried 90-98; a third-rate 64-84; a fourth-rate usually 50-60, but *Mediator* was a fourth-rate of 44 guns, effectively a heavy frigate

2 Collingwood to his sister Mary (February 1793) Hughes 16, London. In this letter he admits he would happily never sail in a frigate again, though he does not say why

3 Warner 1968: 15

4 Collingwood to Sir Edward Blackett (December 1793) Hughes 20, *Prince*, Spithead

5 'Captain Aubrey belonged to the school of Douglas and Collingwood, men who believed that a ship's prime purpose was to bring cannon within range of the enemy and then to fire with extreme speed and accuracy.' *The Ionian Mission*

6 Collingwood to his sister Mary (August 1793) Hughes 18, *Prince*, Spithead

7 See Ireland 2000: 45 for a diagram, and Davies 2002 for a detailed description

8 Davies 2002: 38

9 Each tackle would, using two pulley blocks, exert a three or four times mechanical advantage. This made the gun slower but easier to pull, and meant extra yards of rope trailing across the deck

10 Ireland 200: 49

11 Uglow 2002: 253

12 Collingwood to the Secretary of the Admiralty (May 1793) Hughes 17 supplementary, *Prince*, Hamoaze

13 ibid. Thomas Huntley to Captain Collingwood (May 1793) *St Albans*, Spithead

14 Collingwood to Sir Edward Blackett (July 1793) Hughes 17, *Prince*, Spithead. Sir Edward was Sarah's uncle

15 Pope 1981: 209ff

16 Cronin 1971: 70

17 Naval Chronicle II 297–303

18 Ireland 2000:125

19 Collingwood to Sir Edward Blackett (March 1794) Hughes 21, *Barfleur*, Spithead

20 ibid

21 Padfield 2003: 82

22 see Introduction

23 To use Davies' excellent phrase 2002:62

24 Collingwood to Sir Edward Blackett (June 1794) Hughes 23, *Barfleur*

25 ibid

26 Padfield 2003: 101

27 Collingwood to Sir Edward Blackett (June 1794) Hughes 23, *Barfleur*

28 Warner 1968: 51

29 Newnham-Collingwood 1828: 24

30 ibid

31 Collingwood to Sir Edward Blackett (June 1794) Hughes 24, *Barfleur*

32 Collingwood to Dr Alexander Carlyle (July 1794) Hughes 25, *Barfleur*, Spithead

33 Collingwood to Sir Edward Blackett (June 1794) Hughes 24, *Barfleur*

34 Collingwood to Dr Alexander Carlyle (July 1794) Hughes 25, *Barfleur*, Spithead

35 'The sharp point of misfortune is broken by exposure.' Collingwood to Mrs Stead (October 1809) Hughes 190, *Ville de Paris* off Barcelona

36 Collingwood to Dr Alexander Carlyle (July 1794) Hughes 25, *Barfleur*, Spithead

37 Collingwood to Sir Edward Blackett (August 1794) Hughes 27, *Hector*, Portsmouth

38 Collingwood to Dr Alexander Carlyle (July 1794) Hughes 25, *Barfleur*

39 Collingwood to Dr Alexander Carlyle (March 1795) Hughes 33, *Excellent*

CHAPTER SIX

Two thunderbolts of war 1795–1799

1 Collingwood to Sir Edward Blackett (March 1796) Hughes 36, *Excellent*

2 Jean-Jacques Rousseau (1712-78). His political masterpiece, *The Social Contract*, appeared in 1762

3 Brady and Pottle 1955: 185

4 Gregory 1985: 57

5 This stone cannot now be found, though the inscription was recorded at the time: Nicolas ii: 77

6 Nelson to Collingwood (August 1795) Vado Bay: Nicolas ii: 77

7 ibid

8 Gregory 1985: 143

9 See also his letter on Corsica quoted above in Chapter One

10 Collingwood to Sir Edward Blackett (March 1796) Hughes 36, *Excellent*

11 Collingwood to Sir Edward Blackett (August 1796) Hughes 39, *Excellent*

12 Newnham-Collingwood 1828: 27

13 Collingwood to Sir Edward Blackett (August 1796) Hughes 39, *Excellent*

14 Gregory 1985: 134–5

15 Paoli died in London in 1807 at the age of eighty-two. There is a bust of him in Westminster Abbey

16 'Spiking' a gun entailed driving a nail into its touch hole to prevent its being fired; spike is an alternative name for a nail. De-spiking a gun involved a delicate operation with a gimlet-like instrument

17 Nelson to Collingwood. 20 November 1796. Nicolas ii: 304

18 Davies 2002: 73

19 Padfield 2003: 117

20 Padfield 2003: 118ff

21 Collingwood to Sir Edward Blackett (January 1797) Hughes 40, *Excellent*, Lisbon. Portugal, though passive, was Britain's last continental ally

22 Newnham-Collingwood 1828: 56

23 Newnham-Collingwood 1828: 125. It is stated here that this figure relates to the *Dreadnought* in 1805; but most commentators accept that it probably applied equally to *Excellent*, which Collingwood commanded for nearly five years. Some cite the rate as three broadsides in a minute and a half, but this must surely be a mistake. Three in five minutes was considered very good practice

24 Parsons 1843: unnumbered

25 ibid. Marriage to the gunner's daughter was a euphemism for being seized to a gun and thrashed

26 *Duo fulmina belli*: two thunderbolts of war. This is taken from Vergil: *Aeneid* 6, 843, referring to the Generals Scipio, of Corsica and Carthage fame. Vergil himself borrowed the phrase from Lucretius, *de rerum natura*

27 Nicolas ii: 337

28 Collingwood to Dr Alexander Carlyle (February 1797) Hughes 41, *Excellent*, Lagos Bay

29 Newnham-Collingwood 1828: 37

30 Collingwood to Dr Alexander Carlyle (February 1797) Hughes 41, *Excellent*, Lagos Bay

31 Newnham-Collingwood 1828: 43

32 ibid

33 ibid p. 41

34 Pope 1981: 150

35 Padfield 2003: 131

36 ibid p. 133

37 Naval Chronicle xi, 269-272

38 Collingwood to Dr Alexander Carlyle (June 1794) Hughes 42, *Excellent*

39 Newnham-Collingwood 1828: 45

40 ibid p. 50

41 ibid

42 ibid p. 55

43 Collingwood to his sister Mary (August 1797) Hughes 43, *Excellent*, off Cadiz

44 Kamperduin: a small village in Noord-Holland, close to the town of Alkmaar

45 Collingwood to Dr Alexander Carlyle (December 1797) Hughes 44, *Excellent*, Lisbon

46 Newnham-Collingwood 1828: 64

47 Collingwood to Sir Edward Blackett (December 1798) Hughes 45, *Excellent*, Spithead

48 Newnham-Collingwood 1828: 71

CHAPTER SEVEN

Hope of peace alone 1799–1802

1 Collingwood to Dr Alexander Carlyle (February 1799) Hughes 48, Morpeth

2 ibid

3 Jane Austen: *Persuasion*, Volume II Chapter xii

4 Newnham-Collingwood 1837: i, 99

5 An earlier reform of naval ranks had instituted ten levels of admiral, based on the existence of three squadrons: red, white and blue, of which red was the senior. The most junior admiral was a rear-admiral of the blue squadron; the second grade was vice-admiral. Admiral of the red was the senior operational admiral in theory, with only the admiral of the fleet above. Nelson died a vice-admiral of the white, Collingwood a vice-admiral of the red. There were ninety-nine admirals of all ranks

6 Collingwood to Dr Alexander Carlyle (April 1799) Hughes 49, Morpeth

7 ibid

8 Tooke (1736–1812) was a radical Wilkesite cleric who was tried for high treason in 1790 and acquitted. *DNB*

9 Collingwood to Sir Edward Blackett (May 1799)

Hughes 50, Morpeth

10 *Triumph* was launched in 1764, a year before *Victory*

11 Collingwood to his sister (September 1799) Hughes 53, *Triumph*, Torbay

12 Collingwood to Dr Alexander Carlyle (December 1799) Hughes 56, *Triumph*

13 ibid

14 Collingwood to Sir Edward Blackett (December 1799) Hughes 57, *Triumph*, Plymouth

15 Collingwood to Sir Edward Blackett (January 1800) Hughes 58, *Triumph*, Cawsand Bay

16 Quoted by Cronin 1971: 225

17 Collingwood to Sir Edward Blackett (April 1800) Hughes 59, *Barfleur*, Torbay

18 Warner 1968: 97, footnote

19 Oliver 1831: 177

20 Newnham-Collingwood 1828: 80

21 ibid

22 Newnham-Collingwood 1828: 83–4

23 Collingwood to Dr Alexander Carlyle (August 1801) Hughes 69, *Barfleur*, off Brest

24 Newnham-Collingwood 1828: 82

25 ibid p. 83

26 ibid p. 84

27 ibid

28 Brontë is an estate in eastern Sicily. Patrick Brunty, the parson of Haworth in Yorkshire, was so taken by the title that he changed his surname, and that of his famous children, to Brontë

29 Newnham-Collingwood 1837: i, 114

30 ibid p. 113

31 Newnham-Collingwood 1828: 86

32 Collingwood to his sister (November 1800) Hughes 62, *Barfleur*

33 Newnham-Collingwood 1828: 86

34 ibid p. 87. William Ireland, his long-serving steward, later became a burden as his increasing wealth was spent on drink, and by 1805 Collingwood had replaced him. Warner 1968: 139

35 Collingwood to his sister (November 1801) Hughes 70, *Barfleur*, Bearhaven, Bantry Bay

36 Collingwood to Mrs Stead (November 1801) Hughes 71, *Barfleur*, Bantry Bay

37 ibid

38 Collingwood to Mrs Stead (January 1802) Hughes 72, *Barfleur*, Portsmouth

39 Ireland 2003: 163

40 Collingwood to his sister (April 1802) Hughes 74, Torbay

41 ibid

CHAPTER EIGHT
Exemplary vengeance 1803–1805

1 Jane Austen might have been thinking of Collingwood when she portrayed her Admiral Baldwin: 'I never
saw so wretched an example of what a sea-faring life can
do; but to a degree I know it is the same with them all:
they are all knocked about, and exposed to every
climate, and every weather, till they are not fit to be
seen. It is a pity they are not knocked on the head at
once, before they reach Admiral Baldwin's age.' Jane
Austen, *Persuasion*: Volume I Chapter iii

2 Crawford 1999: 119. This was the description
recorded by Abraham Crawford when he met Collingwood in 1806

3 Clark Russell 1891: preface, xii

4 Newnham-Collingwood 1828: 91

5 Collingwood later wrote, 'If the country gentlemen
do not make it a point to plant oaks every where they
will grow, the time will not be very far distant when, to
keep our Navy, we must depend entirely on captures
from the enemy... I wish every body thought on this
subject as I do; they would not walk through their farms
without a pocketful of acorns to drop in the hedgesides,
and then let them take their chance.' Newnham-
Collingwood 1837: i, 141–2

6 *Newcastle Courant*, 5 Feb 1803

7 *Newcastle Courant*, 26 Feb 1803

8 *Newcastle Courant*, 12 March 1803

9 Secretary to the Board of Admiralty since 1795

10 Collingwood to Dr Alexander Carlyle (March 1803)
Hughes 82, Morpeth

11 ibid

12 *Newcastle Courant*, 26 March 1803

13 Earl St Vincent had famously told the House of
Lords: 'I do not say, my Lords, that the French will not
come. I only say that they will not come by sea.'

14 Oliver 1831: 177

15 Padfield 2003: 193 The purchase included the territories which now encompass Arkansas, Missouri, Iowa,
Nebraska, North and South Dakota and parts of several
other states

16 Naval Chronicle xiii: 351

17 Collingwood to J.E. Blackett (October 1803) Hughes
85, *Venerable*

18 ibid

19 Jane Austen, *Persuasion*: Volume I Chapter viii

20 Newnham-Collingwood 1837: i, 131–2

21 Clark Russell 1891: 116

22 Hay 1953: 69–70

23 Collingwood to Dr Alexander Carlyle (June 1804)
Hughes 88, *Prince*, off Ushant

24 Collingwood to Dr Alexander Carlyle (August 1804)
Hughes 89, *Dreadnought*

25 ibid

26 Collingwood's words. Quoted by Hughes 1957: 157

27 Collingwood to Nelson (December 1804) Hughes 90,
Dreadnought, Cawsand Bay

28 Newnham-Collingwood 1837: i, 143

29 Newnham-Collingwood 1837: i, 136

30 Padfield 2003: 220

31 It had been languishing in the library of a Californ-
ian university, before being purchased by the National
Maritime Museum

32 Secret Letter Book MS 76/001 National Maritime
Museum: Letter 4: Collingwood to William Marsden, 27
May 1805, *Dreadnought* off Cape Finisterre

33 Collingwood to Dr Alexander Carlyle (July 1805)
Hughes 91 *Dreadnought*, off Cadiz

34 Newnham-Collingwood 1837: i, 151

35 Nelson to Collingwood (July 1805) Nicolas v: 57

36 Collingwood to his sister (August 1805) Hughes 92,
Dreadnought, off Cadiz

37 Naval Chronicle xv: 369

38 William Cosway, who later became attached to one
of Collingwood's daughters, but who was subsequently
terribly injured in a coaching accident

39 ibid

40 Robinson 1858: 43

41 Newnham-Collingwood 1837: i, 158–9

42 Coleman 2001: 317 According to ADD MS 33,963,
Nelson gave the plan to his captains a day after he sent it
to Collingwood, on 10 October

43 Newnham-Collingwood 1837: i, 162–3

44 Nicolas vii: 71

45 Nicolas vii: 93

46 Warner 1968: 146

47 Newnham-Collingwood 1837: i, 166

48 ibid p. 167

49 Robinson 1858: 205–6

50 Newnham-Collingwood 1837: i, 173–4

51 Robinson 1858: 206

52 Newnham-Collingwood 1837: i, 174 – this anecdote
was probably reported to the biographer by William
Cosway, the Admiral's secretary, who would have been
in close attendance on him during the battle

53 Naval Chronicle xv: 119

54 Newnham-Collingwood 1828: 125

55 Quoted by Warner 1968: 150

56 Vangs were the backstays of the mizzen gaff yard;
from aft they looked like an inverted V

57 Robinson 1858: 206

58 Clark Russell 1891: 139

59 Robinson 1858: 206

60 Newnham-Collingwood 1837: i, 289

61 ibid p. 227

62 Quoted by Lewis 2000: 171

63 Quoted by Clark Russell 1891: 159

64 Newnham-Collingwood 1837: i, 185–6

65 Blackwood's Magazine 1833: 13

66 Robinson 1858: 208. Villeneuve returned to France in the spring of 1806. He was found stabbed to death in an inn in Rennes; either by his own hand, or that of one of Napoleon's men. Collingwood said of him, 'He has nothing in his manners of the offensive vapouring and boasting which we, perhaps too often, attribute to Frenchmen.' Newnham-Collingwood 1837: i, 237

67 ADM MS 76/001, now in the Caird Library at the National Maritime Museum in Greenwich

68 Because of the importance of the document, the two draft letters are transcribed in full in Appendix 1. Where they differ from the published version the text has been highlighted

69 Part of the King's letter to the Admiralty, in response to the Dispatch, ran as follows:

Every tribute of praise appears to His Majesty due to Lord Nelson, whose loss he can never sufficiently regret; but His Majesty considers it very fortunate that the command, under circumstances so critical, should have devolved upon an officer of such consummate valour, judgement and skill, as Admiral Collingwood has proved himself to be, every part of whose conduct he considers deserving his entire approbation and admiration. The feeling manner in which he had described the events of that great day and those subsequent, and the modesty with which he speaks of himself, whilst he does justice, in terms so elegant and so ample, to the meritorious exertions of the gallant officers and men under his command, have also proved extremely satisfactory to the King. Newnham-Collingwood 1828: 157

70 Warner 1968: 154 note

CHAPTER NINE

Giddy with the multiplicities 1806–1808

1 Indebted properties brought to him through his wife's family. They are estates at the north end of the Cheviot hills, very close to the Scottish border. Part of Collingwood's amusement was that he had never heard of them, and was fairly certain Sarah had not either

2 Horace Epistles II ii 200. *Utrum nave ferar magna an parva ferar unus et idem.* The full sentence translates something like this: 'Be my vessel large or small, I am

carried against them, always one and the same.' It was traced and translated by Warwick Adams

3 Warner 1968: 163. Curtis was blamed by Collingwood for the infamous second letter written after the battle of the Glorious First of June

4 Collingwood to his sister (January 1806) Hughes 98, *Queen*

5 Newnham-Collingwood 1828: 167–8

6 Newnham-Collingwood 1837: i, 226

7 Collingwood to Sir Thomas Pasley (December 1805) Hughes 97, *Queen*, off Cartagena

8 The Ottoman court at Constantinople. Its derivation is seventeenth century, from the French *La Sublime Porte*, 'the Exalted Gate' – a translation of the Turkish for the central office of government. New Oxford Dictionary

9 Gravina, the commander of the Spanish fleet, was also wounded, and died on 9 November

10 Newnham-Collingwood 1837: i, 207–8

11 Secret Letter Book, entry 11. ADM MS 76/001. *Euryalus*, 27 October 1805

12 Newnham-Collingwood 1837: i, 211

13 Secret Letter Book: 40. ADM MS 76/001

14 ibid p. 243

15 ibid

16 Collingwood to his sister (January 1806) Hughes 98, *Queen*

17 Though set at the time of the Risorgimento around 1860, *The Leopard* gives a flavour of decadent aristocracy which, unable or unprepared to defend itself, the British tried to rouse in the period after Trafalgar

18 Messina proved equally vital for the Allied invasion forces in 1943

19 Newnham-Collingwood 1837: i, 255. Author's translation from the French

20 ibid p. 263. Author's translation

21 ibid pp. 269–70

22 i.e. the Algerian Regency, not the English

23 Newnham-Collingwood 1837: i, 281–2

24 Such incidents made it easier, under pressure from France, to deny port facilities to British ships on the Portuguese mainland

25 Newnham-Collingwood 1837: i, 301

26 ibid p. 274

27 ibid p. 291. As Collingwood wrote to Grey, the Foreign Secretary. Collingwood thought such weapons 'un-English': their chief effect was to terrorise and injure civilians, and if the English used them, might not the enemy retaliate with similar weapons

28 Collingwood to his brother John (September 1806) Hughes 116, *Ocean*

29 Newnham-Collingwood 1837: i, 307

30 ibid p. 366

31 Collingwood to his sister Bess (April 1806) Hughes 106, *Ocean*, off Cadiz

32 Collingwood to Rear-Admiral Purvis (February 1809) Hughes 170, *Ocean*, Malta

33 Collingwood to his sister (May 1806) Hughes 107, *Ocean*

34 Robinson 1858: 48–9

35 Collingwood to his brother John (September 1806) Hughes 116, *Ocean*

36 ibid

37 Newnham-Collingwood 1828: 264

38 Collingwood to his sister (November 1806) Hughes 119, *Ocean*, off Cadiz

39 Newnham-Collingwood 1828: 262

40 Act II scene iii. Identified by Warner 1968, and by John Fisher during invaluable discussions on Bounce

41 Newnham-Collingwood 1828: 269–70

42 Collingwood to Rear-Admiral Purvis (September 1806) Hughes 114, *Ocean*

43 Newnham-Collingwood 1828: 272

44 ibid pp. 284–5

45 Collingwood to his sister (June 1807) Hughes 128, *Ocean*

46 See, for example, *The Mauritius Command*: Chapter Two

47 Collingwood to John Davidson (June 1807) Hughes 129, *Ocean*

48 The Anglo-American war lasted from 1812–14, ending, more or less, when *Shannon* and *Chesapeake* met outside Boston harbour in an episode fictionalised in O'Brian's *The Fortune of War*. Collingwood thought the policy of searching American ships 'exceedingly improvident and unfortunate, as in the issue it may involve us in a contest which it would be wisdom to avoid.' Newnham-Collingwood 1837: ii, 74

49 Pope 1981: 221

50 Officially starting was forbidden by the Admiralty in 1809 after the court martial of the notoriously brutal Captain Robert Corbett

51 Newnham-Collingwood 1828: 349. Collingwood estimated his complete strength at thirty ships of the line, the rest made up of frigates, brigs, sloops, bombs and the like

52 Newnham-Collingwood 1837: ii, 47–50

53 At this time the Russians were still negotiating in apparent concert with the British

54 ibid pp. 51–3

55 Collingwood to his sister (April 1809) Hughes 175, *Ville de Paris*

56 Newnham-Collingwood 1828: 307

57 The gentleman in question was Collingwood's old school friend, Lord Eldon

58 i.e. Arbuthnot, the English Ambassador

59 Collingwood to his sister (December 1808) Hughes 167, *Ocean*

60 Collingwood to his sister (October 1807) Hughes 143, *Ocean*, off Sicily

61 Collingwood to his sister ((December 1808) Hughes 167, *Ocean*

CHAPTER TEN

Viva Collingwood 1808–1810

1 Collingwood to his sister (March 1808) Hughes 153, *Ocean*, off Sicily

2 Collingwood's Mediterranean Journal 1807–1810: 2 January 1808

3 Newnham-Collingwood 1837: ii, 90

4 ibid pp. 97–8

5 Andrews and Brown 2002: 271

6 The port of Taranto lies right inside the 'instep' of the Italian boot

7 The very heavy casualty figures for both leading ships provide ample justification for Collingwood's misgivings; see Chapter Eleven

8 Collingwood to his sister (July 1808) Hughes 160, *Ocean,* off Cadiz

9 Newnham-Collingwood 1828: 348–9

10 Collingwood to Rear-Admiral Purvis (April 1808) Hughes 156, *Ocean*, off Sicily

11 Padfield 2003: 271

12 Collingwood to his sister (June 1808) Hughes 157, *Ocean*, off Cadiz

13 Newnham-Collingwood 1828: 375; author's note

14 ibid p. 376

15 Newnham-Collingwood 1837: ii, 227

16 Clark Russell 1891: 240

17 Newnham-Collingwood 1837: ii, 202

18 ibid pp. 180–81

19 ibid p. 211

20 ibid pp. 204–5

21 See Introduction; Mrs Currell was a friend of Sarah Collingwood's in Newcastle

22 Newnham-Collingwood 1837: ii, 206

23 Sarah Collingwood to Miss Mary Woodman (March 1813). Hope Dodds and Hall (Eds) 1954

24 Newnham-Collingwood 1837: ii, 355

25 Collingwood to his sister (October 1808) Hughes 165, *Ocean*, off Toulon

26 Lord Mulgrave to Collingwood, quoted by Collingwood in a letter to his sister (December 1808) Hughes 167, *Ocean*

27 Newnham-Collingwood 1837: ii, 285–6

28 Collingwood to Mary Moutray (November 1808) Hughes 166, *Ocean*, off Toulon

29 Collingwood to his sister (December 1808) Hughes 167, *Ocean*

30 Collingwood to his sister (March 1809) Hughes 172, *Ocean*

31 ibid

32 Collingwood to his sister (February 1809) Hughes 171, *Ocean*, off Sicily

33 Collingwood to his sister (February 1809) Hughes 171, *Ocean*, off Sicily

34 Crawford 1999: 192–3

35 Collingwood to his sister (February 1809) Hughes 171, *Ocean*, off Sicily

36 Collingwood to Rear-Admiral Purvis (May 1809) Hughes 177, *Ville de Paris*, off Toulon

37 Newnham-Collingwood 1837: ii, 331

38 ibid p. 342

39 Collingwood to Mrs Stead (May 1809) Hughes 176, *Ville de Paris*, off Toulon

40 Collingwood to Mrs Stead (April 1809) Hughes 174, *Ville de Paris*

41 Collingwood to Mrs Stead (October 1809) Hughes 190, *Ville de Paris*, off Barcelona

42 Crawford 1999: 184

43 Warner 1968: 224

44 The Duke of Northumberland to Collingwood (January 1810) Hughes Appendix: 13, Teignmouth

45 Maxwell 1903: ii, 161. Thomas Creevey (1768–1838) was a Whig politician and diarist, author of the Creevey Papers, edited by Sir Herbert Maxwell. See Chapter Eleven

46 Collingwood to his sister (August 1809) Hughes 184, *Ville de Paris*, off Toulon

47 Collingwood to Vice-Admiral Purvis (December 1809) Hughes 196, *Ville de Paris*, Port Mahon

48 Mackesy 1957: 395

49 Crawford 1999: 153

50 ibid p. 175

51 Collingwood to his brother John (March 1810) Hughes 200, *Ville de Paris*, Mahon

52 ibid, enclosure

53 Newnham-Collingwood 1837: ii, 427

54 Hope Dodds and Hall 1954: letter 11

CHAPTER ELEVEN

Fame's trumpet

1 Newnham-Collingwood 1837: ii, 9

2 Collingwood's Trafalgar dispatch. See Appendix 1

3 Miss Elizabeth Ord was Creevey's stepdaughter. Her mother was the daughter, coincidentally, of Charles Brandling, MP for Newcastle upon Tyne

4 Maxwell 1903: ii, 161

5 Thackeray 1869: 127

6 A list of Collingwood's commissions is presented in Appendix 2

7 Collingwood to his sister (June 1796) Hughes 37, *Excellent*, off Toulon

8 Referring to the incident in which the captain of the *Leopard* had pressed deserting British sailors from the USS *Chesapeake*, he had written: 'It may involve us in a contest which it would be wisdom to avoid.' Newnham-Collingwood 1837: ii, 74

9 Hope Dodds and Hall 1954: letter 18

10 Newnham-Collingwood 1838: i, 195ff

11 Sir John Laughton. DNB 1887

12 Naval Chronicle xv: 369

13 Hibbert 1994: 399

14 Figures adapted from Pope 1999: 333ff

Collingwood's Trafalgar dispatch

Where the published dispatch differs from the draft, **bold** text indicates a passage excised from the draft, and [brackets] indicate an addition in the published version. It may be noticed that one or two of Collingwood's statements and reports are mistaken: these were corrected in later reports.

To William Marsden, Esq, Admiralty.
Euryalus, off Cape Trafalgar,
October 22nd, 1805

Sir,

The ever to be lamented death of Vice-Admiral Lord Viscount Nelson, who in the late conflict with the enemy, fell in the hour of victory, leaves to me the duty of informing my Lords Commissioners of the Admiralty, that on the 19th instant it was communicated to the Commander in Chief from the ships watching the motions of the Enemy in Cadiz, that the Combined Fleet had put to sea. As they sailed with light winds westerly, his Lordship concluded their destination was the Mediterranean, and immediately made all sail for the Streights' entrance with the British squadron, consisting of twenty-seven ships, three of them sixty-fours, where his Lordship was informed by Capt. Blackwood, (whose vigilance in watching, and giving notice of the enemy's movements, has been highly meritorious,) that they had not yet passed the Streights.

On Monday the 21st instant, at daylight, when Cape Trafalgar bore E. by S. about seven leagues, the Enemy was discovered six or seven miles to the eastward, the wind about west, and very light; the Commander in Chief immediately made the signal for the fleet to bear up in two columns, as they are formed in order of sailing; a mode of attack his Lordship had previously directed, to avoid the inconvenience and delay in forming a line of battle in the usual manner. The enemy's line consisted of thirty-three Ships (of which eighteen were French and fifteen Spanish), commanded by Admiral Villeneuve; the Spaniards, under the direction of Gravina, wore, with their heads to the northward, and formed their line of battle with great closeness and correctness; but as the mode of attack was unusual, so the structure of their line was new; – it formed a crescent convexing to leeward – so that, in leading down to their centre, I had both their van and rear abaft the beam. Before the fire opened, every alternate Ship was about a cable's length to windward of her second a-head and a-stern, forming a kind of double line, and appeared, when on their beam, to leave a very little interval between them; and this without crowding their ships. [Admiral] Villeneuve was in the *Bucentaure* in the centre, and the *Prince of Asturias* bore Gravina's flag in the rear; but the French and Spanish ships were mixed without any regard to order of National squadron.

As the mode of [our] attack had been previously determined on, and communicated to the Flag-officers and Captains, few signals were necessary, and none were made except to direct close order as the lines bore down.

The Commander in Chief in the *Victory* led the weather column; and the *Royal Sovereign*, which bore my flag, the lee.

The Action began at twelve o'clock, by the leading Ships of the columns breaking through the Enemy's line, the Commander in Chief about the tenth Ship from the van, the Second in Command about the twelfth from the rear, leaving the van of the enemy unoccupied; the succeeding Ships breaking through in all parts, a-stern of their leaders, and engaging the Enemy at the muzzles of their guns, the conflict was severe. The Enemy's Ships were fought with a gallantry highly honourable to their Officers, but the attack on them was irresistible; and it pleased the Almighty Disposer of events to grant His Majesty's arms a complete and glorious victory. About three **o'clock** P.M. many of the Enemy's Ships having struck their colours, their line gave way; Admiral Gravina, with ten Ships, joining their Frigates to leeward, stood towards Cadiz. The five headmost Ships in their van tacked, and standing to the southward to windward of the British line, were engaged, and the sternmost of them taken; the others went off, leaving to His Majesty's squadron nineteen Ships of the line, (of which two are first-rates, the *Santissima Trinidada* and the *Santa Anna*,) with three Flag Officers; viz. Admiral Villeneuve, the Commander in Chief; Don Ignatio Maria d'Alava, Vice-Admiral; and the Spanish Rear-Admiral, Don Balthazar Hidalgo Cisneros.

After such a victory it may appear unnecessary to enter into encomiums on the particular parts taken by the several commanders; the conclusion says more on the subject than I have language to express; the spirit which animated all was the same; when all exert themselves zealously in their country's service, all deserve that their high merits should stand recorded; and never was high merit more conspicuous than in the battle I have described.

The *Achille* (a French 74), after having surrendered, by some mismanagement of the Frenchmen took fire, and blew up; two hundred of her men were saved by the Tenders.

A circumstance occurred during the Action, which so strongly marks the invincible spirit of British seamen, when engaging the enemies of their country, that I cannot resist the pleasure I have in making it known to their Lordships. The *Téméraire* was boarded by accident, or design, by a French ship on one side, and a Spaniard on the other: the contest was vigorous; but in the end the Combined ensigns were torn from the poop, and the British hoisted in their places, **forming a glorious group**.

Such a battle could not be fought without sustaining a great loss of men. I have not only to lament, in common with the British Navy and the British Nation, in the fall of the Commander-in-Chief, the loss of a hero whose name will be immortal, and his memory ever dear to his Country; but my heart is rent with the most poignant grief for the death of a friend, to whom, by many years' intimacy, and a perfect knowledge of his virtues of his mind, which inspired ideas superior to the common race of men, I was bound by the strongest ties of affection; – a grief to which even the glorious occasion in which he fell, does not bring the consolation which perhaps it ought: his Lordship received a musket ball in his left breast about the middle of the Action, and sent an Officer to me immediately with his last farewell, and soon after expired.

I have also to lament the loss of those excellent Officers, Captains Duff of the *Mars* and Cooke of the *Bellerophon*: I have yet heard of none others.

I fear the numbers that have fallen will be found very great when the returns come to me; but it having blown a gale of wind ever since the Action, I have not yet had it in my power to collect any reports from the ships, **and when their Lordships consider that I have 23 infirm ships, 18 of them hulks, without a stick standing, and scarce a boat in the fleet, I am sure that they will have due consideration for the slowness with which all that kind of duty**

must necessarily be done, but as I feel the great importance of those reports to the Service, and to individuals, they may trust that I shall leave nothing undone to obtain them speedily.

The *Royal Sovereign* having lost her masts, except the tottering foremast, I called the *Euryalus* to me, while the Action continued, which Ship lying within hail, made my signals, a service Captain Blackwood performed with great attention. After the Action I shifted my flag to her, that I might more easily communicate my orders to, and collect the Ships, and towed the *Royal Sovereign* out to seaward. The whole fleet were now in a very perilous situation; many dismasted; all shattered; in thirteen fathoms water, off the shoals of Trafalgar; and when I made the signal to prepare to anchor, few of the Ships had an anchor to let go, their cables being shot; but the same good Providence which aided us through such a day preserved us in the night, by the wind shifting a few points, and drifting the Ships off the land, except for **four** of the captured dismasted Ships, which are not at anchor off Trafalgar, and I hope will ride safe until those gales are over.

Having thus detailed the proceedings of the fleet on this occasion, I beg to congratulate their Lordships on a victory which, I hope, will add a ray to the glory of His Majesty's crown, and be attended with public benefit to our country.

I am, &c,

C. COLLINGWOOD

THE ORDER IN WHICH THE SHIPS OF THE BRITISH SQUADRON
ATTACKED THE COMBINED FLEETS ON THE 21ST OCTOBER 1805

VAN

Victory

Témeraire

Neptune

Conqueror

Leviathan

Ajax

Orion

Agamemnon

Minotaur

Spartiate

Britannia

Africa

FRIGATES:

Euryalus   *Naiad*

Sirius   *Pickle* Schooner

Phoebe   *Entreprenante* Cutter

REAR

Royal Sovereign

Mars

Belleisle

Tonnant

Bellerophon

Colossus

Achille

Polyphemus

Revenge

Swiftsure

Defence

Thunderer

Defiance

Prince

Dreadnought

Euryalus,

October 24th, 1805

SIR, In my letter of the 22nd, I detailed to you, for the information of my Lords Commissioners of the Admiralty, the proceedings of His Majesty's Squadron on the day of the Action, and that preceding it, since which I have had a continued series of misfortunes, but they are of a kind that human prudence could not possibly provide against, or my skill prevent.

On the 22nd, in the morning, a strong Southerly wind blew, with squally weather, which however did not prevent the activity of the Officers and Seamen of such Ships as were manageable from getting hold of many of the Prizes (thirteen or fourteen), and towing them off to the Westward, where I ordered them to rendezvous round the *Royal Sovereign*, **now** in tow by the *Neptune*; but on the 23rd the gale increased, and the sea ran so high, that many of them broke the tow rope, and drifted far to leeward before they were got hold of again; and some of them, taking advantage of the dark and boisterous night, got before the wind, and have perhaps drifted upon the shore and sunk. On the afternoon of that day the remnant of the Combined Fleet, ten sail of Ships, who had not been much engaged, stood up to leeward of my shattered and straggled charge, as if meaning to attack them, which obliged me to collect a force out of the least injured Ships, and form to leeward for their defence. All this retarded the progress of the Hulks, and the bad weather continuing, determined me to destroy all the leewardmost that could be cleared of the men, considering that keeping of the Ships was a matter of little [consequence] **importance** compared with the chance of their falling again into the hands of the Enemy: but even this was an arduous task in the high sea which was running. I Hope, however, it has been accomplished to a considerable extent. I entrusted it to skilful Officers, who would spare no pains to execute what was possible. The Captains of the *Prince* and *Neptune* cleared the *Trinidad* and sunk her. Captains Hope, Bayntun, and Malcolm, who joined the Fleet this moment from Gibraltar, had the charge of destroying four others. The *Redoutable* sunk astern of the *Swiftsure* while in tow. The *Santa Anna*, I have no doubt, is sunk, as her side was almost entirely beat in; and such is the shattered condition of the whole of them, that unless the weather moderates, I doubt whether I shall be able to carry a Ship of them into Port - **if I had anchored such as had good cables, they (having all their crews on board) would certainly have cut them, and run for Port in the stormy weather; and there were 10 sail, and five frigates, ready to come to their assistance in fair weather, so that** I hope their Lordships will approve of what I (having only in considera-tion the destruction of the Enemy's Fleet) have thought a measure of absolute necessity. **I am under the most serious apprehensions for several of the ships of my squadron - the *Bellisle* is the only one totally dismasted, but the *Victory, Royal Sovereign, Témeraire,* and *Tonnant* are in a very decrepid state.**

I have taken Admiral Villeneuve into this Ship. Vice-Admiral Don Alava is dead. Whenever the temper of the weather will permit, and I can spare a Frigate (for there were only four in the action with the Fleet, *Euryalus, Sirius, Phoebe* and *Naiad*; the *Melpomene* joined the 22nd, and the *Eurydice* and *Scout* the 23rd), I shall collect the other Flag Officers, and send them to England with their Flags, (if they do not all go to the bottom) to be laid at His Majesty's feet.

I cannot discover what the destination of the Enemy was, but if the *Bucentaure* is above water when the gale abates, I will endeavour to do it. There were four thousand Troops embarked, under the command of General Contamin, who was taken with Admiral Villeneuve in the *Bucentaure*.

I am, Sir, &c

C. COLLINGWOOD

Collingwood's commissions
1761-1810

Year	Ship	Rate	Rank	Station	CO	Actions
1761	Shannon	Frigate – 28	volunteer	Atlantic/Home		
				Atlantic/Home/Med		
	Gibraltar	Frigate – 24				
1766			midshipman			
1767	Liverpool	Frigate – 28	master's mate			
1771						
1772	Lennox	74 guns		Portsmouth	Roddam	
1773	Portland	50 guns		WI – Jamaica		
	Princess Amelia				Berkeley	
1773	Preston	50 guns		N. America		
1774					Graves	
1775			Lieutenant			Charlestown
1776	Somerset	64 guns		England – ashore	Le Clas	
1777	Hornet	sloop – 14		WI – Jamaica	Haswell	
1778	Lowestoffe	Frigate – 32			Locker	
	Bristol	50 guns	2nd lieutenant			
	Badger	brig – 14	Commander		Parker	San Juan R.
1779	Hinchinbroke	Frigate – 28	Post Captain			
1780						
1781	Pelican	Frigate – 24		West Indies	Hughes?	
1782						
1783	Sampson	64 guns		Home briefly		
	Mediator	44 guns		Leeward Islands	Hughes	Nav Acts
1786				England – ashore		
1790	Mermaid	Frigate – 32		West Indies	Cornish	
1791				England –ashore		

Year	Ship	Rate	Rank	Station	C.O.	Actions
1793	*Prince*	98 guns	Flag Captain		Bowyer	
1794	*Barfleur*	98 guns				Glor 1st June
1794	*Hector*	74 guns				
1795	*Excellent*	74 guns		Mediterranean	Jervis	
1797						Cape St Vincent
1798			Commodore			
1799				England – ashore		
	Triumph	74 guns	R-Adm: white	Med/Home	Keith	
1800	*Barfleur*	98 guns				
	Neptune	98 guns				
1800	*Barfleur*	98 guns		Home/Plymouth		
1801			R-Adm: red			
1802				Home/ashore	Cornwallis	Treaty of Amiens
1803	*Diamond*	Frigate		Brest blockade	Cornwallis	
	Venerable	74 guns				
1803	*Minotaur*	74 guns				
	Venerable	74 guns				
1804	*Culloden*	74 guns				
	Prince	98 guns				
	Culloden	74 guns	V-Adm: blue			
	Dreadnought	98 guns				
1805				Cadiz blockade	Gardner	Cadiz
	Royal Sovereign	100 guns			Nelson	Trafalgar
			V-Adm: red			
1806	*Queen*	98 guns	C-in-C	Mediterranean		
	Ocean	80 guns				
1809	*Ville de Paris*	110 guns				Ionian Islands
						Rosas Bay
			Major-General			
1810			Royal Marines			

Bibliography

Abram, D. *The Rough Guide to Corsica*. Rough Guides 2000

Andrews, R. and Brown, J. *The Rough Guide to Sicily*. Rough Guides 2002

Austen, J. *Persuasion*. Penguin 1998

Ayling, S. *George the Third*. Collins 1972

Baugh, D. A. Why did Britain lose command of the sea during the war for America? In Black, J. and Woodfine, P. (eds) *The British Navy and the Use of Naval Power in the Eighteenth Century*. Leicester University Press 1988

Bowker, R. M. and Bligh, Lt. W. *Mutiny Aboard HM Armed Transport Bounty in 1789*. Bowker and Bertram 1978

Brady, F. and Pottle, F. A. *Boswell on the Grand Tour: Italy, Corsica and France 1765–1766*. Heinemann 1955

Breen, K. Divided Command: the West Indies and North America, 1780-81, in Black, J. and Woodfine, P. (eds) *The British Navy and the Use of Naval Power in the Eighteenth Century*. Leicester University Press 1988

Carrington, D. *The Dream Hunters of Corsica*. Phoenix 1996

Clark Russell, W. *Admiral Lord Collingwood*. Methuen 1891

Coleman, T. *Nelson*. Bloomsbury 2001

Collingwood, C. *Sailing Logs 1770-1773*. Unpublished, private collection 1773

Collingwood, C. *Secret Letter Book 1805-1808*. Unpublished. National Maritime Museum. MS 76/001 1808

Collingwood, C. *Mediterranean Journal 1807-1810*. Unpublished. University of Durham 1810

Country Life *The Country Life Book of Nautical Terms Under Sail*. Country Life 1978

Crawford, Captain A. *Reminiscences of a Naval Officer*. Chatham 1999

Cronin, V. *Napoleon*. History Book Club 1971

Cunningham, A. E. *Patrick O'Brian: Critical Appreciations and a Bibliography*. British Library

1994

Davies, D. *A Brief History of Fighting Ships*. Robinson 2002

Esdaile, C. *The Peninsular War*. Penguin 2003

Finley, M. I., Mack Smith, D. and Duggan, C. J. H. *A History of Sicily*. Chatto and Windus 1968

Firth, C. H. (Ed) 1908 Naval Songs and Ballads. *Navy Records Society 33* 1908

Fraser, C. M. and Emsley, K. *Tyneside*. David and Charles 1973

Gill, C. S. *The Old Wooden Walls, an abridged edition of Falconer's Marine Dictionary*. Foyles 1930

Gilmour, D. *The Last Leopard: A Life of Giuseppe Tomasi di Lampedusa*. Collins Harvill 1990

Glover, R. Britain at Bay: Defence against Bonaparte 1803-14. *Historical Problems, Studies and Documents, 20*. George Allen and Unwin 1973

Gregory, D. *The Ungovernable Rock: A History of the Anglo-Corsican Kingdom 1793–1797*. Fairleigh Dickinson University Press 1985

Gregory, D. *Sicily, the Insecure Base. A History of the British Occupation of Sicily, 1806–1815*. Fairleigh Dickinson University Press 1988

Gregory, D. *Minorca, the Illusory Prize: a History of the British Occupation of Minorca between 1708 and 1802*. Fairleigh Dickinson University Press 1990

Hay, M. D. (Ed) *Landsman Hay: the Memoirs of Robert Hay 1789–1847*. Rupert Hart-Davis 1958

Hattendorf, J. B. (Ed) British Naval Documents 1204–1960. *Navy Records Society 131* 1993

Hibbert, C. *Nelson: a Personal History*. Viking 1994

Hope-Dodds, M. and Hall, A. H. The Letters of Lady Collingwood and Others to Miss Mary Woodman. *Archaeologia Aeliana*, Fourth Series, 32 (1954), 30-64 1954

Howarth, D. *Trafalgar: the Nelson Touch*. Collins 1969

Hughes, E. *North Country Life in the Eighteenth Century: the North-East 1700-1750*. Oxford University Press 1952

Hughes, E. *The Private Correspondence of Admiral Lord Collingwood*. Navy Records Society 1957

Ireland, B. *Naval Warfare in the Age of Sail*. HarperCollins 2000

Jackson, T. Sturges Logs of the Great Sea Fights 1794–1805. *Navy Records Society 16 & 18* 1900

James, W. *Naval History of Great Britain*. 6 volumes. London 1826

Jones, J. R. Limitations of British Sea Power in the French Wars. In Black, J. and Woodfine, P. (eds) *The British Navy and the Use of Naval Power in the Eighteenth Century*. Leicester University Press 1988

Kennedy, L. *Nelson and his Captains*. Fontana 1975

Ketchum, R. M. *Decisive Day: the Battle for Bunker Hill*. Owl Books 1962

Lawson, W. *Tyneside Celebrities* 1873

Lee, P. *The Rough guide to Menorca*. Rough Guides 2001

Leech, S. *A Voice from the Maindeck*. Chatham 1999

Lewis, J. E. *The Mammoth Book of Life Before the Mast*. Robinson 2000

Lincoln, A. L. J. and McEwen, R .L. (Eds) *Lord Eldon's Anecdote Book*. Stevens and Sons 1960

Mackesy, P. *The War in the Mediterranean 1803–1810* 1957

Mains, B. and Tuck, A. (Eds) *Royal Grammar School Newcastle upon Tyne. A History of the School in its Community*. Oriel Press 1986

Mata, M. *Conquests and Re-conquests of Menorca*. Barcelona, Juvenil 1984

Maxwell, H. (Ed) *The Creevey Papers*. 2 volumes. John Murray 1903

Middlebrook, S. *Newcastle upon Tyne: its Growth and Achievement*. Newcastle Chronicle and Journal 1950

Morgan, W. J. (Ed) *Naval Documents of the American Revolution 3: 1775–1776* 1968

Morgan, W. J. (Ed) *Naval Documents of the American Revolution 5: May 1776–July 1776* 1969

Morrisey, B. *Boston 1775*. Osprey 1993

Murray, G. *The Life of Admiral Collingwood* 1936

Newnham-Collingwood, G. L. *A Selection from the Public and Private Correspondence of Vice-Admiral Lord Collingwood, Interspersed with Memoirs of his Life*. 3rd Edition. London 1828

Newnham-Collingwood, G. L. *A Selection from the Public and Private Correspondence of Vice-Admiral Lord Collingwood, Interspersed with Memoirs of his Life*. 5th Edition. London 1837

Nicolas, Sir H., *The Dispatches and Letters of Vice-Admiral Lord Viscount Nelson*. Chatham 1997

Nicholson, D. V. *English Harbour: the First 2000 years*. Antigua, The Dockyard Museum 2002

Oliver, T. *A Picture of Newcastle upon Tyne*. Dover 1831

Padfield, P. *Maritime Power and the Struggle for Freedom 1788–1851*. John Murray 2003

Palmer, A. and V. *The Chronology of British History*. Century 1992

Parsons, G. S. *Nelsonian Reminiscences: Leaves from Memory's Log*. Saunders and Otley 1843

Pocock, T. *The Terror before Trafalgar*. John Murray 2002

Pope, D. *Life in Nelson's Navy*. Chatham 1981

Pope, D. *Decision at Trafalgar*. Owl Books 1999

Raigersfeld, J. Baron de. *The Life of a Sea Officer*. Cassell 1929

Robinson, Rear-Admiral H. *Sea Drift*. Pitman 1858

Robinson, W. *Jack Nastyface: Memoirs of an English Seaman*. Naval Institute Press 1973

Rodger, N. A .M. *The Wooden World: an Anatomy of the Georgian Navy.* Fontana 1986

Rodger, N. A. M. Honour and Duty at Sea, 1660–1815. *Historical Research*, vol. 75, no. 190: 425-447 2002

Stephenson, D. F. *Admiral Collingwood and the Problems of the Naval Blockade after Trafalgar* 1948

Syrett, D. The Failure of the British Effort in America, 1777. In Black, J. and Woodfine, P. (eds) *The British Navy and theUse of Naval Power in the Eighteenth Century.* Leicester University Press 1988

Thackeray, W. M. *The Four Georges.* John Murray 1869

Thomas, D. *Cochrane: Britannia's Sea Wolf.* Cassell 1978

Thursfield, Rear-Admiral H. G. (Ed) Five Naval Journals 1789–1817. *Navy Records Society* XCI 1951

Tough, D. L. W. *The Last Years of a Frontier: A History of the Borders During the Reign of Elizabeth 1.* Sandhill Press 1987

Twiss, H. *The Public and Private Life of Lord Chancellor Eldon.* 3rd Edition. 2 volumes. John Murray 1846

Uglow, J. *The Lunar Men.* Faber and Faber 2002

Vaitilingam, A. *The Rough Guide to Antigua and Barbuda.* Rough Guides 2001

Warner, O. *The Life and Letters of Vice-Admiral Lord Collingwood.* Oxford University Press 1968

Warner, O. *A Portrait of Lord Nelson.* Reprint Society 1958

Index

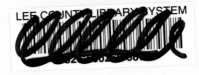
9/05